D0881191

METRICS-DRIVEN ENTERPRISE SOFTWARE DEVELOPMENT

Effectively Meeting Evolving Business Needs

SUBHAJIT DATTA

J.ROSS
PUBLISHING

Copyright ©2007 by Subhajit Datta

ISBN-13: 978-1-932159-64-6

Printed and bound in the U.S.A. Printed on acid-free paper
10 9 8 7 6 5 4 3 2 1

Library of Congress Cataloging-in-Publication Data

Datta, Subhajit.
  Metrics-driven enterprise software development : effectively meeting
evolving business needs / By Subhajit Datta.
    p. cm.
  Includes index.
  ISBN 978-1-932159-64-6 (hardcover : alk. paper)
  1. Computer software—Development. 2. Computer software—Quality
control.
I. Title.
  QA76.76.D47D364 2007
  005.3—dc22   2007018289

DEDICATION

To my parents —
It is amazing how much you taught me without ever teaching.
You also let me be myself.

TABLE OF CONTENTS

LIST OF TABLES
AND FIGURES

PREFACE

Bell (1937) begins the introduction to his *Men of Mathematics*: "This section is headed *Introduction* rather than *Preface* (which it really is) in the hope of decoying habitual preface-skippers into reading...." I can assure you no such artifice is at play here. This is headed a preface, and this is a preface.

I am an avid reader of prefaces. Fowler (2003) says, "...writing a book is so hard and so compulsive"; prefaces give some hint why someone would want to do it. Authors use different styles for prefaces. Some are diffident — yet another book on so and so subject needs such and such explanations, some defiant — the world needs *this* book, and some distinct — "this book almost seemed to write itself" (Graham et al. 1994). Some say how or why the book came to be; others are filled with anecdotes and wisecracks.

All who write a book for fun should agree that bookmaking is an organic experience. (I am not sure, though, why *bookmakers* are dubiously linked with games of chance but *filmmakers* and *homemakers* have exalted pursuits.) The act of writing is just a culmination; thoughts and ideas germinate long before they come to the finger. But only when one writes do many of these crystallize. I thought about a book like this for a long time, but not until I started writing did I fully feel my thoughts.

Software engineering is a young discipline. It has been thousands of years that humans have built magnificent buildings, and clever devices of locomotion have been around for a few hundred years, but only a few decades that software has been built on a scale that affects our lives in powerful and profound ways. Booch (2006) calls it "...a tremendous privilege as well as a deep responsibility to be a software developer." Much of the wisdom of building smart, efficient, and beautiful software still lies buried in people's heads and in folklore of the trade. I joined the software industry in the twilight of the last millennium. I have since marveled at the scope of writing software engineering presents. We are still searching for first principles and basic laws, even as we build more and more complex systems: the accompanying trepidation, tension, and triumph are the stuff of literature.

This is a practice-oriented book, meant to share experience, observation, and insight with other practitioners. This book presents a set of metrics to help make enterprise software systems easier to develop and smoother to enhance. The ideas and their applications are simple; you might think, "I could have thought of that." I hope you do, as that is the whole point. Only when we feel we can do something do we actually want to try it out. I want you to try out the ideas in this book, make them your own, modify and improve upon them. I have applied many of the ideas and have lived to tell the tale! Chapter 1 goes deeper into the theme of the book, provides a reading plan, and discusses who should read it (if you have come this far, let me assure you that *you* should), among other topics. Writing this book sharpened my own sense of what I know about the subject and made me rewind and relearn some of the much I do not.

Writing the book has been exciting. It took me back to another book-writing project of which I was partly a part, what seems eons ago. My father was an engineer, an accountant, and a man of many other interests. We always thought he could write books. A few years after he had successfully set up his own management consultancy practice, he finally got down to writing one. It was titled *ISO 9000: A Roadmap for Design, Installation and Implementation of Quality Management Systems* and was accepted by a leading publisher. As he wrote the book, he often asked my opinion on one aspect or another. I was all too eager to offer opinions. A sophomore, I felt equal to commenting on his style of writing and organization of the chapters. After submitting the manuscript, my father was admitted to a hospital for treatment of some minor symptoms. He asked me to borrow a few books for him from the local British Council Library to help plan his next book as he "served out" the hospital time. I did. Three weeks later, I sifted through the pages of those books, pulled out the bookmarks, and returned them to the library. My father was no more.

Any reflective work takes us back to our roots. I share my enthusiasm for this book with my mother — who is both a mother and a father now. My brothers have always remained for me acmes of original thinking and sources of much encouragement.

Most of this book was written during the first year of my marriage. A distracted husband is no recipe for early nuptial bliss; that bliss abounds goes to the credit of Reshmi — a very old friend and a very new wife. She gave me love, understanding, and sumptuous food and took away the cares of functioning.

I wrote this book while we lived in Tallahassee. Tallahassee, in addition to Florida sunshine, offers a delicious detachment. But my unsocial grain has not gained me fully, only because Dr. Tapas Bhattacharyya is here. He gave me enriching company, use of his laser printer, and took the photo for the author biography. In general, being mired in this book has helped me to take life's major and minor irks with greater humor.

I make it a point to forget the origins of best ideas I come across. Then it is easy to believe they were originally mine. This habit prevents a list of acknowledgments. I hope originators of best ideas are too deep into worthwhile things to mind.

Whatever the reader finds sublime or useful in this book cannot be claimed to be mine; it comes from the chemistry of circumstances shaping my life. Whatever the reader finds feckless speaks of my inability to make the best of what came my way.

Along the lines of what the pilot says as the plane taxies toward the arrival gate, I understand you had many choices but picked up this book, and I appreciate your indulgence (actually the pilot says *business*, but I am chary of sounding too gross). Thank you for trying out *Metrics-Driven Enterprise Software Development: Effectively Meeting Evolving Business Needs.*

Subhajit Datta
Tallahassee, Florida
subhajit.datta@gmail.com

REFERENCES

Bell, E. T. (1937). *Men of Mathematics*. Simon and Schuster.

Booch, G. (2006). *Handbook of Software Architecture*. http://www.booch.com/architecture/index.jsp.

Fowler, M. (2003). *Patterns of Enterprise Application Architecture*. Addison-Wesley.

Graham, R. L., Knuth, D. E., and Patashnik, O. (1994). *Concrete Mathematics: A Foundation for Computer Science*. Addison-Wesley.

ABOUT THE AUTHOR

 **Subhajit Datta** has a master of science in computer science and an undergraduate degree in electrical engineering. He is an IBM Certified Specialist for Rational Unified Process v2003 and has additional certification in object-oriented analysis and design with Unified Modeling Language (IBM Test 486).

Mr. Datta has wide experience in developing enterprise software systems. He worked as a software engineer with IBM Global Services in roles of technical lead, business systems analyst, release manager, and application developer. One of his papers was published as intellectual capital in the IT Process Model knowledge network of IBM's ICM AssetWeb.

Mr. Datta is currently working on his doctoral dissertation at Florida State University. His research interests include software architecture, design tools and techniques, metrics, and requirements, and he has several research publications. He is also involved in teaching courses on Internet technologies and Java.

Mr. Datta is a member of Upsilon Pi Epsilon, the international honor society in the computing and information disciplines, the Institute of Electrical and Electronics Engineers (IEEE), and the Association for Computing Machinery (ACM).

Reading, writing, and travel are among Mr. Datta's interests. He may be reached at subhajit.datta@gmail.com.

Free value-added materials available from
the Download Resource Center at www.jrosspub.com

At J. Ross Publishing we are committed to providing today's professional with practical, hands-on tools that enhance the learning experience and give readers an opportunity to apply what they have learned. That is why we offer free ancillary materials available for download on this book and all participating Web Added Value™ publications. These online resources may include interactive versions of material that appears in the book or supplemental templates, worksheets, models, plans, case studies, proposals, spreadsheets and assessment tools, among other things. Whenever you see the WAV™ symbol in any of our publications, it means bonus materials accompany the book and are available from the Web Added Value Download Resource Center at www.jrosspub.com.

Downloads available for *Metrics-Driven Enterprise Software Development: Effectively Meeting Evolving Business Needs* consist of a metrics-driven software development presentation and a quick reference glossary of important metrics.

INTRODUCTION

1.1. OVERVIEW

In this chapter, we will discuss along broad, general lines what this book is about, for whom the book is meant, how the book is organized, and a reading plan. All of this is meant to get you, the reader who has come this far, sufficiently interested to carry on further. In addition, there are some reflections on why and when the narration uses "I" instead of "we" and vice versa. Lastly, I relate the reasons why I wrote this book in the first place.

1.2. WHAT IS THIS BOOK ABOUT?

This is not a book about how enterprise software should be built. This is a book about how enterprise software is built and how metrics can help make a difference. (In the next chapter, the meaning of the terms *enterprise software* and *metrics* is clarified; for the moment, let us understand them in their usual sense.) There are many books that harp on the "should" of enterprise software development. The fact that there are *many* books implies: (a) there are many strong feelings about the subject and (b) there is very little consensus. This book illustrates how simple and intuitive techniques can go a long way toward better meeting customer expectations and building systems that are easier to evolve and improve while causing developers less pain and penance.

A set of metrics and artifacts is presented which will help software engineering practitioners do their jobs better. However, no formulas are given.

In 1998, Amartya Sen won the Bank of Sweden Prize in Economic Sciences in Memory of Alfred Nobel, better known as the Nobel Prize in Economics. Sen was awarded the prize "for his contributions to welfare economics" (nobelprize.org 1998). Although Sen is a world citizen in the most eclectic sense, teaching and lecturing all over the globe, Kolkata (Calcutta), India, takes him to be very much her own. Euphoria was abounding when the news of Sen's Nobel Prize reached there. A neighbor of mine remarked with much veneration, and not a little patriotic pride, "This is such great news! But what is Professor Sen's *formula*? None of the newspapers reported it."

A formula is a nifty little thing, and formulas for happiness are in strong demand. Regrettably, formulas of such sweeping width and utility are not easy to come up with, so no such promise is made here. This book deals with mechanisms that will help you decide one way or the other as you negotiate the quagmires of building quality enterprise software. Giving you a set of heuristics or rules of thumb is very much the aim. These will complement your best judgment, and constrict your worst, but in all cases call upon your active involvement.

It is often said that a software product is never complete in the way a building or a car is. The very *softness* of software, what may be called its plasticity (refer to Section 3.2.3), ensures that software is ever caught in the quest for improvement. Thus it is no wonder the ideas in this book concerning the development of enterprise software should have room for continual refinement. Based on my own experience, I am sanguine this book's ideas will give you results. Just as I remain eager to learn from readers how they have found this book useful, I remain as receptive to know when a technique became a bottleneck or some circumstance where things did not work well. I would like readers to read this book, absorb and use the ideas, make them their own, and feel free to modify and improve them. In this era of global connectivity, a book has a new role to play. It is no longer a static repository of facts or an eternal fount of wisdom; a book now is more an instigator of interaction. In an ideal state, the interplay of ideas never had borders; the Web has just made that real. Through the Web Added Value™ downloads on the publisher's Web site (www.jrosspub.com), I plan to keep the material in this book current and remain responsive to your feedback.

In sum, this book presents a set of ideas to help practitioners build enterprise software systems that are easier to develop and better tuned to customer expectations. Many of these ideas have been applied in practice. This is meant to be a practice-oriented book which will help you understand things better and, more significantly, help you *do* things better.

The next question which begs our attention is: Who is this book meant for? Or to put it more personally: Should you be reading this book?

1.3. INTENDED AUDIENCE

Every author pines to pen a book that will become *the book* — everything for everybody. In one of Sukumar Ray's (1962) nonsense rhymes, the narrator rhapsodizes about his *notebook*. It is a compendium of every fact and all wisdom — the number of legs a grasshopper has, the diet of a cockroach, why glue feels sticky to the touch, whether jaggery goes into making soap or a firecracker, why soda has fizz but chili tastes hot, the dynamics of snoring, and what have you. The notebook's author has compiled all of these on his own, with occasional doubts cleared by pestering an elder brother. The poem ends with the readers being chided for their ignorance, which the narrator says is expected, as they have yet to read his book. Such a notebook, alas, is too big a project for our limited means. We have to be happy with subsets.

The book you have in your hands is intended for software engineers with a few years behind them in the industry — senior enough to have seen how things work and junior enough to believe things can be made to work better. Software engineers at such a level in organizations are actively involved in analysis and design and in overall charge of implementation, testing, and delivery of a software project. This role is variously named *technical lead, project leader,* or more grandly *architect.* Individuals in these roles have the independence to try out this book's ideas in their projects, along with the onus of making them work. But this does not mean you should not be reading this book if you currently do not find yourself in such a role.

If you have just entered the exciting world of enterprise software development, you will soon find yourself making decisions that will directly impact the quality and timing of customer deliverables. This book will prepare you to make those decisions with greater confidence, replicate the success when decisions go right, and when they go wrong (as they sometimes will) glean the deepest and most durable lessons. On the other hand, if you are no longer a technical lead or project leader or if the sublime tasks of an architect no longer appeal to you (in which case you have probably moved up the so-called "value-chain" and into management), this book will help you appreciate the lot of many of those with whom you need to work closely, be better equipped to help them make better software, and keep abreast of the evolving ways of software development so that some hotshot "techie" cannot take you for a ride.

I hope to interest readers at either end of a spectrum whose center makes up the core audience. For the new entrants to the industry, programming is still the entire cosmos; they sincerely believe that the success of software projects depends solely on consummate coding. This book will give them a more holistic view of software engineering. For those into the management of software projects who have been technical leads or project leaders, the book will evoke many memories. Hopefully, the dé-jà vu will foster a culture where individuals and teams can be creative with their use of metrics-based techniques.

Whenever a book is written and a publisher sought, the author faces the question whether the book can be used as a textbook in any course. I happen to feel strongly about how engineering textbooks should be written, having seen many that embody ways they should not be. A textbook in engineering is different from textbooks in other disciplines. Engineering is about doing, and engineering textbooks should ultimately talk about getting things done. It is vital to discuss the theory that goes behind the practice and equally vital to point out that practice is different from theory. To succeed, every engineer needs to learn tricks of the trade which go far beyond any textbook. This book illustrates many such tricks, which I hope will contribute to the nascent but growing collection of software engineering heuristics. Thus this book can serve as an important companion edition to software engineering course materials in any undergraduate or graduate curriculum.

I have made a conscious effort to keep jargon to a minimum; nothing puts me off more than arcane wordplay. If you do not know what a "third normal form" is, feel intimidated by the very mention of "inner classes," or are blind to the power of "pair programming," rest assured that this book will not spring such things on you without adequate reason or motivation. I only assume that the reader appreciates standard software engineering practices and the scale and complexities of enterprise software systems. Whenever subtle or involved ideas are introduced (to wit, *abstraction* in software design), I have taken care to ease things up beforehand.

If you are neither a software engineering practitioner nor a student, and do not plan on becoming either soon, even then this book might be of value to you. Software permeates our lives today as no single technology has done in the history of mankind. The story of how software is built in the large — software that handles our money, safeguards our health, lets us go safely from place to place, etc., determining our very quality of life in near transparent ways — will engage anyone with a general interest in history, society, and culture.

The books I like, irrespective of subject, have some features in common: they are written without affectations of the topic's difficulty or the author's unique gifts, they are written about circumstances the author has *lived* and not just *learned*, and they are written with simplicity and humor. These are not easy traits to emulate. In writing this book, I have been sincere in striving toward them.

1.4. ORGANIZATION OF THE BOOK

In terms of the organization of content, this book has three logical parts — Part 1: Context (Chapters 3 to 5), Part 2: Constructs (Chapters 6 to 11), and Part 3: Case Study (Chapters 12 to 16). Chapters 1 and 2 simply precede Part 1 as introductory and background material and are not numbered as a part.

Following the introductory chapter is Chapter 2, titled "Schmoozing with the Ideas." It is kind of an up-front glossary of the main themes of the book. As I find that I seldom read glossaries, I have tried to make this chapter readable. In addition to introducing the ideas, this chapter also shows how one relates to the other in our scheme of things. Some of the words which have already been bandied about several times (metrics, enterprise software, heuristics) are clarified there in their contexts.

Part 1 serves as the overall background for the book. In Chapter 3, "Software Engineering and Metrics," software is placed in the pantheon of engineering disciplines, the software metrics odyssey over the last few decades is discussed, and the approach of this book is summarized. Chapter 4, "Key Themes in Software Measurements," goes over a hit parade of how software metrics should and should not be viewed or used. This is a digest of conventional wisdom, with an occasional spin from me. In Chapter 5, "Taking Your Project the Metrics Way," the discussion focuses on some of the very real but "nontechnical" issues in taking a project to the metrics culture and making it drink. This chapter takes up such juicy issues as metrics and politics and presents a metrics charter for a project.

Part 2 presents the core ideas of this book. It covers desiderata of the major software development life cycle activities: requirements, analysis and design, implementation, and testing. For each set of activities, metrics and artifacts are introduced which help practitioners leverage the feedback mechanism of the iterative and incremental model and moderate the course of development.

Chapter 6, "Iterative and Incremental Development: A Brief Background," goes over the salient features of this development paradigm and briefly compares it with the waterfall and agile methodologies. In Chapter 7, "Requirements: The Drivers of Software Development," the *Correlation Matrix* and the *Mutation Score* are introduced. The former maps the artifacts of a software development project to specific requirements while the latter is a measure of how much a requirement changes over a set of iterations. Chapter 8, "Analysis and Design: On Understanding, Deciding, and Measuring," one of the longer chapters, takes a look at how metrics can help the highly interactive and reflective pursuits of analysis and design. It introduces the *Meshing Ratio* (a measure of how closely the analysis components, called *players*, link with the requirements), *AEI Score* (which reflects the extent to which a design conforms to the canons of *abstraction, elision,* and *indirection*), and *Morphing Index* (which indicates how much a design is changing between iterations). Chapter 9, "Implementation: It Takes Some Doing," is about where the rubber meets the road — when a developer gets down to writing code, line by line. It unveils the *Specific Convergence* (which measures how much of the total development effort is covered in an iteration as compared to what must finally be covered across all iterations) and the *Interface Map* (which specifies the dependencies between chunks of functionality, called *Implementation Units*, delegated to teams or individuals). Chapter 10, "Testing: Hunt for a Litmus Paper for Software," talks about the importance of testing and the gaps in conventional testing metrics. As I usually try not to be critical about something for which I cannot suggest an alternative, our take on testing differs from conventional software testing metrics: the *Exception Estimation Score* gives an idea of the likelihood the implementation of a major functional area (a *Deliverable Unit,* in our parlance) may have serious "showstopping" exceptions. The title of Chapter 11, "Putting It All Together," pretty much explains things; this chapter puts into perspective the whole of Part 2, with directions on when and how to use the metrics and artifacts.

Ideas such as those introduced in Part 2 are best explained by illustration. Part 3 is a case study that follows an enterprise software project from inception onward and shows how the techniques in Part 2 can be put into practice. The context of and characters in the case study are fictitious. To use a popular phrase, any resemblance to reality is purely accidental. But I am sure the discerning eye will find many a parallel to the "usual" circumstances of enterprise software building. (As Gerald M. Weinberg [1971] says in the preface of his *The Psychology of Computer Programming,* "…some of these experiences have had to be fictionalized to protect the innocent, and sometimes the guilty.") The chapters in Part 3 have playful names — "The Plot Thickens," "Getting into the Groove," "Diving at the Deep End," "Building Time," and "Feel of the World" — and deliberately so; because Part 3 is much storytelling, a lighter mood is not entirely out of place.

Finally, the epilogue gets into some grand rumination in the spirit of a coda and places the book in its context.

1.5. READING PLAN

Executive summaries are very hot in the software industry. You may have reams of documents detailing many subtleties, but until there is a "one-pager" that digests the whole, you are not considered done. I believe, rather naively, that the phrase "executive summary" has its roots in the kinds of summaries executives like, given their constraints on time and attention. Indeed, having the right thing summarized for the right executive can get you far. Unfortunately, however, not everything can be executively summarized or summarily executed. The author R. K. Narayan is believed to have once riposted to a reporter's request for a short summary of his latest novel, saying there is no way he could shorten something he has taken eighty thousand words to say in the first place. The best reading plan an author can offer for his or her book is to read the whole book, from start to finish.

Yet as I often find in technical nonfiction, authors prescribe that readers go over Chapter X and then "feel free" to skip a few chapters and rejoin the trail in perfect harmony in Chapter Y. In keeping with that fashion, I offer the following advice to readers who want to avoid committing to read the whole book on the first go.

To get acquainted with the ideas with which this book will be mainly concerned, you need to read the next chapter, "Schmoozing with the Ideas." If you want to know about the general state-of-the-art of software metrics, and how this book says something new or looks at something old in a new way, Chapter 3, "Software Engineering and Metrics," is your destination. That is the first chapter in Part 1. The two other chapters in Part 1 build the context for Part 2. To verify whatever there is new in this book, you need to plunge into Part 2. The chapters in Part 2 are the most closely knit, and I would certainly encourage reading them in sequence. (For example, you cannot implement before you design, or at least should not, so reading Chapter 9, "Implementation: It Takes Some Doing," before Chapter 8, "Analysis and Design: On Understanding, Deciding, and Measuring," may not give you the best results.) If Part 2 fires up your imagination, which I am sure it will, but leaves you slightly skeptical, which I surmise it may, proceed to Part 3. Everything that is prescribed in Part 2 is illustrated by example in Part 3. In addition, Part 3 is also a tongue-in-cheek take on the ecosystem of an enterprise software development project. As in all interesting situations, understanding the ecosystem is often the foremost step in understanding the system. I have deliberately tried to make Part 3 go beyond the mere play of the metrics. Many practitioners will find many circumstances in Part 3 familiar, and this should breed an interest in the destiny of the case study project presented there. Adventurous readers may try reading Part 3 first and as their interest is piqued rewind to Parts 1 and 2, but the usual risks of adventure come with taking this route.

I have tried to make the cross-references as precise and the index as detailed as possible to help readers swing back and forth without losing their way. For those who will use the ideas in this book in their work, rereading parts of it will be helpful after an initial browse.

What I said above should qualify as a reading plan, but it does not offer you a way to absorb everything in the book in an hour and a half. This book is not like another whose title I will not mention which promised in the preface to be able to be read in its entirety during a flight from Washington, D.C. to New York.

Every reader makes his or her own reading plan to make the most out of a book. A book, in that sense, is the most customizable commodity.

1.6. OF I AND WE, AND OTHER SENSITIVITIES

Neil Armstrong's famous remark about a small step for *man* might have been cited for gender insensitivity, had the times been less lax or the occasion less exhilarating. Throughout this book I use the neuter plural "they" in talking about issues far more mundane than what Armstrong had to say. The protagonist in the case study in Part 3 is Tina, a representative of the very many young women working with such distinction in the global software industry. Many men are doing that too. I just made a random choice.

A thornier issue with the narrative has been "I" versus "we." One of the first term papers I wrote for a class had a liberal peppering of the first-person singular because I thought term papers were graded on originality. The professor called me into his office and said I should use "we." "But there is only I. No one else is in this," I interjected. "Still, we must use 'we.' 'We' sounds more academic." I smarted at the dilution of my identity at that time, but have since come to note the subtle difference in mood that "I" and "we" impart. It is usual for academic writing to assume an air of speaking *on behalf* of a putative brotherhood of believers (even if it is a gang of one), so "we" is the custom. "I" definitely has an egotistic ring to it; too much of it jars the sensibilities and makes one a spectacle, an "I specialist" that is. In this book, I do not want to sound academic or become a spectacle. As a middle ground, whenever I say something for which I solely wish to assume responsibility, I say "I." In all other cases, including when I am talking about opinions or experiences that are widely held in the software engineering community, I say "we." And when I want to be politically correct, I use neither, sending the good old passive voice to the rescue.

1.7. WHY I WROTE THIS BOOK

This chapter ends with reflections on why and how this book came to be. Writing a book is a major undertaking, especially as most books are written part-time. Moonlighting sounds very romantic, reminiscent perhaps of the *Moonlight* Sonata, but it needs much motivation. (Was Beethoven moonlighting when he came up with the eponymous sonata? Probably not.) Being too honest with the motivations may end up seeming too crass, so allow me a little discretion.

A book usually has a mission; the author may be clever or coy enough not to be forthright with it. Enlightening the readership surely qualifies as one mission, but often there are more covert ones. I first started thinking about this book almost two years ago. From that first flicker of thought to the time the book comes out as a product, there has been and will be many modifications, morphings, and modulations. And this is all in the game. All of this change allows some ideas to crystallize and others to vaporize, and finally leaves one with a core set of notions and their interconnections to explore in the book. For me, writing is very much a process of learning (I find William Zinsser's [1993] thesis in *Writing to Learn* very apt and very neglected in curricula across the world), and this book helped me see many of the things I have written about in a much clearer light.

I have written mostly about situations in enterprise software development which I experienced. This seems a very natural way to write, but there are certain difficulties. To write from experience, one has to first decide how to handle the baggage that comes with every experience. The way the past has dealt with us often colors the way we deal with the future, and this comes in the way of an objective point of view. I give many anecdotes in this book, from my own experience or hearsay from sources I trust, but I try to avoid making conclusions or, worse, judgments based on them. My experiences with building enterprise software from the bottom up in the trenches are by no means unique, and the familiarity other practitioners will recognize while reading the book should interest them more in it.

The very fact that my experiences spurred me to write a book shows there was something about them which I thought could or should have been different. Software engineering is young, in fact infant, by the standards of the other engineering disciplines (structural, mechanical, and even electrical). We do not yet have anything near the common body of knowledge which these disciplines have accumulated. Yet software engineers find themselves building critical and complex systems which influence our lives in diverse ways and even stand to affect life-and-death situations in the straightforward meaning of the term. The only way we can scale our skills to the level of preparation necessary to address such criticality and complexity is by honing a set of heuristics. Heuristics do not appear in dreams; they have to be consciously harvested from the relentless cycles of trials and errors, failures and successes that every engineer needs to go through. To do this, software engineers need to have awareness, discipline, and, curiously, a sense of history, but I had not seen these elements in many software engineers and mostly in myself. This book seeks to recoup some of that loss.

All of my experiences with building software systems and teaching and reading about them have helped me write this book. I have tested many of the techniques I describe on real-life software development projects. The results have convinced me that every metric or software development artifact has a scope of continual improvement. To improve, we must start from somewhere. Writing this book also helped me unearth many such starting points.

Lastly, through this book I hope to start a process of dialogue (and perhaps some diatribe, too!) with like- and unlike-minded people who think, talk, or do enterprise software development. The contact will certainly enrich me and may also end up helping others and furthering the discipline.

1.8. SUMMARY

This chapter is much a potpourri. We went over such meta information as what the book is about, the intended audience, organization of the chapters, a reading plan, some of the quirks of the narrative, and the author's reasons for writing this book. If you are interested in enterprise software development by passion or profession, and want to know how simple, intuitive metrics can help make software easier to build and more useful to use, you have hit upon the right book. Read on.

In the next chapter, readers are familiarized with the main ideas in this book and their interconnections.

REFERENCES

nobelprize.org (1998). The Sveriges Riksbank Prize in Economic Sciences in Memory of Alfred Nobel 1998. http://nobelprize.org/nobel_prizes/economics/laureates/1998.

Ray, S. (1962). *Abol Tabol,* 9th ed. Signet Press.

Weinberg, G. M. (1971). *The Psychology of Computer Programming.* Van Nostrand Reinhold.

Zinsser, W. K. (1993). *Writing to Learn.* HarperCollins.

2

SCHMOOZING
WITH THE IDEAS

2.1. OVERVIEW

The major ideas of this book and how they relate to one another are introduced in this chapter. Some of the words and phrases which will be frequently encountered are explained and their contexts clarified. This chapter may be viewed as an informal and readable glossary of the themes with which we will be mainly concerned going forward.

2.2. IDEAS AND THEIR RELATIONS

Every book is a book of ideas. We may use facts, figures, and opinions to contradict or corroborate, but ultimately we are trying to establish ideas. Ideas in isolation are exciting, but really exciting things begin to happen when ideas relate to one another. Each of us has our own "eureka" moments, when hitherto disparate notions click together in congress. Books enrich us by uncovering some of this clicking together and somehow convincing us that relating ideas is not such an esoteric game after all. Some reflection and discipline can get us there, which they surely can.

I sometimes think the very attitude toward books has changed with the popularity of the Web and the ubiquity of information it has brought with it. We rely less and less on books for our facts; the onus of books has shifted to presenting new ideas or at least relating existing ideas in novel or insightful ways.

This chapter is kind of an *idea map* for this book. Here you will be introduced to some of the keynote ideas you will need to live with from now on. Certain words and phrases will recur in this book, and this chapter will ensure we are all on the same page about their meanings and insinuations. Usually, a glossary does something like that, but it comes at the end of a book. As I am too lazy to flip back and forth, I usually find myself assuming meanings of words and phrases and reading on, only to find later that the author meant very differently. The reverse is also true at times; two ideas may be very closely related, but I suffer by assuming they are gulfs apart. Once I was reading the requirement specifications for a large project, with a pressing need to make sense of them. I frequently came across "users" and "merchants" and got confused about their overlapping roles, only to realize later they were one and the same business entity. Reading the glossary might have helped, or might not have. Unfortunately, reading glossaries is no fun, just as reading dictionaries is not, no matter how rich their content is. Therefore, I decided to front-end the glossary idea and throw in some more verbiage, so that you have a fair idea what the book is about before taking the plunge. Hopefully, acquaintance with the themes up front will also help you absorb the narrative better. In the next few sections, quick summaries of the ideas in this book are given, followed by an effort to tie the threads together. Before that, however, let us savor two instances where ideas separated by eons and disciplines have come together in hair-raising harmony. These have always motivated me in ferreting around for relations amongst ideas.

In 1936, Alan Turing (1936) published the paper "On Computable Numbers, with an Application to the Entscheidungsproblem." Turing introduced the notion of what subsequently became known as the "Turing machine." Turing was exploring the ideas of computability, and his Turing machine was initially a thought construct to illustrate his arguments. Bewitchingly simple in conception, a Turing machine is ultimately a symbol-manipulating device that consists of an infinite-length tape, a head (which can move left or right) to read and write symbols at box-like locations or cells on the tape, and a table of instructions. It has since become manifest that a Turing machine is a complete model for the basic operations of a computer. But this relation of ideas, from a pure thought construct to the ubiquitous utility of computers as we know them today, does not end the story of Turing machines. DNA — the genetic character sequences regarded as the "blueprint" of life — has been married to the Turing machine idea in recent research into the feasibility of DNA computers (Parker 2003; Johnson 2000). This serves as just one instance of how ideas are not bound by provenance or politics.

Turning to another area, a Bose-Einstein condensate is a phase of matter formed by bosons (particles having integer spin, named after Bose) cooled to temperatures very near to absolute zero (0 Kelvin or –273.15 degrees Celsius). This was first predicted in 1925 through the work of Albert Einstein and Satyendranath Bose. It was produced seventy years later by Eric Cornell and Carl Wieman (1995) at the University of Colorado in Boulder. Tim Berners-Lee (1999), while working as a software engineer at CERN, the European Particle Physics Laboratory, in Geneva in the 1980s and early 1990s, conceived, built, and refined the infrastructure of what was to become the World Wide Web. The evolution and dynamics of the Web have been the subject of much scrutiny, leading to the startling question: Could the Web or the Internet represent a gigantic Bose condensate (Barabasi 2001)? This is another example of confluence of ideas from fields seemingly far apart.

These examples wake us to the gregariousness of ideas. Even if we cannot see every thread in its full light (in all honesty, DNA and that condensate stuff are far beyond me), we can appreciate the beauty and, more often than not, the utility of the braid. The trope of a braid in describing the intermingling of ideas has been powerfully exploited in the Pulitzer Prize–winning book *Gödel, Escher, Bach: An Eternal Golden Braid* (Hofstadter 1979).

We will now look at the ideas in this book and their connectedness. After this chapter, whenever reference is made to a word or phrase to which a subsection is devoted here (like *enterprise software* or *metrics*), we will implicitly take it to have the meaning and context described below.

2.3. THEMES IN THIS BOOK

2.3.1. Enterprise Software Systems

Enterprise software systems are in a way the very *raison d'être* of the software engineering profession. The phrase will be encountered many times as we go deeper. How are enterprise software systems characterized?

Enterprise software systems usually support business processes; they need to respond to changing user needs, they are bound by business and technological constraints, and their soundness of design and implementation is of *material* interest to different groups of stakeholders. To the above must be added another feature which is becoming increasingly common to these systems: their scope of operation ranges across a diverse spectrum of geography, nationality, and culture. Fowler (2003), in his book *Patterns of Enterprise Application Architecture*, says enterprise applications are characterized by persistent data, concurrent data access, lots of "user interface screens," needs to integrate with other enterprise applications, needs to bridge conceptual dissonance between diverse business processes, and complex business "illogic." This is indeed a very insightful list; the last two points in particular deserve some elaboration.

Conceptual dissonance is an apt expression for the great (and grave) diversity of interests every enterprise system has to reasonably resolve. An enterprise application is usually a confluence of many business processes, none of which is obligated to align with others. These nonaligned, often contradictory interests are represented by different stakeholders, all of which stand to gain or lose materially from the success or failure of the system. The gains and losses, however, are very different in nature and extent. Building and maintaining enterprise software systems is about balancing very many tugs and pulls in very many directions to minimize losses and maximize gains for every stakeholder.

Fowler also hits the nail on the head when he talks about the illogic of business logic. Business logic is about business; it is not about logic. Logic is an overloaded and overworked word, with such exalted trappings as reason and syllogism. "Business rules" would be a better name for the instincts and credos that drive any business. They have no reason to be logical or at least logical in the sense software engineers (let alone logicians) understand the term. A major challenge of enterprise software development is to capture the capriciousness of business rules in the formal structure of design and ultimately code.

Enterprise software systems usually do not involve complex mathematical operations on data. It would be highly unlikely to have such a system solve differential equations. Enterprise systems do, however, deal with very large amounts of data and their storage, display, and simple manipulations. Another aspect of enterprise software is that the users of such systems are different than the developers, and these two groups are different from those who commission the building of the software. This is of much consequence, as we have at least three different groups associated with the systems, which speak three different languages and yet must talk to one another.

Thus, in essence, enterprise software systems are software applications which are commissioned to support business processes that involve diverse groups of stakeholders. These systems may have a scope of development and operation that ranges across a variety of technological, geographical, and cultural domains.

We will next be more precise about the stakeholders.

2.3.2. Stakeholders

The *Merriam-Webster Online Dictionary* (2006) defines *stake* as "an interest or share in an undertaking or enterprise." (We will ignore other less germane definitions, one of which is the device for burning dissonant individuals in less tolerant times.) And we have just been talking about *enterprise* software systems! Simply put, stakeholders are people whose material interests stand to be affected, for better or for worse, by an undertaking with which they associate. Material interest is different from such spiritual passions as the joy of discovery, the love of humanity, or the bliss of doing something well. Very often, material interest means immediate financial gain. Sometimes the connection may not be that quick, but stakeholders are always in the game for some worldly gain. There is a time in everyone's life when worldly gains seem so gross. Then we are able to take a more practical view of the world. This view is very important for those in the business of developing enterprise software.

Some stakeholders are easy to identify. In an enterprise software project, the customer (represented by a small group from the customer organization) is a stakeholder; the customer is pumping money into the project in the hope it will help bring back more money. The development team (a group of individuals assigned to the project by the organization contracted by the customer) is a stakeholder; if the project goes well, the team wins accolades, which may eventually translate to enhanced responsibility and a higher pay packet for its members. The users (for an online application, the multitude of individuals who access it over the Web, to send, fetch, or review information) are stakeholders; they are spending time and energy, and maybe money, on the application in the hope of being adequately recompensed. These are just the overt stakeholders. There may be other covert ones too. What about competing companies or groups within the same company whose interests are not best met if the project succeeds? What about other business entities curious to see how the system impacts the users, so their strategies can be accordingly tuned? Thus, stakeholders exist at many levels of visibility and invisibility. The development team, a stakeholder itself, has the job of reconciling the stakes of all other stakeholders. The overt ones are paramount, but it pays to keep an antenna open to the covert ones too.

Let us now examine a special kind of stakeholder: the practitioners.

2.3.3. Practitioners

Practitioners may or may not preach, but they are professionally obligated to practice. Engineering to a large extent is a practitioner's profession. Things must be made to actually work, even if they should work in theory. When we talk about practitioners in this book, we will be referring to individuals or groups who are expected to carry out the techniques described. Practitioners certainly have a significant stake in the success of what they practice, so they are stakeholders too. However, it was imperative to give them another, more specific name, as this book is mainly practice oriented. Whatever idea is put forward, if it is worth its salt, should help practitioners somewhere do their jobs better.

So far we have dwelt upon the system and its players. Let us now limn another key word in the title of this book: metrics.

2.3.4. Measure-Measurement-Metrics

Even within the software engineering context, there is hardly any consensus as to what measure, measurement, or metrics truly means. Discord is good, as it usually signifies independent thinking. Pressman (2000) says "a measure provides a quantitative indication of the extent, amount, dimension, capacity, or size of some attribute of a product or process" and "measurement is the act of determining a measure." The IEEE (1990) Software Engineering Standards define metric as "…a quantitative measure of the degree to which a system, component, or process possesses a given attribute." In this book, whenever we talk about metrics, we take it to cover the entire gamut of measure, measurements, and metrics. We will concern ourselves more with the utility of a metrics-driven approach to enterprise software development and less with its pedagogical aspects. The chapters in Part 1 are devoted to a general review of metrics in software engineering, as well as some key themes in software measurements. We now take a passing glance at how metrics relate to our lives.

Nothing is truer than Mah and Putnam's words: "We manage things 'by the numbers' in many aspects of our lives.…These numbers give us insight and help steer our actions" (Pressman 2000). Inflation rate indicates the state of an economy, blood cholesterol level signifies the state of one's heart, and money is a measure of one's station in life. All three of these work on certain assumptions. Inflation takes into account only a "basket" of goods and services, cholesterol level is just one among many factors that make or break a heart, and money cannot buy happiness. Yet policies are based on the inflation rate, care goes into keeping cholesterol in check, and the pursuit of money is deemed a worthy endeavor. Thus the assumptions behind these metrics, though certainly not sweepingly true, are apt enough under certain situations. These are just some of the metrics which guide decisions on national, societal, and personal levels. Metrics give us some numbers upon which we base the branching logic of our decision trees. While it is important to remain mindful of the limitations the assumptions of every metric place upon it, it is equally important to understand that metrics can and do help traverse the maze of complex decision making in our lives.

Decision making is an intriguing process, tied closely as it is to the very functioning of the human mind. Decisions come out of a chemistry of observation and perception, facts and hunches, objectivity and subjectivity. Use of metrics streamlines the decision-making process to a large extent, clearly delineating the subjective and the objective aspects and their interfaces. In this book, it will be illustrated how metrics help us make expedient choices in the software development process. I always find it easy and useful to view metrics as some kind of *heuristic*. This brings us to the next important idea of this book.

2.3.5. Heuristics

Maier and Rechtin (2000), in the second edition of their seminal work *The Art of Systems Architecting,* treat *heuristics* as "abstractions of experience." The word "heuristics" certainly has a Greek origin, but different authors give different shades to its original meaning. Maier and Rechtin (2000) say the Greek word *heuriskein* means to "'find a way' or 'to guide' in the sense of piloting a boat through treacherous shoals." According to Luger (2004), the original word means "to discover." Luger offers a down-to-earth take on a heuristic as "a useful, but potentially fallible problem-solving strategy..." and adds that "much of what we commonly call intelligence seems to reside in the heuristics used by humans to solve problems." According to Polya (1945), in his classic *How to Solve It: A New Aspect of Mathematical Method*: "Heuristic, as an adjective, means 'serving to discover'...The aim of heuristic is to study the methods and rules of discovery and invention."

Cutting through these thickets of definitions, the notion of a heuristic is familiar to many of us. To cite some of the instances mentioned by Luger (2004), checking to see if an appliance is plugged in before complaining that it does not work is a heuristic, as is the strategy of "castling" in chess to fortify your king. Doctors and car mechanics use heuristics all the time. Nausea and stomach pain? Likely diagnosis: food poisoning. Too much smoke and low gas mileage? The car may be due for an engine tune-up. Every professional has his or her own bag of heuristics, which are refined and expanded with experience. We are also taught many heuristics in school. The sum of the angles of a triangle is 180 degrees is one of the earliest and most widely used heuristics in geometry. It helps in the deduction of many clever things about a triangle, given specification of some of its sides and angles. Many of the heuristics we use in getting through an average day at home, work, or school are so ingrained in our education, culture, or just general awareness that we hardly notice the ways they make us smarter, helping us avoid past mistakes and make better judgments. In fact, in our everyday lives, much of what is feted as sterling "common sense" is actually a subconscious collection of heuristics interlinked and annotated for quick recall and application.

But heuristics are not eternal truths. Luger's comment on their potential fallibility is significant. Many a time a doctor's or car mechanic's diagnosis goes wrong (in spite of their most sincere efforts): nausea and stomach pain may not just be food poisoning, malodorous smoke and low gas mileage may be due to the demise of one or more engine cylinder, and the angles of a triangle will not add up to 180 degrees if the triangle is described on the surface of a sphere. Thus heuristics come with certain assumptions about scope and context, and one needs to remember these when using heuristics.

In spite of this fallibility, the state of heuristics indicates a discipline's maturity. Maier and Rechtin (2000) give a list of "heuristics for systems-level architecting" in their book, classifying each heuristic as *prescriptive* or *descriptive*. Culled from the literature and the authors' own research, almost all are very pithy and some quaintly aphoristic: "Success is defined by the beholder, not by the architect"; "one person's architecture is another person's detail"; "if you can't analyze it, don't build it"; and so on. Polya (1945) devotes more than three-quarters of his book to what he calls the "Short Dictionary of Heuristic," which contains sections such as "Can You Derive the Result Differently?," "Decomposing and Recombining," and "Have You Seen It Before?" Both works, set apart by half a century and different disciplines, share the commonality of purpose in compiling a set of useful heuristics for practitioners.

Heuristics closely relate to something of a more homely name: rules of thumb. In my area of undergraduate study, electrical engineering, we had Fleming's left and right hand rules, where the thumb *really* entered into the rules. In general, rules of thumb are quick and easy judgment aids (although the thinking that went into them might have been neither quick nor easy) that can be widely applied. In his *The Timeless Way of Building,* Alexander (1979) explains how design involves calling forth rules of thumb gathered through experience and practice. He goes on to add that "...each one of us, no matter how humble, or how elevated, has a vast fabric of rules of thumb, in our minds, which tell us what to do when it comes time to act."

Sets of time-tested heuristics or rules of thumb are still evolving for software engineering. Metrics can go a long way in enriching this body of common knowledge. The formulation of a metric encapsulates much reflection, awareness, and experience. Applying it in a given scenario lets us leverage the background wisdom without going through the motions again. A good metric goes much beyond being just a number; it becomes a heuristic for guiding software development through the "treacherous shoals" of changing user requirements, technological and business constraints, and ever-gnawing competition.

In this book, we will build some metrics and show how they can be applied. The thrust of the discussion will be toward distilling the scope and aptitude of the metrics into heuristics. The heuristics should be useful even without the scaffolding of metrics derivation.

But for any metric, heuristic, or rule of thumb to work for the better, one needs a closed-loop system, that is, a system with feedback.

2.3.6. Feedback

Feedback is one of the most fundamental techniques of engineering. Like all fundamental techniques, it goes beyond a discipline and spreads across life. Feedback is one of those tenets that seems to work because it is so intuitive and seems so intuitive because it works. In the simplest of terms, feedback is a mechanism for controlling an activity by regulating the input based on the output.

Feedback is nearly everywhere. We use it all the time, often without realizing it. Pressing on the accelerator increases the speed of a car: the visual perception of the car's speed is processed back to the foot, to modify the pressure and control the speed. If you are hungry after a hard day, you ingest food rapidly and in large servings, but nearing the level of satiety, the quantity and celerity of intake go down until you stop altogether. This happens as signals from the stomach go back to the brain, which controls the hand that feeds the mouth. Autopilot systems on aircraft monitor altitude and other parameters and feed them back to the system to generate required levels of thrust to maintain the plane on an even keel. As mentioned earlier, often the phrase "closed-loop system" is used to denote a system which has a feedback path from the output to the input. A comparator mechanism gauges the actual output vis-à-vis the desired output and adjusts the input accordingly. Success of a feedback mechanism hinges on a few key factors. We must be able to measure the input and output and have a clear notion of what the output needs to be. Feedback techniques are not yet sufficiently mature in enterprise software development. Metrics can play a crucial role in harnessing this classic engineering stratagem in software building.

But do software development processes allow for feedback loops? Not all do, but the iterative and incremental development model does.

2.3.7. Iterative and Incremental Development

Larman and Basili (2003), in their paper "Iterative and Incremental Development: A Brief History," highlight how the roots of iterative and incremental development (or IID, as the authors abbreviate it, true to software's acronymic culture) go far deeper and are older than the recent interest in "agile" methods. Among the most interesting insights, we learn how Royce's (1987) article titled "Managing the Development of Large Software Systems," widely considered to be the waterfall manifesto, in fact contains germs of iterative and incremental development. "If the computer program in question is being developed for the first time, arrange matters so that the version finally delivered to the customer is actually the *second* version insofar as critical design/operations areas are concerned" (italics added). How close in spirit this advice is to Brooks's (1995) credo — "Plan to throw one away; you will, anyhow" — which Raymond (2001), in his classic essay *The Cathedral and the Bazaar,* explains as "...you don't really understand the problem until after the first time you implement a solution....So if you want to get it right, be ready to start over *at least* once. Brooks (2000), in his keynote speech at the 1995 International Conference on Software Engineering, declared: "The waterfall model is wrong!" In his 2000 Turing lecture "The Design of Design," Brooks (2000) goes a step further and titles one of his slides "The Waterfall Model Is Dead Wrong"!

Instead of being too judgmental, I have found that it helps to regard both the waterfall and the iterative and incremental approaches to software development as being complementary in a subtle and useful manner. What goes on inside an iteration is often not very different from the waterfall tenets. The acts of analyzing, designing, building, and testing a software system *must* have an element of sequential linearity; one cannot analyze after testing (although testing before building, or at least thinking and talking about testing before building, is recommended in some circles). The most marked departure of the iterative and incremental worldview from the waterfall is the recognition of the inherently evolutionary nature of software. Gilb (1977), in his book *Software Metrics* (arguably the first book on software metrics and undoubtedly the first juxtaposition of "software" with "metrics," thus coining the phrase), was basically promoting iterative and incremental development when he talked about how complex systems have a better chance of success when implemented in "small steps," each step having a "clear measure of successful achievement as well as a 'retreat' possibility to a previous successful step upon failure." He also underlined the scope of receiving "feedback from the real world" and how this helps better allocation of resources and correction of errors. Retreat and feedback are the key concepts in iterative and incremental development.

As Campbell (1984) observed in his *Grammatical Man* — a book which brilliantly matches depth, width, and concision — evolution in the natural world, contrary to popular belief, is far from a unidirectional ascent from lower to higher forms of life. The path is replete with false starts, cul-de-sacs, peaks, and plateaus. An ineluctable feedback mechanism is continuously at play, moderating the journey through countless repeats and revisits toward deeper levels of perfection. The iterative and incremental model takes its lesson from these evolutionary trends.

Very interestingly, the co-evolution model (Brooks 2000) seeks to establish how the evolution of the problem space is influenced by the evolution of the solution space. Among the key benefits of the iterative and incremental model is that it allows for the inevitable changes in the problem domain and helps tune the solution domain to the latest realities of the problem.

Chapter 6, the first chapter in Part 2, is devoted to discussion of the dynamics of the iterative and incremental model in detail. The techniques presented in this book are all geared toward facilitating feedback and hence applicable when software is built iteratively and incrementally. Although iterative and incremental development is hard to understand and harder to apply (it takes more than one iteration to get used to, believe me!), it remains the most expedient software development philosophy. We will have many occasions to explore its innards in this book.

Iterative and incremental development as a process works so well for software even as it is absurd in other conventional engineering disciplines. The reasons lie in the peculiarities of software as an industrial artifact, some of which are described in Chapter 3. Information technology, or IT, is *ITerative,* and the industry has more or less awakened to this truth. Yet much confusion still lurks regarding the place of processes in the software sun. Why and where does software development need processes?

2.3.8. Process

A process is a set of predefined and coordinated activities prescribed to practitioners — in teams or individually — with the intention of fulfilling an objective. The second edition of *The Unified Modeling Language User Reference* defines a software development process simply "as the steps and guidelines by which to develop a system" (Rumbaugh et al. 2005). More specifically, a software development process has been called "the set of activities needed to transform a user's requirements into a software system" (Jacobson et al. 1999). Processes ensure consistent levels of quality and repeatability in any industrial production. Awaking to the need for processes in enterprise software production marks a milestone. It comes with the crucial recognition of software as a product of engineering, bound by the usual demands of reliability, consistency, safety, and usability that set apart good engineering from bad. It is good that "process" in software engineering has come to have overtones related to discipline, quality, and such salutary traits. References to "process-driven approaches" nowadays are often taken to mean ways of doing things that are not just ad hoc or instinctive but include time-tested techniques and the wisdom from past successes and failures. When process is mentioned in this book, we are talking about some standardized way of doing some software development activity.

Processes are great things. They allow for teams of practitioners with very different preparation and perception (or even political views!) to work together and produce consistent results. They allow for smart integration of technology and human skills toward the generation of superior software. But processes are not everything. There are certain areas — and in many of these lies much that is enchanting in software development — where processes cannot help and may also hinder. In the 2000 Turing Award Lecture, Brooks (2000) makes the compelling point that great designs come not from processes but from great designers. And where do great designers come from? Brooks says great designers need to be grown deliberately and managed imaginatively. He adds another sly and sapient slant: "We have to protect them [great designers] *fiercely.*" The next bullet reads: "From managers." And the next: "From managing." The message comes through loud and clear. The most reflective and thoughtful activities of software development need undistracted efforts of the mind. Processes cannot give us great ideas, but they can guide us as to how best to use a great idea or make the best of a not-so-great idea. Processes can help turn ideas into ubiquitous utility — so ubiquitous and so utilitarian that we no longer wonder about them, like the lightbulb, air travel, or even the Web. We make best use of processes when we are sensitive to both their strengths and limitations.

Practitioners in the enterprise software development business often love and hate processes at the same time. It is charming to see processes align a diverse set of individuals and technology toward a common goal. It is equally maddening to share the frustration and angst of going over the facile motions of process for the sake of process. I am increasingly led to believe that, just like antipatterns, there may be antiprocesses, sets of activities which never should have been *processized* to begin with. In general, metrics play an important role in identifying the facility or fatuity of processes.

Software engineering processes are sometimes prone to what I call the "unicorn effect"; it is easy to get very excited about great processes without ever getting to see one. This is a dangerous circumstance for enterprise software development. To ensure this does not happen, artifacts come in handy.

2.3.9. Artifacts

Kruchten (2004), in his book *The Rational Unified Process: An Introduction,* calls an artifact "a piece of information that is produced, modified or used by a process." An artifact usually manifests as a textual or pictorial record of the output of one or a set of related tasks mandated by a process. The word has an artistic ring to it; in fact, it derives from the Latin *arte* by skill (ablative of *art-*, *ars* skill) + *factum,* neuter of *factus,* past participle of *facere* to do (Merriam-Webster 2006). Artifacts are produced when the skill of extraneous (as human) agency is applied to environmental ingredients. The brilliant Altamira cave paintings (most memorably the charging bison) created by predecessors to modern man, whose drawing skills used the ingredients around them (the cave walls, the color pigments, maybe some flesh-and-blood inspiration bison), are certainly artifacts on one level. (The artifact product has far outlived the process which was used to arrive at it, and herein lies its triumph; processes are only remembered when something went wrong with them.) On another level, a piece of software design — boxes and lines scribbled on the back of an envelope or a sequence diagram with all annotations — is also an artifact. It creates a new way of thinking, gleaning new information from existing information such as user needs and technological and business constraints. Artifacts are easily confused with documents. All artifacts need to be documented if they are to be preserved for review and reuse, but artifacts are ultimately the thinking that goes behind the mere recording.

There are conflicting views on whether code qualifies as an artifact. In my opinion, it does. Code is essentially new information created from the synergy of all the factors affecting software development. In fact, code is by far the most flexible — in terms of both structure and function — artifact that the software development life cycle produces. The techniques described in this book will lead to the recording of new information such as metrics data or classification of entities; these are all artifacts.

2.4. THREADS AND BRAIDS

In the last section, we reflected on the major ideas of this book and saw how one leads to another. Some aspects of interplay of these ideas must already be clear. How this book tries to bring together the threads in a braid is discussed next.

As mentioned earlier, the harmony of different, even seemingly contrasting ideas has been illustrated to great effect in Hofstadter's book *Gödel, Escher, Bach: An Eternal Golden Braid.* Hofstadter (1979) says: "I realized that to me, Gödel and Escher and Bach were only shadows cast in different directions by some central solid essence. I tried to reconstruct the central object, and came up with this book." The book is a significant work and deals with issues deep and resonant. I borrow the construct of a braid to underline the intermingling of the ideas in this book.

Enterprise software systems are the field of our interest. We are not focusing on software that is built for instructional purposes (such as classroom projects), for highly specific scientific computing, or for mere pleasure. Some of our discussions may be pertinent to such types of software families, but they certainly are not our main concern. Enterprise software systems have *stakeholders* associated with them, usually several different groups. *Practitioners* are a special class of stakeholders; the practice of their profession involves building enterprise software systems and resolving the (often conflicting) stakeholders' demands from the system. We seek to establish how *metrics* can help practitioners do their job better; we take "metrics" to cover the whole gamut of measure, measurements, and metrics. The application and interpretation of metrics lead to more general and intuitive *heuristics* — rules of thumb which allow practitioners to make informed judgments as they go about enterprise software development. Metrics and heuristics facilitate *feedback* in the development process, a crucial factor in ensuring the solution stays aligned to the ever-evolving problem. The *iterative and incremental development* model has built-in feedback mechanisms which use inputs from the real world (user responses) to better tune the objective and course of development. Iterative and incremental development is a particular kind of *process,* a set of guidelines for the construction, delivery, and maintenance of software systems. *Artifacts* are outputs from processes; they embody the information that is produced, modified, or consumed by process activities. Some of the methods in this book call for a special way of arranging and interpreting information from the development activities; we also call such products artifacts.

This interplay of these ideas has strongly influenced the organization of the book (Figure 2.1) and the suggested reading plan in Chapter 1.

2.5. SUMMARY

This chapter reflected on the significant ideas permeating this book and their interactions. As we go deeper, we will discover more related concepts and other interesting ways how all of these play with one another. Some of these ideas are actually collections of ideas; they are grouped together so that they can be referred to easily later, to explain, refine, or dissect further.

We are now ready to get into the meat of our matter. Let us proceed to Part 1; the next chapter gives an overview of the place of metrics in software engineering.

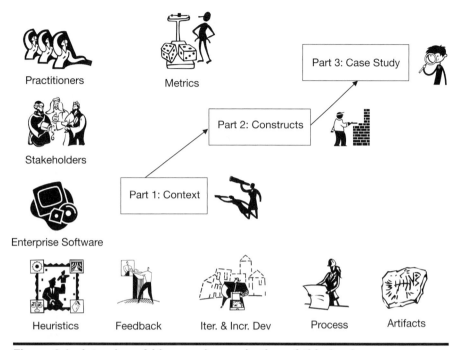

Figure 2.1. Interplay of ideas and organization of this book

REFERENCES

Alexander, C. (1979). *The Timeless Way of Building.* Oxford University Press.

Barabasi, A.-L. (2001). The Physics of the Web. http://physicsweb.org/articles/world/14/7/9.

Berners-Lee, T. (1999). *Weaving the Web: The Original Design and Ultimate Destiny of the World Wide Web by Its Inventor.* Harper San Francisco.

Brooks, F. P. (1995). *The Mythical Man-Month: Essays on Software Engineering, 20th Anniversary Edition.* Addison-Wesley.

Brooks, F. P. (2000). The Design of Design, A. M. Turing Award Lecture. http://www.siggraph.org/s2000/conference/turing/index.html.

Campbell, J. (1984). *Grammatical Man: Information, Entropy, Language and Life; The Story of the Modern Revolution in Human Thought.* Penguin Books.

Cornell, E. and Wieman, C. (1995). BEC home page. http://www.colorado.edu/physics/2000/bec/.

Fowler, M. (2003). *Patterns of Enterprise Application Architecture.* Addison-Wesley.

Gilb, T. (1977). *Software Metrics.* Winthrop Publishers.

Hofstadter, D. (1979). *Gödel, Escher, Bach: An Eternal Golden Braid.* Harper San Francisco.

IEEE (1990). IEEE Software Engineering Standards, Standard 610.12-1990, pp. 47–48. standards.ieee.org/software/.

Jacobson, I., Booch, G., and Rumbaugh, J. (1999). *The Unified Software Development Process.* Addison-Wesley.

Johnson, R. C. (2000). Time to Engineer DNA Computers. http://www.nature.com/embor/journal/v4/n1/full/embor719.html.

Kruchten, P. (2004). *The Rational Unified Process: An Introduction,* 3rd ed. Addison-Wesley.

Larman, C. and Basili, V. R. (2003). Iterative and incremental development: A brief history. *Computer,* 36(6):47–56.

Luger, G. F. (2004). *Artificial Intelligence: Structures and Strategies for Complex Problem Solving,* 5th ed. Addison-Wesley.

Maier, M. W. and Rechtin, E. (2000). *The Art of Systems Architecting,* 2nd ed. CRC Press.

Merriam-Webster (2006). *Merriam-Webster Online Dictionary.* http://www.m-w.com.

Parker, J. (2003). Computing with DNA. http://www.nature.com/embor/journal/v4/n1/full/embor719.html.

Polya, G. (1945). *How to Solve It: A New Aspect of Mathematical Method.* Princeton University Press.

Pressman, R. S. (2000). *Software Engineering: A Practitioner's Approach.* McGraw-Hill.

Raymond, E. S. (2001). *The Cathedral and the Bazaar: Musings on Linux and Open Source by an Accidental Revolutionary.* O'Reilly.

Royce, W. W. (1987). Managing the development of large software systems: Concepts and techniques. In *ICSE '87: Proceedings of the 9th International Conference on Software Engineering,* pp. 328–338. IEEE Computer Society Press.

Rumbaugh, J., Jacobson, I., and Booch, G. (2005). *The Unified Modeling Language User Reference,* 2nd ed. Addison-Wesley.

Turing, A. (1936). On Computable Numbers, with an Application to the Entscheidungsproblem. http://web.comlab.ox.ac.uk/oucl/research/areas/ieg/e-library/sources/tp2-ie.pdf.

PART 1.
CONTEXT

3

SOFTWARE ENGINEERING AND METRICS

3.1. OVERVIEW

This chapter covers the background material for the book. In the first two sections, software engineering is placed in the context of the other engineering disciplines and the saga of software metrics is briefly reviewed. We then segue into how there is a need for something more. The salient features of the approach in this book are described next, followed by concluding remarks.

Much of what is said in the first two sections has been discussed elsewhere, so there will be copious references. What is covered here is by no means a complete history of software metrics. To the best of my knowledge, such a seminal work is yet to be written. The software engineering community eagerly awaits the author who will take on the task.

3.2. THE SOFT AND HARD OF SOFTWARE ENGINEERING

When I decided to take a job as a software engineer after receiving a degree in electrical engineering, an acquaintance congratulated me upon graduation and added as a caveat: "But this is soft engineering." The gentleman was an engineer from the old school — the "hard" school, he called it. He said his first job was at a blast furnace, where temperatures ran into the thousands of degrees and tempers often followed suit. There seemed to be every symptom that something worthwhile was happening all the time. *"That* was fun. *Real* engineers do not sit at desks," he concluded, almost questioning the whole point of the software engineering profession. There is much confusion within the engineering disciplines as to why and how software engineering is called engineering. (Throughout the book, "conventional" or "other" engineering disciplines will sometimes be referred to vis-à-vis software engineering. Too much should not be read into this figure of speech; I fully accept that every engineering discipline, no matter how long it has been around, has much scope for exciting, unconventional, or even nonconventional breakthroughs.)

The term *software engineering* was probably used for the first time in public discourse at the 1968 NATO Software Engineering Conference held in Garmisch, Germany (Bauer et al. 1968). The literature is peppered with pithy and prosaic comments on how software engineering came to be. What was that magic moment when *writing* computer programs came to be viewed as *engineering* software? Some authors feel software engineering was born when software started to be used by people who did not necessarily write it. To others, when writing software became too involved for hardware engineers to fully attend to marks the birth of software engineering.

There are very many definitions of software engineering; almost every author who gets his or her say on the subject comes up with a new one. IEEE Standard 610.12 says software engineering is "(1) the application of a systematic, disciplined, quantifiable approach to the development, operation, and maintenance of software, that is, the application of engineering to software" and "(2) the study of approaches as in (1)." In the prologue (titled "Software Engineering Is a Verb") to Whitmire's (1997) *Object-Oriented Design Measurement,* software engineering is called a "slippery term." The author goes on to give a "working definition" of software engineering as "...the science and art of designing and building, with economy and elegance, software systems and applications so they can safely fill the uses to which they may be subjected." The author makes a notable distinction between *design* and *building* and introduces the key themes of economy and elegance. These are deeply engineering *attitudes*: the separation of design and implementation and the concern for achieving an end with the most optimal organization of the means — economy and sensitivity — or what Alexander (1979) calls "the quality without a name" and Whitmire has called "elegance."

Over the next few subsections, I briefly highlight how software fits and does not fit the standard engineering stereotypes. Similar discussions are widely covered in the literature; I only underscore areas which connect strongly with the material in the following chapters.

3.2.1. Software Engineering Is Not Supported by Laws of Software, at Least Not Yet

One of those rare statements which do not become cliché even after endless repetition is that software engineers have no laws to fall back on. Every other engineering discipline is underpinned by laws of physics or chemistry, which serve as scaffoldings upon which the engineers build their structures. Laws can be either codifications of phenomena of Nature, such as Newton's laws of motion, or insightful observations about the behavior of synthetic systems, such as Moore's law. They may even be a commentary on the quirks of human or organizational behavior, such as Parkinson's law. Software lacks these types of laws, most significantly the first type.

Laws often are not formulated through mere cogitation; large collections of empirical data play an important role in understanding and formalizing them. Similar efforts to collect data for software engineering projects have just begun: Booch (2006) has commenced work on a *Handbook of Software Architecture,* whose mission is "to fill this void in software engineering by codifying the architecture of a large collection of interesting software-intensive systems, presenting them in a manner that exposes their essential patterns and that permits comparisons across domains and architectural styles." On the handbook Web site, Booch quotes from Christopher Alexander's *The Nature of Order* in which he and his colleagues "made observations, looked to see what worked, studied it, tried to distill out the essentials, and wrote them down." With these efforts afoot, it may not be long before the first vestiges of software laws appear. But until then, we must remain mindful of the fact that software development does not have laws to constrain and guide it. And we must make the best of these circumstances.

3.2.2. Software vis-à-vis a Cheeseburger

DeMarco and Lister's (1987) classic *Peopleware* has a chapter titled "Make a Cheeseburger, Sell a Cheeseburger" and begins with the credo "development is inherently different from production." Using the *production* of a cheeseburger as a metaphor, the authors make powerful (and, as is the hallmark of this great book, seemingly playful) points about how making software is inherently different from assembly line production of any other engineering artifact. (A cheeseburger, in the way it is made and sold by fast-food chains, is indeed an engineering artifact!)

DeMarco and Lister's points of view remain fresh even twenty years later. Although making software is engineering, and the phrase *software factory* is sometimes bandied about without understanding its implications, software is developed and not produced. What is this great divide between production and development? Production, in the conventional engineering context, can be thought to be the repetitive application of well-established rules and techniques toward the manufacture of a clearly defined product. The act of production at its most sophisticated does not need human presence (humans may need to monitor or manage, though); robots can do it, as they extensively do now in car factories and the like. Software cannot be produced in the same way, as the rules and techniques are not yet well established. More importantly, however, the end product for software is seldom well defined up front. This is because people who want the software developed for them often do not know exactly what they want from the software. This overweening human element in software engineering makes it so different, so challenging, and so rewarding. Software engineers are not just *resources,* as they are often referred to by management; they are human individuals whose very human traits like powers of judgment, gut feelings, preferences, and prejudices strongly influence the software they are making. Over the past ten years, we have heard about how software soon will not be written anymore but rather composed "Lego-like" from off-the-shelf components, or even more chimerically, there will be software to write software. We are still far short of such *Star Trek* stuff. Without speculating if and when we will reach that, it is better now to focus on honing the most important ingredient of software making — people and their skills.

What makes me so enamored of software engineering is linked to a memory from an electrical engineering class in my sophomore year. A friend of mine made it a point to ask half a dozen sharp but sincere questions each class. Some of the professors encouraged it, while others got aggravated. One of them once said, pretty indulgently, "It is good you ask so many questions, but what we learn here in class are standard practices that have been in use half a century now. They are in use so long because they are so good; they are so good because they have withstood so many questions like yours. Save your questions for later, when you will do cutting-edge research." He emphasized "cutting," which to a bunch of budding electrical engineers seemed hopelessly afar. But for software engineers, the cutting edge is never that far; neither it is something one can get to only by doing research. Just because things have not had the chance to standardize as yet over half a century, there is scope for thinking new and making the new thoughts work.

3.2.3. The Plasticity of Software, or Why a Software Product Is Never Complete

A piece of software is never complete, in the sense a building or a car is. To modify a building or a car, often the easiest way is to make a new building or a new car. Software, on the other hand, always seems so tantalizingly close to a quick tweak which will make new and great things happen. This apparent attribute is what may be called the *plasticity* of software in the sense of "flexibility" (Maier and Rechtin 2000).

It is true; changing one line of code in a thousand lines can cause the behavior of a software system to change cataclysmically, for better or for worse. But how much should we use such a facility, for better or for worse? This is a big question. There is a tendency, driven by economics, lack of discipline, or just the spirit of adventure, to keep on changing code to make it do more and more different things. It works spectacularly for a while (Great! The patch is doing just what we wanted. That was easy, wasn't it?) and then fails just as spectacularly.

Code has to be worked on to make it better and worked on in a streamlined and disciplined way. The idea of *refactoring*, propounded and practiced by many and crystallized by Fowler (2006) in his book *Refactoring: Improving the Design of Existing Code* and subsequent work, is something essentially unique to software. It is absurd to try to think of something similar about a building or a bridge or a car. The very need for software to be refactored points to the fact that its design degenerates as it runs — another peculiarity of the software product. For other engineering products, wear and tear result in degradation of their physical condition, and better design can prevent, preempt, or postpone such decay. Design, for other engineering disciplines, is something born and bred on the drawing board, to be subsequently translated into making the product. For software, however, design is a whole new animal. In addition to the initial *intent* — which is obscured in no time by changing circumstances of use, software design has to budget for the countless tweaking the system will have to undergo over its lifetime.

Software is perhaps the only engineering artifact which is customarily applied for purposes widely different from the intents of its original design and expected to deliver in ever-new circumstances at original or heightened levels of performance. The absurdity of a family sedan doubling as a Mars rover is pretty obvious, but similar range of versatility is often demanded from software systems. The Y2K confusion in the last years of the last millennium showed how "legacy" software written decades earlier could still be in active service. Such software was successfully supporting vital business and other services way beyond the context and capacity envisaged when it was built.

Thus software design is a continuum rather than a one-off task, and software never stops being built. This sets engineering software apart from other engineering disciplines, and this difference is vital. A large proportion of practicing software engineers today were trained in other engineering disciplines. The perspective from conventional engineering is very useful for a software engineer. There have been countless occasions when I felt lucky to have learned electrical engineering, even as I was using none of the specific skills it taught me. But when practitioners trained in the other engineering disciplines engage in software building, they need to remain mindful of a significant cultural shift. Certain things can and are customarily done with software which are absolute no-nos in other engineering disciplines, and the favor is similarly returned.

Ultimately, software's plasticity is what makes creating it so much fun and more than a little challenging.

3.2.4. The Macro and the Micro States

Although engineering usually deals with the macro state of things, conventional engineering disciplines also have a very good understanding of the micro states that contribute toward a macro state. Take, for example, the case of Joule heating, which is the phenomenon of temperature increase of a conductor due to the resistance it offers to the passage of electric current through it. Many mechanical and electrical engineering products and processes make use of this occurrence. The use is helped by the fact that the phenomenon can be explained at the molecular level, that is, from the micro point of view.

Similar connections between the macro and the micro levels in software are not yet as widely or deeply understood. In an insightful little book, charmingly titled *Mother Nature's Two Laws: Ringmasters for Circus Earth,* Kirwan (2000) gives an example which may be taken to show how the macro and micro states do not readily correspond in the software world. He talks about activating a computer, launching a word-processing program, and on the blank screen typing the word "entropy" and then deleting it. Before the word was typed and after it is deleted, the screen is seen to be blank, and evidently the macro states are the same. But are the micro states contributing to the same macro state before and after the word was typed and deleted the same? Hardly so. Simply clicking "undo edit" or "control-Z" may bring "entropy" back on the screen, so the information was somewhere in what is loosely called the computer's memory even when it was not on the screen. One of the conclusions the author draws from the observation is: "In principle, all macrostates are observable or distinguishable; that is, each can be assigned a unique name. Microstates may either be distinguishable or indistinguishable."

Software engineers still have a shallow understanding of the plethora of micro states that go into the making of a macro state of a working program. We know for sure that everything is ultimately stored and transported via 0s and 1s, but what goes on between that primal level and the various facilities offered by the high-level programming languages seems an unfathomable maze.

I am reminded of an occasion when a software engineer friend of mine was trying to placate a customer manager who complained that the system was too "slow." After trying out several of what he called explanations, and the manager called excuses, my friend pulled out an ace: "After all, it finally depends on the internal bus speed." The manager said, "Oh! Does it?" and left it at that. The micro state seemed too strong and too subtle to delve into deeper.

A far from even reasonably complete understanding about the macro and micro states sets software apart from the other engineering disciplines in a deep, and potentially insidious, way.

3.2.5. Software Engineering and Communication, or Why Software Engineers Need to Listen

In *The Psychology of Computer Programming,* published in 1971 and one of those rare books which, like wine, become better as they age, Weinberg (1971) lays down the book's purpose as "to trigger the beginning of a new field of study: computer programming as a human activity, or, in short, the psychology of computer programming." In the three and a half decades since these visionary words were written, computer programming has graduated to software engineering, yet the human aspects of building software systems remain little understood (or worse, misunderstood) and ignored.

I feel the central theme of this "human activity" viewpoint is communication. In corporate circles, communication is often confused with public relations or even marketing. For a software engineer, communication plays a deeper and more fundamental role. When a building is commissioned, for office, hospital, school, residential, or any other purpose, the users have a clear idea of what the finished product needs to be, how they will use it, and even how they should not use it. This subliminal understanding comes from the fact that human civilization has been using buildings for centuries, if not millennia. Thus the *cognitive gap* between what users want engineered and what can be engineered for them is manageably narrow. However, it has been only a few decades — in fact just one, if the coming of the Web is taken as the watershed — that people who cannot build software themselves have been using software in earnest, so not knowing what they want is a common characteristic of the common software consumer. Accordingly, a software engineer's first task is to listen; listen to hear what is being said, but additionally, a la the solitary reaper, to hear what is not being said. Without honing this skill consciously, no software engineer can be good at his or her job. The real challenge of software specifications lies not in coming up with full (and fool-) proof notations and artifacts, or verifying them automatically — although these are important tasks.

The major obstacle lies in deciphering the user's real needs from the twaddle of wishes, nice-to-have features, and fantasies. Only after adequate separation of signal from noise can we get to a point where specifications can be put to paper. No software engineering curriculum to my knowledge teaches this kind of communication skill, and this is the kind of skill which is better learned than taught. No other engineering discipline needs this degree of human interaction, and software engineering has a place of its own in this respect.

3.2.6. We Cannot Build Software the Way We Build Buildings

In the 2000 Turing Lecture titled "The Design of Design" (seldom is so much wisdom concentrated in so few slides), Brooks (2000) brought to light how building buildings differs from building software. Customers pay for a design phase, have the design approved, and contract its implementation, or a builder pays for the design phase and sells its implementations. According to Brooks, software design has to let go of the "spurious" assumption that "function and performance are what matters about software." He goes on to mention other attributes that matter: reliability, changeability, structure, and testability. Brooks advocates the co-evolution perspective: a conjoint evolution of the problem and solution spaces, the former coming more to light as the latter is progressively explored. This hardly conforms to the design paradigm of, say, civil engineering as discussed in Petroski's (1992) *To Engineer Is Human*.

What Brooks declares so strongly has been felt as strongly by many whose bread and butter is software building. Software development calls for a very fresh outlook, like no other engineering discipline of the past. The experience of studying and practicing other engineering disciplines can and does help software engineers, but learning from the other fields has to be carefully predicated to make it come in handy for software.

3.2.7. The Open-Source Paradigm of Software Building

The whole new way with software is never as spectacularly apparent as in the realm loosely and sometimes confusingly referred to as the "open-source" world. Making the source code "open," that is, distributing it for free and encouraging people to use it for their own ends (thereby allowing limitless revision, modification, and enhancement), is an important if not central characteristic of open-source development. But it goes far deeper than that. Open-source development and its resounding successes (Emacs editor, Linux operating system, Eclipse environment, you name it) have been studied and discussed at length. Perhaps among the earliest, and still the most engaging, discourse can be found in Raymond's (2001) *The Cathedral and the Bazaar: Musings on Linux and Open Source by an Accidental Revolutionary.* Raymond's book is a must-read for anyone delving into the dynamics of software building in the large. The author makes many provocative points, perhaps none as maverick as highlighting that sustained successes of open-source development models have made us "…entitled to wonder what, if anything, the tremendous overhead of conventionally managed [software] development is actually buying us."

The open-source development model is something essentially unique to software. It is impossible for a bridge to be built the way Linux was built, by a plethora of "hackers" (a term whose negative slant Raymond categorically dispels) located far apart, joined only through the Internet and by a nameless passion. Raymond has analyzed at depth what ultimately drives the hackers to contribute to an ever-improving spiral of shared development. In addition to the obvious chimera, open-source development has also proved to be a great practical mechanism to harness the best resources for a project, without geographical or other constraints. That software — durable, reliable, and usable — can be built by teams widely asunder in everything other than a common purpose puts software in a category of its own compared to the other engineering disciplines.

In view of all of software's quirks described above, metrics assume a special significance in software engineering. Metrics in software are used not merely to measure, but also to guide. Software metrics cannot, at least not yet, measure with the same surety as the ohm or the newton. What they can do is let practitioners reuse some of the thought and wisdom others have gained in understanding a situation. Reviewing metrics efforts in software engineering over the past decades gives us a peek into the earlier quests for the Holy Grail — software that is easier to build, maintain, and use. Many of these have become dated due to newer ideas and more advanced technology, but their trail remains instructive. In the next section, we follow this trail.

3.3. SOFTWARE METRICS: A QUICK RECCE

The study of software metrics has come a long way, yet it has a long way to go. Software engineering as a discipline is grappling with deepening complexity; more illuminating metrics are being called upon to aid monitoring, feedback, and decision making. In this chapter, we survey the study — and, to some extent, practice — of software metrics. Table 3.1 summarizes the major trends in software metrics research by decade and highlights the leading works con-

Table 3.1. Software metrics trends

Decade	Major theme
1970s	***Efforts to formulate "laws" of software and complexity measures*** ■ Belady and Lehman (1976, 1979) scrutinize the behavior of large systems and come up with their First, Second, and Third Laws of Program Evolution Dynamics ■ McCabe (1976) introduces the cyclomatic complexity metric ■ Halstead's (1977) book *Elements of Software Science* brings in new vistas in the study of structure and behavior of software systems
1980s	***Building an enterprise-wide metrics culture*** ■ Conte et al. (1986) present an extensive study of how metrics are used toward productivity, effort estimation, and defect detection ■ Grady and Caswell (1987) report their endeavors in establishing a company-wide metrics program ■ DeMarco and Lister's (1987) book *Peopleware* argues strongly in favor of using metrics to enhance organizational productivity
1990s	***Object-oriented measures and quality concerns*** ■ Lorenz and Kidd (1994) present a set of metrics for the design of object-oriented systems ■ Chidamber and Kemerer (1991, 1994) propose the CK suite of object-oriented metrics ■ Whitmire's (1997) *Object-Oriented Design Measurement* builds a rigorous theoretical foundation for object-oriented measurements
2000s	***Measuring across the spectrum: product, people, process, project*** ■ Lanza (2001) introduces the evolution matrix to understand software evolution ■ COCOMO II, building on earlier COCOMO, is proposed as a model for estimating cost, effort, and schedule (CSE 2002) ■ van Solingen (2004) advocates measuring the return on investment of software process improvement

Note: Only some of the important works are cited. This is *not* an exhaustive list.

tributing to each trend. This classification is not exhaustive; the details are discussed in the following sections.

3.3.1. Initial Ideas

Any discussion of software metrics must begin with due deference to the first and arguably still the most *visible* of all software measures, *lines of code* (LOC), or its inflated cousin, *kilo lines of code* (KLOC). LOC is so primal that no definite source can be cited as its origin. It seems natural that counting lines of program instruction was the very first software metric. Lines of program instruction, after all, is the closest software gets to tangibility. LOC or KLOC gives software "size" in a very blunt sense of the term. Counting the number of stones in the Pyramids of Giza will give an idea of the monuments' size, but to anyone familiar with the brilliance and complexity of the Pyramids, the vacuity of such an idea will be apparent. Strangely, and somewhat sadly, to this day many measures of software are sought to be normalized by somehow bringing in the LOC angle. LOC was a helpful metric when software systems were less complex and understanding of the dynamics of working software was far shallower. In all but trivial systems of the present, there is almost nothing insightful LOC can measure. Misgivings about LOC abound in the current literature. As an example, Armour (2004) cautions against "counting" LOC and highlights how it is now high time the so-called estimation of system size through LOC gave way to more mature quests for measuring knowledge content.

One of the reasons why software development is so less amenable to precise measurements is the absence of physical laws that underpin other sciences and engineering disciplines (see Section 3.2.1). As Humphrey (2005) explains so succinctly: "Physicists and engineers make approximations to simplify their work. These approximations are based on known physical laws and verified engineering principles. The software engineer has no Kirchoff's law or Ohm's law and no grand concepts like Newtonian mechanics or the theory of relativity."

Ironically, it was the very quest for laws of software that started initial explorations in software measurement. Belady and Lehman (1976, 1979) scrutinized the behavior of large systems and came up with their First, Second, and Third Laws of Program Evolution Dynamics, which may be paraphrased as:

1. **Law of continual change** — A system is modified and used until it makes more business sense to retire it and commission a new system.
2. **Law of increasing entropy** — The structure of a system degenerates over time (that is, its entropy increases) unless effort is given to contain or reverse this trend.
3. **Law of statistically smooth growth** — "Growth trend measures" of system parameters may seem stochastic in local scope, but statistically, they exhibit clear long-range trends.

It speaks to the credit of these laws that three decades after their conception, the ideas appear so intuitive. The authors backed up their assertions with empirical data and introduced techniques for understanding and documenting the behaviors of large systems.

In a paper evocatively titled "Metrics and Laws of Software Evolution: The Nineties View," Lehman et al. (1997) review their earlier notions twenty years later. Using results from case studies, the authors conclude: "…The new analysis supports, or better does not contradict, the laws of software evolution, suggesting that the 1970s approach to metric analysis of software evolution is still relevant today."

McCabe's (1976) *cyclomatic complexity* is one of the most widely referenced (and strongly contended) quantitative notions of software complexity. It seeks to measure how difficult testing for a particular module is likely to be; empirical studies have also established correlations between the McCabe metric and the number of errors in source code. (In Chapter 10, the *Exception Estimation Score* is introduced on a related idea, but with a very different treatment.) The derivation of cyclomatic complexity is based on graph theory and considers factors like the number of independent paths through code. Using real-life project data, McCabe concluded that a value of 10 for cyclomatic complexity serves as an upper limit for module size. McCabe has given a more recent perspective on software complexity in a paper in *Crosstalk* (McCabe and Watson 1994).

Arguably, the first book devoted entirely to software engineering metrics is Gilb's (1977) *Software Metrics.* The author, quite aware of his pioneering position, says in the preface: "...I have had few examples to build on, and felt very alone during the preparation of the text." As the first attempt to structure a nascent discipline, the book treats the subject with maturity, even touching upon areas such as "motivational" metrics for human communication and automating software measurement. It ends with reflections on measuring abstract notions such as information, data, evolution, and stability. The author also provides code snippets and examples to corroborate his points. In subsequent years, Gilb has gone on to become a metrics guru, propounding many interesting ideas.

Halstead's (1977) book *Elements of Software Science* introduced new vistas in the study of structure and behavior of software systems. The book highlights attributes such as *program length* (N), *program volume* (V), relations between operators and operands, and, very interestingly, a quantification of "Intelligence Content." Taking n_1, n_2, N_1, and N_2 to respectively denote the number of distinct operators, number of distinct operands, total number of operator occurrences, and total number of operand occurrences in a program, Halstead shows that

$$N = n_1 \log_2 n_2 + n_2 \log_2 n_2$$

and

$$V = N \log_2 (n_1 + n_2)$$

According to Halstead, program volume varies with programming language and indicates the volume of information in bits needed to describe a program.

The work illustrates that theoretically a minimum volume must exist for a particular algorithm; volume ratio is defined as the ratio of the most compact form of a program to the volume of the actual program. The rigor of this work's mathematical treatment is notable, and some of the ideas have remained fresh. However, consistent with the contemporary view of software systems being merely computer programs, the author's treatment is overly algorithmic at times. Thus some of the results have become dated in the light of more recent challenges in concurrency, data volume, performance demands, usability criteria, etc. that enterprise software systems face.

Cavano and McCall (1978) can be credited with the first organized quest for a software quality metric. They identify quality dimensions as *product operations, product revision,* and *product transition* and factors within these dimensions as correctness, reliability, efficiency, integrity, usability, maintainability, and testability. The major contribution of this work is the framework, though rudimentary, that is introduced for measuring software quality. Later in this book, in Chapter 10, the idea of *testing dimensions* is introduced along similar lines.

Albrecht (1979) proposed a function-oriented metric which has gained wide currency: the *function point.* Function points are computed using experimental relationships between the direct measures of the software's information domain and estimation of its complexity on a weighted scale. The information domain values are based on the following criteria: number of user inputs, number of user outputs, number of user inquiries, number of files, and number of external interfaces. Once they are computed, function points are used in a manner similar to LOC to normalize measures for software productivity, quality, and other attributes such as errors per function point, defects per function point, etc. *Feature points*, an extension of the function point idea, were suggested by Jones (1991). This is a superset of the function point measure, and it seeks to expand the former's domain of applicability from business information system applications to general software engineering systems. In addition to the information domain values of function points, feature point identifies a new software characteristic — *algorithms.* Jones defines this as "a bounded computational problem that is included within a specific computer program." The main benefit of the function- and feature-point-based approaches is highlighted as their programming language independence.

3.3.2. Deeper Quests

Somewhat similar to the overall intent of the function point metric, the *bang* metric developed by DeMarco (1982) "is an implementation independent indication of system size." Calculating the bang metric involves examining a set of *primitives* from the analysis model — atomic elements of analysis that cannot be broken down further. Following are some of the primitives that are counted: functional primitives, data elements, objects, relationships, states, transitions, etc. DeMarco asserts that most software can be differentiated into the types *function strong* or *data strong* depending on the ratio of the primitives, relationships, and functional primitives. Separate algorithms are given for calculating the bang metric for these two types of applications. After calculation, a history of completed projects can be used to associate it with time and effort.

Conte et al. (1986) present an extensive study of the state-of-the-art of software metrics in the mid-1980s. Given when it was written, the introductory parts expectedly cover arguments and counterarguments for regarding software as engineering vis-à-vis science. The only development methodology considered is the waterfall model, and the authors base their metrics view on the *physical* attributes of code such as size and volume. The book also introduces some models for productivity, effort estimation, and defect detection.

Grady and Caswell (1987) report their endeavors to establish a company-wide metrics program at Hewlett-Packard in the 1980s. The book underscores many of the challenges large organizations face in producing industrial software and how a metrics culture can help deliver better solutions. Additionally, this works is often cited as the first exposition of the FURPS approach to classifying requirements, which is now a de facto industry standard. Some extensions to this idea through a metrics-based technique are given by Datta (2005).

DeMarco and Lister's (1987) *Peopleware* is the fount of much lasting wisdom of the software trade. The first chapter's title is something of a shibboleth: "Somewhere Today, A Project Is Failing." *Peopleware* unravels the chemistry of diverse factors — technological, social, political, and interpersonal — that go into the making of successful software. The authors come up with many schemes to measure various dimensions of the development process. Though often lacking in rigor, these measures are intuitive and easy to use. The *Environmental Factor* or *E-Factor* is a good example. In discussing the effect of environmental factors on the quality of developer effort, the E-Factor is defined as a ratio of "uninterrupted hours" to "body-present hours." Empirical data cited by the authors show large variation of E-Factor values from site to site within the same organization, and higher values closely correspond to instances of higher personnel productivity. Twenty years later, *Peopleware* remains a software engineering classic.

3.3.3. Newer Concerns

Baker et al. (1990), calling themselves the "Grubstake Group," present a serious view of the state of software measurements. The authors are convinced of the need to create an environment for software measures, which can only be done within a formal framework for software measurement, and one which is appreciated by all stakeholders. The paper applies notions of measurement theory to software metrics, stressing the need to identify and define among other things "attributes of software products and processes, formal models or abstractions which capture the attributes, important relationships and orderings which exist between the objects (being modeled) and which are determined by the attributes of the models." The authors highlight the role of sound validation schemes in the reliability of a software measure. In sum, the paper establishes that software metrics should and can be developed within a measurement theory framework.

Card and Glass (1990) defined three software design complexity measures: *structural complexity, data complexity,* and *design complexity.* The structural and design complexity measures use the *fan-out* idea to indicate the number of modules immediately subordinate to a module, that is, which are directly invoked by the module. System complexity is defined as the sum of the structural and data complexities. The authors conjecture that as each of these complexities increases, overall architectural complexity of the system also increases, leading to heightened integration and testing efforts.

Similar to Grady et al.'s report on initiating a metrics program at their organization discussed earlier, Daskalantonakis (1992) recounted the experience of implementing software measurement initiatives at Motorola. Based on the practical issues faced during implementation, the author concludes that metrics can expose areas where improvement is needed. Whether or not actual improvement comes about depends entirely on the actions taken on the results of analyzing metrics data. This paper highlights the important fact that metrics are only the means to an end; the ultimate goal of improvement comes through measurement, analysis, and feedback.

Based on his experience introducing metrics in a large organization, Grady (1992) points to the twin benefits of using metrics: expedient project management and process improvement. He first takes up the tactical application of software metrics in project management and follows it up with the strategic aspects in process improvement. The book gives rare insight into the human issues of applying metrics in a chapter titled "Software Metrics Etiquette," which has a number of enduring messages, most notably: metrics are not meant to measure individuals. Lack of understanding of this credo has led, and still leads, to the failure of many metrics initiatives. Some related issues and the politics of metrics are discussed in Chapter 5.

Layout appropriateness is a metric proposed by Sears (1993) for the design of human-computer interfaces. The metric seeks to facilitate an optimal layout of graphical user interface (GUI) components that is most suitable for the user to interact with the underlying software. Sears's work stands out as one of the few metrics to explore human-computer interfaces.

Davis et al. (1993) suggest a set of metrics for gauging the quality of the analysis model, based on corresponding requirement specifications: *completeness, correctness, understandability, verifiability, internal and external consistency, achievability, concision, traceability, modifiability, precision,* and *reusability.* Many of these attributes are usually seen as deeply qualitative. However, the authors establish quantitative metrics for each. As an example, specificity (that is, lack of ambiguity) is defined as the ratio of the number of requirements for which all reviewers had identical interpretation to the total number of requirements.

Summarizing his experience with implementing metrics programs in a large organization, Grady (1994) puts forward a set of tenets in his article "Successfully Applying Software Metrics." He highlights four main areas of focus which contribute substantially to the outcome of the overall metrics effort: project estimation and progress monitoring, evaluation of work products, process improvement through failure analysis, and experimental validation of best practices. In conclusion, Grady recommends project managers involved in a metrics initiative: define success goals early and monitor progress toward them, decide timing of product release based on defect data trends, and use complexity measures to facilitate design decisions.

Paulish and Carleton (1994) report results of measuring software process improvement initiatives in Siemens software development organizations. The authors' recommendations include: using the Capability Maturity Model, initiating software process improvement programs, implementing a small set of process improvement methods assiduously, and attending to the implementation of the method as closely as the method itself.

Lorenz and Kidd (1994) present a set of metrics for the design of object-oriented systems as well as projects that develop such systems. Building up from fundamental ideas like inheritance and class size, the authors introduce metrics to better understand and control the development process. A selection of the metrics includes *class size, number of operations overridden by a subclass, number of operations added by a subclass,* and *specialization index.* Some metrics are backed up by empirical results from projects implemented in languages such as Smalltalk and C++.

One of the most widely referenced sets of object-oriented metrics was put forward by Chidamber and Kemerer (1991, 1994) in two related papers. The set has come to be called the *CK metrics suite* and consists of the six class-based design metrics with explanatory names: *weighted methods per class, depth of inheritance tree, number of children, coupling between object classes, response for a class,* and *lack of cohesion in methods.* In the latter paper, the authors provide analytical evaluation of all the metrics and claim that "this set of six metrics is presented as the first empirically validated proposal for formal metrics for OOD." The paper also mentions several applications of these metrics in the development of industrial software.

Weller (1994) tackles the practical and contentious issue of using metrics to manage software projects. Three levels of project management are identified, highlighting how metrics can help each of them. The author concludes that defect data should be used as a key element to improve project planning. However, he acknowledges the biggest bottleneck of the approach to be the reluctance of developers to share defect data with management.

Fenton (1994), in his paper "Software Measurement: A Necessary Scientific Basis," argues strongly in favor of adhering to fundamental measurement theory principles in software metrics. He also asserts that "...the search for general software complexity measures is doomed to failure" and backs up his claim with detailed analysis. The paper reviews the tenets of measurement theory that are closely allied to software measurement and suggests a "Unifying Framework for Software Measurement." Fenton stresses the need to validate software measures and mentions that, in his observation, the most promising formulations of software metrics have been grounded in measurement theory.

Studies on software metrics usually tend to neglect postdelivery woes. Whatever happens in the loosely labeled realm of "maintenance" is seldom subjected to systematic scrutiny. A notable exception is the IEEE-suggested *software maturity index* (SMI) (IEEE 1994) that reflects on the level of stability of a software product as it is maintained and modified through continual postproduction releases. Denoting the number of modules in the current release, the number of modules in the current release that have been changed, the number of modules in the current release that have been added, and the number of modules from the preceding release that were deleted in the current release as, respectively, M_T, F_c, F_a, and F_d, the formula is given as:

$$SMI = [M_T - (F_a + F_c + F_d)]/M_T$$

As SMI approaches 1.0, the product begins to stabilize. Although maintenance issues can arise independent of the modules added or modified (lack of user awareness, environmental failures, etc.), the SMI is helpful for quantifying postdelivery scenarios of enterprise software systems.

Binder (1994) underscores the importance of metrics in object-oriented testing. Software testing, due to its easily quantifiable inputs (effort in person-hours, number of units being tested, etc.) and outputs (number of defects, defects per unit, etc.), is seen as the development activity easiest to measure.

More on this can be found in Chapter 10 in Part 2 and Chapter 16 and Part 3.

Cohesion and coupling describe some important characteristics of components and their interaction. In a way, they are the *yin* and *yang* of software design, contrary yet complementary forces that influence component structure and collaboration. Bieman and Ott (1994) studied cohesion of software components in great detail. They present a set of metrics, defined in terms of the notions of *data slice, data tokens, glue tokens, superglue tokens,* and *stickiness.* The authors develop metrics for *strong functional cohesion, weak functional cohesion,* and *adhesiveness* (the relative measure to which glue tokens bind data slices together). All of the cohesion measures have values between 0 and 1. Dhama (1995) proposed a metric for module coupling subsuming data and control flow coupling, global coupling, and environmental coupling. The module coupling indicator makes use of some proportionality constants whose values depend on experimental verification.

Basili et al. (1994) adapted the Goal Question Metric approach to software development. According to the authors, an organization "...must first specify the goals for itself and its projects, then it must trace those goals to the data that are intended to define those goals operationally, and finally provide a framework for interpreting the data with respect to the stated goals." This model has three levels: conceptual level (goal), operational level (question), and quantitative level (metric). In the general context of software quality, this approach suggests a mechanism for defining and measuring operational systems.

Churcher and Shepperd (1995) make an interesting point regarding the preoccupation with *class* as the main entity in object-oriented measurements. Citing Wilde et al. (1993), they observe that methods are small in terms of number of instructions and logical complexity, which in turn suggests that "...connectivity structure of a system may be more important than the context of individual modules." On a similar note, in Chapter 8 it is argued that software design can be viewed as components and their collaborations. Related to the conclusions of Churcher and Shepperd and Wilde et al., the work of Lorenz and Kidd (1994) defines three simple metrics that analyze the characteristics for methods: *average operation size, operation complexity,* and *average number of parameters per operation.*

Berard (1995) examines the special place object-oriented metrics have in the study of software metrics. He identifies five points that set apart object-oriented metrics as localization, encapsulation, information hiding, inheritance, and object abstraction techniques. In the introductory part of the article, the author asserts that software engineering metrics are seldom useful in isolation; "...for a particular process, product, or person, 3 to 5 well-chosen metrics seems to be a practical upper limit, that is, additional metrics (above 5) do not usually provide a significant return on investment." This point is elaborated on in Section 4.3.2.

Humphrey's *Personal Software Process* (PSP) (Humphrey 2005) and *Team Software Process* (TSP) (Humphrey 2006) are methodologies for enhancing productivity of practitioners and teams. In a paper titled "Using a Defined and Measured Personal Software Process," Humphrey (1996) demonstrates how measurements can assist in the enhancement of individual skills and expertise. A cornerstone of Humphrey's techniques is in continual monitoring of the development process.

Garmus and Herron (1996) introduce functional techniques to measure software processes. Their approach is based primarily on function point analysis, which is customized toward process measurement. The chapter on the success stories in applying these methods certainly adds weight to the arguments.

Whitmire's (1997) *Object-Oriented Design Measurement* is a seminal work in the study of object-oriented metrics. The author is rigorous in his treatment: putting measurement into context, building up the theoretical foundations, and deriving metrics to capture design characteristics. Whitmire proposes metrics for *size, complexity, coupling, sufficiency, completeness, cohesion, primitiveness, similarity,* and *volatility*. Within each area, motivations and origins, empirical views, formal properties, empirical relational structures, and application areas are discussed. Whitmire gives original perspective on many aspects of software measurements. The most important contribution of the book is establishing a sound mathematical framework for understanding and measuring software design. However, practitioners are stretched thin by production deadlines typical of enterprise software projects. They hardly have the latitude to master the theory needed to fully understand and apply Whitmire's constructs.

Harrison et al. (1998) reviewed a set of object-oriented metrics referred to as the *MOOD Metrics Set* (Abreu 1995). It includes *method inheritance factor, coupling factor,* and *polymorphism factor*. The reviewers examine these metrics in light of certain criteria (information hiding, inheritance, coupling, and dynamic binding) and conclude that the six MOOD metrics can be shown to be valid measures.

In a keynote address titled "OO Software Process Improvement with Metrics," Henderson-Sellers (1999) underlines vital links between product and process metrics. He also explores the interconnections of measurement and estimation and outlines his vision for a software quality program. This work will be referred to again in Section 4.3.11.

Wiegers (1999), in an article titled "A Software Metrics Primer," gives a list of "appropriate metrics" for three categories of software engineering practitioners: individual developers, project teams, and development organization. For the first, second, and third categories respectively, some of the suggested metrics are "work effort distribution, estimated vs. actual task duration and effort…"; "product size, work effort distribution, requirements status (number approved, implemented, and verified)…"; and "released defect levels, product development cycle time, schedule and effort estimating accuracy…." Though far from exhaustive, this list provides a starting point for metrics orientation. Wiegers also gives several tips for succeeding with metrics: start small, explain why, share the data, define data items and procedures, and understand trends.

3.3.4. Evolving Odyssey

Demeyer et al. (2000) propose a set of heuristics to detect refactorings by "…applying lightweight, object-oriented metrics to successive versions of a software system." Relations between metrics and heuristics and the facilities of building software over successive versions (that is, iterative and incremental development) were discussed in detail in Chapter 2. Demeyer et al. make certain assumptions, such as decrease in method size is taken to be a symptom of method split, change in class size indicates shift of functionality to sibling classes, etc. (In Section 4.3.3, the role of assumptions in metrics is examined.) While these assumptions can be contended (for example, a method may shrink in size due to the introduction of a smarter algorithm, not necessarily indicative of method split), the authors show important correlations between refactoring and design drift and how metrics can aid in identifying and understanding them.

Pressman (2000) treats the discipline of software metrics deeply in his wide-ranging book *Software Engineering: A Practitioner's Approach*, the standard text for many graduate courses. Pressman makes a distinction between the so-called *technical* metrics which seek to capture the progression and behavior of the software product vis-à-vis the metrics relevant for project management and process compliance. The book also devotes an entire chapter to metrics related to object-oriented systems.

Sotirovski (2001) points out the pitfalls of iterative software development: "If the iterations are too small, iterating itself could consume more energy than designing the system. If too large, we might invest too much energy before finding out that the chosen direction is flawed." To tackle this, the author highlights the role of heuristics in iteration planning and monitoring. As discussed in Section 2.3.5, wisdom from metrics is best encapsulated in heuristics, and in the absence of physical laws to fall back on, heuristics are our best bet to better enterprise software.

Lanza (2001) takes an unconventional approach toward a metrics-based understanding of software evolution. The author proposes the *evolution matrix* to describe the evolution of classes in a system: its columns show versions of the software and rows represent different versions of the same class. Classes are categorized into groups, some with stellar names: *pulsar, supernova, white dwarf, red giant, stagnant, dayfly, and persistent.* Based on case study data, Lanza delineates phases in a system's evolution characterized by specific categories of classes.

Understanding the effects of change on enterprise software systems remains an important concern of software engineering. It is interesting to note how Kabaili et al. (2001) have tried to interpret cohesion as a changeability indicator for object-oriented systems. The authors seek to establish a correlation between cohesion and changeability. The paper concludes that coupling vis-à-vis cohesion appears to be a better changeability indicator. This study shows how design characteristics may reveal more than they are initially intended to.

Mens and Demeyer (2001), in their paper "Future Trends in Software Evolution Metrics," underscore the relevance of predictive analysis and retrospective analysis in studying software evolution. They cite some of the promising fields of future metrics research as: coupling or cohesion metrics, scalability issues, empirical validation and realistic case studies, long-term evolution, detecting and understanding different types of evolution, data gathering, measuring software quality, process issues, and language independence.

Ramil and Lehman (2001) study the relevance of applying measurements to long-term software evolution processes and their products. An example using empirical data from the *Feedback, Evolution, and Software Technology* (FEAST) program is presented. The example illustrates the use of a sequential statistical test on a suite of eight evolution activity metrics. The authors underscore the need for *precise* definition of metrics, as small differences in defining can lead to inordinately large divergence in the measured values.

Rifkin (2001) gives a perspective on why software metrics are so difficult to put into practice, given the business needs enterprise software has to fulfill first. Four different software development domains are reviewed and their attitudes toward measurements compared: Wall Street brokerage house, civilian government agency, computer services contractor, and the nonprofit world. The author advocates a *measurement strategy* suited to each type of organization and concludes that "a whole new set of measures" has to be devised "for all those customer-intimate and product-innovative organizations that have avoided measurement thus far."

Fergus, in his book *How to Run Successful Projects III: The Silver Bullet* (O'Connell 2001), the title of which evidently alludes to Brooks's (1995) classic "no silver bullet" essay, discusses how measurement techniques can make a great difference in the outcome of projects. His *probability of success indicator* metric is especially insightful.

Measurement initiatives in a software organization usually focus on the concrete: LOC, developer productivity, etc. Buglione and Abran (2001) investigate how creativity and innovation at an organizational level can be measured. Based on the structure of commonly used software process improvement models such as Capability Maturity Model Integration (CMMI) and People Capability Maturity Model (P-CMM), the authors view how both process and people aspects of creativity and innovation can be measured.

COCOMO and COCOMO II are primary among several models for estimating cost, effort, and schedule of software development activity (CSE 2002). These are useful in the planning and execution of large software projects. COCOMO consists of three submodels: application composition, early design, and postarchitecture. The original COCOMO was published by Boehm (1981) and remains the best introductory reference to the model. The COCOMO model has been kept current by regular updates and refinements, as software engineering has matured since 1981.

Clark (2002), in his article "Manager: Eight Secrets of Software Measurement," enumerates some tricks for making a software measurement scheme work. Some of the eight "secrets," not unexpectedly, are cliché, but the author makes some perceptive points, like "…measurement is not an end in itself; it's a vehicle for highlighting activities and products that you, your project team, and your organization value so you can reach your goals."

Fenton et al. (2002) argue that the typical way of using software metrics is detrimental to effective risk management. They identify two specific roles of software measurement as quality control and effort estimation and point to complexity measures, process maturity, and test results as the most commonly used factors to assess software while it is being developed. The problems with widely used regression models are discussed. The authors recommend a Bayesian network-based defect-prevention model and explain details of the *AID* (assess, improve, decide) tool built on it. The authors see the dawn of "an exciting new era" in software measurement with wider applications of Bayesian networks.

Kruchten (2004), in his widely referenced book on the Rational Unified Process, makes an important categorization of measures. He calls *measure* "a concrete numeric attribute of an entity (e.g., a number, a percentage, a ratio)" whereas *primitive measure* is "an item of raw data that is used to calculate a measure." The book only mentions measurement in the context of the project management discipline, which unnecessarily constricts the scope of metrics.

Effective metrics, in addition to facilitating project management, may and can aid in the planning and execution of developer and team activities. This idea is developed in Part 2 and its use is illustrated through a case study in Part 3.

In their book *Software by Numbers,* Denne and Cleland-Huang (2004) introduce concepts like *Incremental Funding Methodology, Minimum Marketable Feature*, etc. to facilitate business decisions in enterprise software development. This work makes a notable attempt to bridge the seemingly "never the twain shall meet" chasm between those who build software and those who commission it.

Eickelmann (2004) makes an interesting distinction between the measurements of maturity and process in the context of the Capability Maturity Model levels. The author underscores that an organization's process maturity can be viewed from multiple perspectives.

Return on investment (ROI) and *software process improvement* are among the most bandied about buzzwords in the industry today. van Solingen (2004) establishes the practicality of measuring the former in terms of the latter. The author bases his discussion on the ROI numbers for several major software development organizations across the world.

Rico (2004) examines how the use of metrics by both project managers and software engineers can lead to better ROI on software process improvement. His book discusses investment analysis, benefit analysis, cost analysis, net present value, etc. and integrates these within the established methodologies such as the Personal Software Process, Team Software Process, Capability Maturity Model, and ISO 9001. Although the author's focus is mainly on process improvement, he offers insights on the positioning of metrics in the "bigger picture" of a development enterprise.

Continuing with the ROI theme, Pitt's (2005) article "Measuring Java Reuse, Productivity, and ROI" uses the *effective lines of code* (ESLOC) metric to measure the extent of reuse in Java code and the resultant ROI achieved. The author reaches some expansive conclusions, but the ESLOC metric may not reflect all the nuances of a software system in the first place. Also, the author's remark that "many elements are generated from an IT project, but arguably the most important element is the source code" can be argued against. With increasing trends toward model-driven development, larger and larger portions of source code are being automatically generated; analysis and design artifacts (that finally *drive* code generation) can very well claim to be the so-called "most important element."

Bernstein and Yuhas's (2005) work takes a matured view of software measurements: metrics should not reflect merely the countable aspects of a software product — like LOC — but must address the spectrum of people, product, process, and project that makes up software engineering in totality. The authors present interesting quantitative strategies on software development. However, some chapters present ready nuggets of wisdom, modulated as "Magic Number" (for example: "The goal for the architecture process is to reduce the number of function points by 40%"), which seem too ready to withstand close scrutiny.

Napier and McDaniel (2006), in their book *Measuring What Matters: Simplified Tools for Aligning Teams and Their Stakeholders,* discuss management techniques to measure seamlessly and painlessly. The book gives several measurement templates.

The preceding sections traced the course of development of software metrics from its earliest forms to the present. As new ways of conceiving and constructing software are being introduced, ways of devising, applying, and interpreting software metrics are also undergoing significant changes.

3.4. THE NEED FOR MORE

The above reconnaissance of software metrics, though quite a mouthful, is certainly not exhaustive, but it is enough to impart a *sense* of the discipline and its growth and direction. Metrics are widely regarded and used as monitoring artifacts. This book suggests the use of metrics from a different angle. As is established in Part 2 and demonstrated in Part 3, metrics have a great role to play in planning and performing iterations. An iteration is the smallest logical unit of software development, and it results in an increment, the smallest physical unit of a software system under development. In addition to aiding a holistic view of software development, metrics can play a meaningful role in guiding the atomic activities of understanding requirements, directing analysis and design, and streamlining implementation and testing. How?

That is precisely what this book is about. The contexts in the software development life cycle where metrics can make a difference are dissected, a set of metrics which will fit the bill is derived, and their use is demonstrated through a case study. As mentioned earlier, *Software Metrics* by Tom Gilb (1977) is arguably the first book on software metrics. In the introduction, Gilb describes the "spirit" of his book as "...all critical software concepts have at least one practical way of being measured." He boldly addresses a critical bridge between ideas and metrics; this is still the keynote theme of any worthwhile exploration of software metrics.

This book gives the reader tools and artifacts to build software better and build better software, but it is ultimately an attempt to explore the many subtleties of software building — that make the pursuit so fascinating and frustrating — through metrics.

3.5. SUMMARY

This chapter discussed some of the reasons why software engineering stands apart from the other engineering disciplines. It then briefly reviewed the journey of software metrics since they became an area of organized study. The chapter concluded with a discussion of how this book brings a new angle to the use of software metrics.

REFERENCES

Abreu, F. B. (1995). The MOOD Metrics Set. In Proc. ECOOP '95 Workshop on Metrics.

Albrecht, A. (1979). Measuring application development productivity. In Proc. Joint SHARE/GUIDE/IBM Application Development Symposium, pp. 83–92.

Alexander, C. (1979). *The Timeless Way of Building*. Oxford University Press.

Armour, P. G. (2004). Beware of counting LOC. *Commun. ACM*, 47(3):21–24.

Baker, A. L., Bieman, J. M., Fenton, N., Gustafson, D. A., Melton, A., and Whitty, R. (1990). A philosophy for software measurement. *J. Syst. Softw.*, 12(3):277–281.

Basili, V. R., Caldiera, G., and Rombach, H. D. (1994). *The Goal Question Metric Approach: Encyclopedia of Software Engineering*. Wiley and Sons.

Bauer, F. L., Bolliet, L., and Helms, H. J. (1968). NATO Software Engineering Conference 1968. http://homepages.cs.ncl.ac.uk/brian.randell/NATO/nato1968.PDF.

Belady, L. A. and Lehman, M. M. (1976). A model of large program development. *IBM Syst. J.*, 15(3):225.

Belady, L. A. and Lehman, M. M. (1979). The characteristics of large systems. In *Research Directions in Software Technology*, pp. 106–138. MIT Press.

Berard, E. V. (1995). Metrics for Object-Oriented Software Engineering. http://www.ipipan.gda.pl/~marek/objects/TOA/moose.html.

Bernstein, L. and Yuhas, C. M. (2005). *Trustworthy Systems through Quantitative Software Engineering*. Wiley-Interscience.

Bieman, J. M. and Ott, L. M. (1994). Measuring functional cohesion. *IEEE Trans. Softw. Eng.*, 20(8):644–657.

Binder, R. V. (1994). Object-oriented software testing. *Commun. ACM*, 37(9):28–29.

Boehm, B. W. (1981). *Software Engineering Economics*. Prentice Hall.

Booch, G. (2006). *Handbook of Software Architecture*. http://www.booch.com/architecture/index.jsp.

Brooks, F. P. (1995). *The Mythical Man-Month: Essays on Software Engineering, 20th Anniversary Edition*. Addison-Wesley.

Brooks, F. P. (2000). The Design of Design. http://www.siggraph.org/s2000/conference/turing/index.html.

Buglione, L. and Abran, A. (2001). Creativity and innovation in SPI: An exploratory paper on their measurement. In IWSM '01: International Workshop on Software Measurement, pp. 85–92, Montreal.

Card, D. N. and Glass, R. L. (1990). *Measuring Software Design Quality.* Prentice Hall.

Cavano, J. P. and McCall, J. A. (1978). A framework for the measurement of software quality. *SIGSOFT Softw. Eng. Notes,* 3(5):133–139.

Chidamber, S. R. and Kemerer, C. F. (1991). Towards a metrics suite for object oriented design. In *OOPSLA '91: Conference Proceedings on Object-Oriented Programming Systems, Languages, and Applications,* pp. 197–211. ACM Press.

Chidamber, S. R. and Kemerer, C. F. (1994). A metrics suite for object oriented design. *IEEE Trans. Softw. Eng.,* 20(6):476–493.

Churcher, N. I. and Shepperd, M. J. (1995). Towards a conceptual framework for object oriented software metrics. *SIGSOFT Softw. Eng. Notes,* 20(2):69–75.

Clark, B. (2002). Manager: Eight secrets of software measurement. *IEEE Softw.,* 19(5): 12–14.

Conte, S. D., Dunsmore, H. E., and Shen, V. Y (1986). *Software Engineering Metrics and Models.* Benjamin/Cummins.

CSE (2002). COCOMO. http://sunset.usc.edu/research/COCOMOII/.

Daskalantonakis, M. K. (1992). A practical view of software measurement and implementation experiences within Motorola. *IEEE Trans. Softw. Eng.,* 18(11):998–1010.

Datta, S. (2005). Integrating the FURPS+ model with use cases — A metrics driven approach. In Supplementary Proceedings of the 16th IEEE International Symposium on Software Reliability Engineering (ISSRE 2005), Chicago, November 7–11, pp. 4-51–4-52.

Davis, A., Overmyer, S., Jordan, K., Caruso, J., Dandashi, F., Dinh, A., Kincaid, G., Ledeboer, G., Reynolds, P., Sitaram, P., Ta, A., and Theofanos, M. (1993). Identifying and measuring quality in a software requirements specification. In Proceedings of the 1st International Software Metrics Symposium.

DeMarco, T. (1982). *Controlling Software Projects.* Yourdon Press.

DeMarco, T. and Lister, T. (1987). *Peopleware: Productive Projects and Teams.* Dorset House.

Demeyer, S., Ducasse, S., and Nierstrasz, O. (2000). Finding refactorings via change metrics. *SIGPLAN Not.,* 35(10):166–177.

Denne, M. and Cleland-Huang, J. (2004). *Software by Numbers: Low-Risk, High-Return Development.* Prentice Hall PTR.

Dhama, H. (1995). Quantitative models of cohesion and coupling in software. In *Selected Papers of the Sixth Annual Oregon Workshop on Software Metrics,* pp. 65–74. Elsevier Science.

Eickelmann, N. (2004). Measuring maturity goes beyond process. *IEEE Softw.,* 21(4): 12–13.

Fenton, N. (1994). Software measurement: A necessary scientific basis. *IEEE Trans. Softw. Eng.,* 20(3):199–206.

Fenton, N., Krause, P., and Neil, M. (2002). Software measurement: Uncertainty and causal modeling. *IEEE Softw.,* 19(4):116–122.

Fowler, M. (2006). Refactoring home page. http://www.refactoring.com/.

Garmus, D. and Herron, D. (1996). *Managing the Software Process: A Practical Guide to Functional Measure.* Prentice Hall.

Gilb, T. (1977). *Software Metrics*. Winthrop Publishers.

Grady, R. B. (1992). *Practical Software Metrics for Project Management and Process Improvement*. Prentice Hall.

Grady, R. B. (1994). Successfully applying software metrics. *Computer,* 27(9):18–25.

Grady, R. B. and Caswell, D. L. (1987). *Software Metrics: Establishing a Company-Wide Program*. Prentice Hall.

Halstead, M. H. (1977). *Elements of Software Science*. Elsevier North-Holland.

Harrison, R., Counsell, S. J., and Nithi, R. V. (1998). An evaluation of the mood set of object-oriented software metrics. *IEEE Trans. Softw. Eng.,* 24(6):491–496.

Henderson-Sellers, B. (1999). OO software process improvement with metrics. In *METRICS '99: Proceedings of the 6th International Symposium on Software Metrics,* p. 2. IEEE Computer Society.

Humphrey, W. S. (1996). Using a defined and measured personal software process. *IEEE Softw.,* 13(3):77–88.

Humphrey, W. S. (2005). *PSP: A Self-Improvement Process for Software Engineers*. Addison-Wesley.

Humphrey, W. S. (2006). *TSP: Leading a Development Team*. Addison-Wesley.

IEEE (1994). *Software Engineering Standards, 1994 edition*. IEEE.

Jones, C. (1991). *Applied Software Measurements*. McGraw-Hill.

Kabaili, H., Keller, R. K., and Lustman, F. (2001). Cohesion as changeability indicator in object-oriented systems. In *CSMR '01: Proceedings of the Fifth European Conference on Software Maintenance and Reengineering,* p. 39. IEEE Computer Society.

Kirwan, A. (2000). *Mother Nature's Two Laws: Ringmasters for Circus Earth — Lessons on Entropy, Energy, Critical Thinking and the Practice of Science*. World Scientific.

Kruchten, P. (2004). *The Rational Unified Process: An Introduction,* 3rd ed. Addison-Wesley.

Lanza, M. (2001). The evolution matrix: Recovering software evolution using software visualization techniques. In *IWPSE '01: Proceedings of the 4th International Workshop on Principles of Software Evolution,* pp. 37–42. ACM Press.

Lehman, M., Ramil, J., Wernick, P., and Perry, D. (1997). Metrics and Laws of Software Evolution: The Nineties View. http://citeseer.ist.psu.edu/lehman97metrics.html.

Lorenz, M. and Kidd, J. (1994). *Object-Oriented Software Metrics: A Practical Guide*. Prentice Hall PTR.

Maier, M. W. and Rechtin, E. (2000). *The Art of Systems Architecting,* 2nd ed. CRC Press.

McCabe, T. (1976). A software complexity measure. *IEEE Trans. Softw. Eng.,* SE-2 (December):308–320.

McCabe, T. and Watson, A. (1994). Software complexity. *Crosstalk,* 7(12):5–9.

Mens, T. and Demeyer, S. (2001). Future trends in software evolution metrics. In *IWPSE '01: Proceedings of the 4th International Workshop on Principles of Software Evolution,* pp. 83–86. ACM Press.

Napier, R. and McDaniel, R. (2006). *Measuring What Matters: Simplified Tools for Aligning Teams and Their Stakeholders*. Davies-Black.

O'Connell, F. (2001). *How to Run Successful Projects III: The Silver Bullet*. Addison-Wesley.

Paulish, D. J. and Carleton, A. D. (1994). Case studies of software-process-improvement measurement. *Computer,* 27(9):50–57.

Petroski, H. (1992). *To Engineer Is Human: The Role of Failure in Successful Design.* Vintage.

Pitt, W. D. (2005). Measuring Java reuse, productivity, and ROI. *Dr. Dobb's J.,* July.

Pressman, R. S. (2000). *Software Engineering: A Practitioner's Approach.* McGraw-Hill.

Ramil, J. F. and Lehman, M. M. (2001). Defining and applying metrics in the context of continuing software evolution. In *METRICS '01: Proceedings of the 7th International Symposium on Software Metrics,* p. 199. IEEE Computer Society.

Raymond, E. S. (2001). *The Cathedral and the Bazaar: Musings on Linux and Open Source by an Accidental Revolutionary.* O'Reilly.

Rico, D. F. (2004). *ROI of Software Process Improvement: Metrics for Project Managers and Software Engineers.* J. Ross Publishing.

Rifkin, S. (2001). What makes measuring software so hard? *IEEE Softw.,* 18(3):41–45.

Sears, A. (1993). Layout appropriateness: A metric for evaluating user interface widget layout. *IEEE Trans. Softw. Eng.,* 19(7):707–719.

Sotirovski, D. (2001). Heuristics for iterative software development. *IEEE Softw.,* 18(3):66–73.

van Solingen, R. (2004). Measuring the ROI of software process improvement. *IEEE Softw.,* 21(4):32–34.

Weinberg, G. M. (1971). *The Psychology of Computer Programming.* Van Nostrand Reinhold.

Weller, E. F. (1994). Using metrics to manage software projects. *Computer,* 27(9):27–33.

Whitmire, S. A. (1997). *Object-Oriented Design Measurement.* Wiley Computer.

Wiegers, K. E. (1999). A Software Metrics Primer. http://www.processimpact.com/articles/metrics_primer.html.

Wilde, N., Matthews, P., and Huitt, R. (1993). Maintaining object-oriented software. *IEEE Softw.,* 10(1):75-80.

KEY THEMES IN SOFTWARE MEASUREMENTS

4.1. OVERVIEW

In this chapter, some of the major ideas in software measurements are highlighted. These will serve as useful guidelines in understanding the metrics culture. They also encapsulate the wisdom emerging from the theory and practice of software metrics in the past few decades. The discussion here serves as a background for the materials in the later chapters.

4.2. MANY AUTHORS, MANY RUBRICS

Almost every author writing about software metrics comes up with his or her own *n* commandments. Baker et al. (1990), Berard (1995), Fenton (1994), Grady (1992), Henderson-Sellers (1999), and Wiegers (1999) are some of those who have done that, and done it well. Bullet points are easy and quick to read and impart a sense of knowing all there is to know, but there is much to be read between the lines. In the following section, I briefly touch upon some of the rubrics I have had occasion to appreciate. What I cover here is by no means exhaustive or all that is essential in measuring software, but it has had major influence on my thinking and working with metrics. It also gives a context to the discussion in the following chapters of this book. Build up the atmosphere, as they say in the world of fiction.

A disclaimer is due here. This chapter is mostly about generalizations, and every generalization can appear too sweeping, given certain specifics. Generalizations, however, give bird's-eye views, and bird's-eye views give useful perspective, provided one remains mindful of missing some details.

4.3. THE ESSENCE OF SOFTWARE MEASUREMENTS

4.3.1. No Silver Bullet

Brooks (1987) began his celebrated essay "No Silver Bullet: Essence and Accidents of Software Engineering" talking about folklore, nightmares, werewolves, and the human craving for "bullets of silver" that can lay these "magically" to rest. Brooks's 1987 essay (first published in 1986) sagely forecasts that there will be no single development in the coming decades which will bring about even one order of improvement in productivity, reliability, or simplicity. More than this soothsaying, the essay is remembered for giving the "no silver bullet" metaphor to the folklore of software engineering. *No silver bullet* is invoked whenever the improbability or impossibility of a magical solution needs to be stressed.

There is no silver bullet in software metrics. It is very unlikely we will have a metric in the foreseeable future which will give us everything we need to know about a software product or development circumstance, a la the credit score, which (alas!) acts as the single-point reference of one's financial health. For reasons discussed in Chapter 3, software lacks universal metrics such as the ohm, the joule, or the calorie. Single software metrics in isolation are seldom, if ever, useful. Efforts to devise useful software metrics are best directed at coming to terms with specific aspects of the process or product and not discovering "the metric" to end all metrics.

Like the six wise men in a poem by Saxe (1850) who are trying to describe an elephant and come up with their own contrasting impressions (which ironically complement one another), software metrics too, in parts, give us parts of the picture. As we still do not understand fully how software evolves and behaves under all circumstances of interest, whatever metric we devise cannot give us the whole picture. It is futile to complain that a particular metric does not say enough; the finesse lies in making the best sense of what it says in the light of what other metrics give us. This observation leads us to the next point.

4.3.2. Metrics Hunt in Groups

As discussed in Section 3.3, in the 1970s software metrics studies were mainly concerned with finding laws of software and complexity measures. McCabe's

(1976) *cyclomatic complexity* metric illustrates the preoccupation of this age: trying to find a know-all metric that revealed the deepest secrets about a particular aspect of software. With the passing decades, as software grappled with deeper complexity, it became clear that single "silver bullet" metrics were unlikely to deliver. This cultural shift is manifested in Chidamber and Kemerer's (1991, 1994) oft-referenced "CK" suite of object-oriented metrics, where the authors defined a set of *related* metrics to describe the design of object-oriented software. Given the continuing quest for the laws of software — fundamental principles like the ones other engineering disciplines have — and the fact that we do not have them yet, metrics have to depend on one another for a so-called "total picture." Returning to the metaphor of Saxe's poem in which six wise men inspect an elephant, each metric is limited in the scope of what it can see. Together, they can help us see the whole. The key attitude is accepting this fact and working with sets of metrics.

Groups of metrics, sometimes called *metrics suites,* which see related objects of interest, although from different angles, have been proven to be far more useful for applying, interpreting, and acting on than single seemingly omniscient metrics.

How do metrics become related? Metrics are related when each tells us something which, though interesting by itself, gives a deeper insight into the problem when taken in context of one another. A quick analogy can be drawn to the idea of mean, median, and mode in simple statistics. Each one of these measures tells us something notable about a data set. But whenever I reported a test score to my parents, I found it helpful to append the mean, median, and modal scores for the whole class. (Usually my test results needed such extenuation!) Thus, mean, median, and mode together give a deeper perspective than each individually does. I have increasingly become chary of one-off metrics; it always makes more sense to me when I see a few trying to work together. Related metrics also share the same or very similar assumptions. This brings us to the inevitability of assumptions.

4.3.3. There Will Always Be Assumptions

When I was first taught Newton's laws of motion, somewhere in the mists of middle school, I had a hard time believing the first law. I could easily see that bodies continued being where they were, without being shoved or pushed, but the part about bodies continuing in uniform motion once set moving baffled me no end. I tried testing it out the easiest way I could: by rolling a ball on the floor. The ball eventually stopped rolling, every time. Obviously, I was overlooking the key assumption about continual uniform motion (or continued rest) being contingent upon the absence of external impressed force. The force of friction was acting on the ball all the while it rolled, finally bringing it to a halt. The moral of this story is not the value of skepticism in early youth. The moral is that all formulations have assumptions.

It is important to be cognizant of assumptions and to guard against getting sold on something with too general — or just plain absurd — assumptions (like all humans are immortal or, worse, all humans are good). Nevertheless, assumptions do exist, and one has to learn to work with or around them. A favorite thrust of academic nitpicking is demolishing assumptions. I have witnessed speakers heckled at conferences by suave members of the audience who find the results "somewhat interesting," but the assumptions "obviously invalid." Any formulation can be stultified by questioning the assumptions, and no assumption holds under every circumstance. In India, a valued metric for academic institutions is the so-called *teacher-student ratio.* A high teacher-student ratio is taken to indicate a better level of instruction. Of course, there are many assumptions in this line of conclusion. Let us play devil's advocate: more teachers do not mean better teaching standards, some teachers help students unlearn a subject more than they help learn, the really bright students are best left to self-learn...*ad nauseam.* All this takes us nowhere. In a practice-oriented book such as the one in your hands, we will consciously avoid trying to sanitize assumptions. There will be assumptions in the metrics and methods suggested in the later chapters, sometimes explicit, sometimes implicit. We will check to see if they are reasonable in our context. If they are, we will remember what we assume and move on.

All software metrics are based on assumptions. The more useful ones have specific and reasonable assumptions. The essence is to extract as much insight as possible within the assumptions.

4.3.4. Be Prepared to Customize a Metric

As discussed in Section 3.2.3, software is a plastic medium. While this is frustrating at times (we do not have the immutable truths of the "hard sciences" or even the conventional engineering disciplines), it also has its benefits. Customization is an idea which software products have reinforced over the last decade or so. Interestingly, it can also be applied to software metrics. The lines of code metric is a case in point. There are countless variations of it, such as kilo lines of code and effective lines of code (Pitt 2005). Many other metrics are also *normalized* with respect to lines of code, such as defect density, development effort, etc. Although I stand by the reservations expressed in Section 3.3 regarding the whole lines of code point of view, it has been *customized* extensively to serve some useful purposes.

Whenever an established metric is used, one needs to remain open to how it can be customized to better suit the specific goal at hand. More often than not, software metrics are amenable to tweaking quite a bit. In fact, I take "tweakability" as a triage of how widely a metric may be used!

As stated in Chapter 1, one of my fervent hopes is that you will take the metrics presented in this book and tweak them to best fit your projects. I do not mind if you customize to the extent these metrics become new ones; the true test of ideas lies in how well they alloy into new ideas. So, there is nothing absolute about software metrics; be ready to do what it takes to make a metric useful to you.

But sometimes you will find that no amount of customization will make a metric fit your bill, or you will find no metric that reflects your way of thinking about a problem or circumstance. This is the time to indulge in what is called "thinking outside the box."

4.3.5. Do Not Be Afraid to Create Your Own Metrics

The power and beauty of metrics hit home the first time for me when I was involved in making and using them to notable effect in my work. It imparted a sense of control (and, rather naively, achievement) which went far beyond what one gets by reading someone else rhapsodize about metrics. I will save the juicy parts of that story for later.

Briefly (and dryly), I was trying to ensure that thirty-two practitioners across six project teams and two continents followed a process to do certain tasks every week. If even one team did not do its bit — and do it per the process, success of all the projects would have been in jeopardy. More importantly, I would have "faced the music." I used entreaty and diplomacy in the first few weeks — without much effect. We then devised a set of metrics to give a numerical measure of how well each team was complying with the process on a weekly basis, as well as the exact areas of each team's delinquency. The numbers were circulated to the teams by 5:00 P.M. every Friday. At 9:00 A.M. each following Monday, we had a conference call "to discuss ways for better compliance." Over the last few weeks of the life cycle of the three-month project, at least four teams had 100% compliance on an average. The projects were released without any major issue. This also taught me some other lessons about metrics, which I will talk about later.

Metrics which help quick, back-of-the-envelope type of calculations are not that difficult to build. True, they may not always conform to the deepest of measurement theory principles (which many authors are sticklers for, as shown in Chapter 3), but they are useful nonetheless. Making and using software metrics call for rigor versus expediency trade-offs. These issues will become clearer as we devise our metrics in Part 2 of this book and illustrate their use in Part 3. I am sanguine those discussions will inspire (or instigate!) readers to try out their own metrics.

So, in the world of software metrics, it is often easier, more fun, and more useful to build your own metrics and apply them. The metrics presented in this book will bring out some of the basic principles of metrics building.

4.3.6. Keep It Simple

I deliberately left out the trailing "S" in KISS — Keep It Simple, Stupid — because it sounds a trifle condescending. In the enterprise software business, we all start stupid, and we can only end wiser if we accept our stupidity with grace and humor. The real point is about keeping it simple.

I was once cornered by a software metric aficionado in the coffee room and asked if I remembered solving double integrals. I had to admit I did not, even doubting whether I had the skill in the first place. The aficionado told me that was a pity, as he had just devised a metric which needed the services of double integrals, but he had forgotten all about them. I concurred it was a pity and suggested he try out Wikipedia. What I did not say, but felt strongly, was, given the endemic comfort level with double integrals, his metric had very little chance of being used widely, if at all.

Metrics must get you to the numbers fast. The more complicated calculating a metric is, the less it will be calculated. It is easy to argue that no calculation is too complex for a neat little computer program. This is true, but practitioners caught in the grind of meeting production deadlines may have neither the will nor the way to write such neat little computer programs. I have found that the most used metrics are calculated on spreadsheets. (I do not necessarily support this approach; formulas on spreadsheets can be hell. Yet it is widely rumored that 90% of *real* business logic — the kind of stuff that gets bandied about in boardrooms — is stored in spreadsheets.) Interpreting metrics is tricky business, and using the interpretations to bring about change is trickier. Thus, if even the calculation is tricky, all this trickery may become too much, and the metric will just be passed on.

But how much can simple metrics tell you? Surprisingly, they can tell you much if the scope is specific and the extent manageable. Remember that software metrics are not used in the hunt for some eternal truth. They serve well as heuristics to develop usable and reliable systems. The metrics in this book rely on basic math to capture some of the key ideas of enterprise software development. As discussed in Chapter 3, the *Environmental Factor* as described in *Peopleware* (DeMarco and Lister 1987) is a great example of what a simple, straightforward metric can be.

A caveat is due here. I am not suggesting that what metrics seek to measure about enterprise software development is simple or open to flagrant dilution to be made simple. Enterprise software development is wickedly complex in parts. The absence of first principles and basic laws makes things more difficult. With insightful choices of parameters and relationships, however, it is possible to greatly simplify metrics making. And what is called "Gilb's Law" is always such a comfort: "Anything you need to quantify can be measured in some way that is superior to not measuring at all" (DeMarco and Lister 1987).

Therefore, when you build your metrics, start simple. Being simple with metrics helps one see quickly and clearly what a metric can give us — and sometimes, more helpfully, what it cannot.

4.3.7. Collect and Compile over Time

Using metrics should be more of a culture than a chore. Whether you use established metrics or build your own, it has to be done over time. Metrics seldom — if ever — work as afterthoughts. The worst way to work with metrics is *a posteriori*. It invariably leads to "what might have been" and attendant recriminations. Metrics work best when collected and compiled over time in a planned manner. Comparing metrics across projects is dangerous; a more sensible approach is to observe metrics and their variation over time for the same or similar projects. The best way to use metrics is to collect data over a period of time across the same scope. It is important to desist from making peremptory judgments before a critical mass of data is reached. The same numbers can be made to mean many things with widely varying overtones. This becomes a serious problem with metrics data collected over too short a time or too narrow a scope. Metrics are often used in what paper reviewers call "toy examples," situations of so limited relevance or so closely controlled conditions they do not in any way reflect the uncertainties, tensions, or complications of real-world scenarios. Unfortunately, many metric studies become mired in such toy examples. Accepting the reality that metrics will not give quick results, it is imperative that projects plan for a sustained metrics program. Such acceptance brings us to several questions.

Who takes charge of collecting and compiling the metrics? Should one or a few of the practitioners be hectored (or lured) into the task over and above their usual responsibilities? Should it be a practitioner(s) external to the team, who has a more objective view of things? In that case, will the customer be willing to support something certainly not *directly* related to the deliverables?

Lack of a satisfactory answer or even lack of sufficient thought given to these questions has been known to scupper many a metric effort. These questions need to be addressed before a project can be expected to start looking into metrics seriously. How to resolve them is a management issue, blissfully beyond our present scope. But automation helps.

4.3.8. Use Automation

Whenever one speaks of metrics to a team stretched thin by carping customers, looming deadlines, and obdurate bosses, the usual responses are sighs, grimaces, or things more colorful. This is understandable: under production pressures of the kind common in the software industry (as many of us know, Yourdon's [2003] "death march projects" are more reality than lore), few have the bandwidth or attitude to commit themselves to collecting and reporting metrics. There are also qualms whether the metrics will come back to haunt the very practitioners who helped calculate them, a crucial issue discussed in the next chapter. In short, I have seen enough metrics initiatives choke due to lack of practitioner latitude to have become a strong supporter of automation.

Automated approaches to metrics come in many flavors. A very involved piece of software might do everything from calculation to collection and interpretation on its own, but it takes a lot of time to build, test, and deploy, and this kind of effort is unlikely to ever be "billable." More modest pieces of software can be built which help make the collection of metrics data easier for each practitioner. For example, when trying to calculate how much development time was being lost due to environmental issues such as power outages, it became much easier for each person to enter their losses on a spreadsheet stored at a common location, from which a little tool extracted the hours lost and calculated what was called the utilization factor.

Thinking about automation should start along with thinking about metrics. If the metrics effort is seen as overhead by the practitioners, their cooperation will not be forthcoming, and without their cooperation, the metrics effort will fail. Only when developers are convinced that the acts of collecting data and calculating the metrics will not lead to significantly more work for them can one count on their interest. Little tools developed for the metrics across projects can be integrated into a tool kit which gradually develops into a "soup-to-nuts" automation suite for metrics collection, calculation, and interpretation.

But who holds the metrics "intelligence"? Is it good if only a few people in the project know the whys and whats of the metrics? Or is it in the greater good to share the knowledge across all the members of the team and even the customer? Which is a better model, the black box or the white box?

4.3.9. Black Box Is Bad: Be Clear about Scope and Workings

I have always found it easier to apply metrics to a project when the purpose, scope, assumptions, and formulas of the metrics are explained to the whole team up front. Software engineers are suspicious of numbers when they do not know how they are arrived at. Metrics are simple strategies to extract more insight from a circumstance than readily meets the eye; there is no thaumaturgy, and they should not be viewed as black magic. If the workings of a metric are not clear, misgivings abound as to its objective, and misgivings can kill a metric. It is best to circulate a brief memo about the metric and hold a tutorial session for the whole team before the metrics initiative starts. The message must go out loud and clear that metrics are meant for the whole team to do its task better, and their dynamics are transparent.

Transparency is crucial, as metrics are sometimes construed to be people-measurement units. Nothing can be more unfortunate.

4.3.10. Never Use Metrics to Measure People

A software engineer friend of mine is rather bitter about metrics. The grouse goes back to her first brush with metrics in an enterprise software project. The technical lead was a great stickler for doing things the right way, which often meant *his* way. In addition, the technical lead was a great believer in the power of metrics. When the project team was forming — and had just begun to "gel," in team jargon, the technical lead sent a circular e-mail detailing all that needed to be done to collect and report metrics. Perhaps to ensure his e-mail was taken seriously, he mentioned that the metrics were going to be used in the team members' yearly appraisals. And in a seeming masterstroke of corporate diplomacy, the manager was copied on the e-mail. At the end of the ten-month project, there were reams of metrics data. The graphs pointed the way they should, every inflection clearly indicating improvement. And as my friend said, all of it meant nothing. Stated discretely, the metrics data were produced by a team whose members were anxious to get a good appraisal at the end of the year. From then on, metrics came to mean manipulation to my friend.

This is a sorry story, sorrier because it is so common. The biggest mistake people make about metrics is trying to evaluate teams and individuals with them. (How do you hold defect density against a team — the higher the number, the worse the team?) Even if such evaluation is finally not carried out, just the fact that it was talked about is enough to put practitioners completely off of metrics. Metrics are finally numbers, and to some misguided minds they seem ready pointers to human performance. "Meeting your numbers" is an oft-repeated rubric in the industry. Whatever it may mean, software metrics should not be in its scope. We need metrics in enterprise software development to guide us in making decisions and better understanding situations. Software metrics are not meant to judge practitioners, and they never should be used toward that end. I find it helpful to assure all practitioners involved in a metrics initiative — up front, in a common forum — that the so-called "numbers" *will not* be held against an individual or group; neither will they be shared with management in a form that makes it possible to recognize whose actions generated which number. And then deliver on the promise. There is a deeply human element in succeeding with software metrics; these issues are discussed at length in the next chapter.

In summary, software metrics will never work without the interest, support, and cooperation of those who build software. Trying to use metrics to "fix" people will generate so much bad blood that not only the metrics initiative but also the project is likely to fail. Whether numbers are needed to appraise individuals or teams is a decision entirely up to an organization's management. Software metrics cannot and should not supply such numbers.

Metrics can only facilitate feedback on a particular aspect of software development. What one does with it is left to one's best judgment. This takes us to the next nugget.

4.3.11. Metrics Give Feedback — The Rest Is Up to You

Henderson-Sellers (1999) in the keynote address to the Sixth International Software Metrics Symposium (METRICS '99), titled "OO Software Process Improvement with Metrics," says: "…instigating a metrics programme does not bring immediate 'magical' answers to all software development.…A metrics programme provides knowledge and understanding; it does not provide quick fixes." I find the words "instigating" and "magical" to be very revealing. In many organizations, serious difficulties with processes, quality, customer satisfaction, or even employee morale "instigate" initiation of a metrics program. In those cases, it is usual to regard the very initiative as a panacea for all ills. But a panacea for all ills exists only in folklore, like the werewolves invoked by Brooks. Thus, the program is not able to deliver the "magical" solutions sought, leading to frustration and despair. Even worse, the metrics are used for "fixing."

Getting the best out of software metrics ultimately depends on how deeply an organization imbibes the metrics culture. Starting a metrics program is just the first step toward that culture. There needs to be a clear follow-up plan as to what will be done with the insights the metrics will reveal. The good things the metrics reflect will need to be made repeatable, consistent, and better. For the not-so-palatable ones, strategies need to be defined for betterment. Metrics by themselves will not give you results; results will come from the actions your organization takes on the metrics. Much metrics data is interred in managers' mailboxes, because it is too hot to handle. To have metrics work for you, you must be prepared to work on the metrics. And this kind of action calls for significant political will. The next chapter takes a look at some of the administrative, practical, interpersonal, and political concerns that crop up in initiating a metrics culture for a project.

4.4. SUMMARY

This chapter went over a hit parade of software metrics wisdom. Many of these ideas have been pointed out by other authors in other contexts. They have come to represent a set of shared sensitivities and sensibilities for using metrics in enterprise software development.

In the next chapter, we will see how these insights translate to the reality of taking a project down the metrics path.

REFERENCES

Baker, A. L., Bieman, J. M., Fenton, N., Gustafson, D. A., Melton, A., and Whitty, R. (1990). A philosophy for software measurement. *J. Syst. Softw.*, 12(3):277–281.

Berard, E. V. (1995). Metrics for Object-Oriented Software Engineering. http://www.ipipan.gda.pl/~marek/objects/TOA/moose.html.

Brooks, F. P. (1987). No silver bullet: Essence and accidents of software engineering. *Computer*, 20(4):10–19.

Chidamber, S. R. and Kemerer, C. F. (1991). Towards a metrics suite for object oriented design. In *OOPSLA '91: Conference Proceedings on Object-Oriented Programming Systems, Languages, and Applications*, pp. 197–211. ACM Press.

Chidamber, S. R. and Kemerer, C. F. (1994). A metrics suite for object oriented design. *IEEE Trans. Softw. Eng.*, 20(6):476–493.

DeMarco, T. and Lister, T. (1987). *Peopleware: Productive Projects and Teams.* Dorset House.

Fenton, N. (1994). Software measurement: A necessary scientific basis. *IEEE Trans. Softw. Eng.*, 20(3):199–206.

Grady, R. B. (1992). *Practical Software Metrics for Project Management and Process Improvement.* Prentice Hall.

Henderson-Sellers, B. (1999). OO software process improvement with metrics. In *METRICS '99: Proceedings of the 6th International Symposium on Software Metrics*, p. 2. IEEE Computer Society.

McCabe, T. (1976). A software complexity measure. *IEEE Trans. Softw. Eng.*, SE-2 (December):308–320.

Pitt, W. D. (2005). Measuring Java reuse, productivity, and ROI. *Dr. Dobb's J.*, July.

Saxe, J. G. (1850). The Blind Men and the Elephant. http://bygosh.com/Features/092001/blindmen.htm.

Wiegers, K. E. (1999). A Software Metrics Primer. http://www.processimpact.com/articles/metrics_primer.html.

Yourdon, E. (2003). *Death March,* 2nd ed. Prentice Hall PTR.

5

TAKING YOUR PROJECT THE METRICS WAY

5.1. OVERVIEW

No matter how good your metrics are on paper, applying them to real-life projects and getting worthwhile results is a very different ball game. Metrics programs often fail not due to the ineptitude of the metrics but on account of the way they were introduced and intended to be used. This chapter explores some of the issues a project needs to resolve to go the metrics way. It also discusses the utility of having a *metrics charter* for a project.

5.2. THE METRICS WAY

In the Indian epic *Mahabharata* (which will be discussed further in the sidebar titled "Abstraction, Elision, Indirection: A Touch of *Mahabharata*" in Chapter 8), Yudhisthira, the exiled prince and eldest of the protagonist brothers — a person of unimpeachable morality, rumored never to have spoken a lie, was asked by a demon: What is a way? Now at that turn of the story, the demon had something of an upper hand. He had killed all four of Yudhisthira's brothers, promising to restore their lives only if his questions were answered. "What is a way?" was one among several loaded questions the demon asked. The exiled prince answered to the best of his judgment, and his judgment was pretty good. To cut a short story shorter, the demon was edified enough to bring the brothers back to life and bless them as a bonus. (In true epical intricacy, it turned out that the demon was a god in disguise, trying to test the prince!) Yudhisthira's take on the question of a way is interesting. He said there is no consensus *what* a way is, so it is best to learn from example and tread the paths of great men and women. What intrigues me most is that the question never was *which is the way* (a la quo vadis), but *what is a way*. The difficulty with applying Yudhisthira's recipe to software metrics is that there is not yet a sufficient collection of ways trodden by great individuals so that one may pick and choose. But still we must take our projects the metrics way.

At many places in this book, we talk about "metrics culture." A metrics culture is usually taken to be at an organizational level, like the efforts to establish a company-wide metrics program as reported by Grady and Caswell (1987). But a metrics culture cannot be created top down. It needs to be built bottom up, one project at a time. One project at a time, like one brick at a time, sounds like a rather onerous way of building something, but the power of hearsay may make one project at a time soon turn into many projects at a time. The success stories with metrics for a project spread via the organizational grapevine quickly. The challenge lies more in committing a project to metrics than metrics to a project. The former is about bringing about changes in the way things are viewed, done, and evaluated. Committing a project to metrics is certainly easy in companies with strong process orientation. It is now fashionable for software development organizations to flaunt their levels of certification on various standards. Surprisingly (perhaps not that surprisingly), organizational certification level may not reflect concomitant awareness or attitude within a particular project team. Certification is always for the organization, but a project team is about individuals. With the high attrition rate in the software industry, who ensures that a practitioner leaving company A at certification level X to join company B at certification level Y (Y is greater than X) is brought up to speed on the differential that should exist between X and Y? Humphrey's (2005, 2006) *Personal Software Process* and *Team Software Process* seek to address these concerns. Unfortunately, very many software engineers do not know of these elegant constructs. This brings us to a very serious issue in the software engineering profession.

Most of today's software engineers have never received formal software engineering training. They are from the other engineering disciplines, mathematics, the sciences, or the arts and learned software building "on the job." I greatly value learning on the job, as I am very much one of these software engineers (I studied electrical engineering as an undergraduate), but I increasingly feel it helps to be formally initiated into software engineering, almost paradoxically, as it has such practical impact. One can pick up skills on the job, even rise to the level of virtuosity, but to be a consummate practitioner one must sense the course of the discipline and be acquainted with the ideas and techniques that have come up in the past. Without these connections, we end up trying to reinvent the wheel at best and at worst repeat the same mistakes *ad nauseam.* It is heartening that countries such as India and China are investing so much resource and attention in software engineering curricula. I would be pretty nervous the next time I fly if I learned the pilot was really trained as a doctor of medicine but picked up flying by sitting in the cockpit a couple of times. Yet we are strangely complacent when software engineers building our banking software actually learned bridge building in school.

These factors impart some peculiarities to software engineering vis-à-vis the other engineering disciplines, as discussed in Chapter 3. Nowhere is this more manifest than when trying to take a project the metrics way.

What does "the metrics way" mean? In a project that takes the metrics way, certain commitments are made. There is agreement to collect information on certain parameters *consistently* throughout the project life cycle, *periodically* collate the information and *apply the metrics formulations* to it, *share* the metrics "numbers" amongst the team members, *interpret* the results in light of the project realities, *identify* areas of improvement, and *take appropriate action.* This is quite a mouthful and may not be practicable to implement without management concurrence or customer knowledge. If the returns are tangible, neither should demur. Assuming both management and the customer see the value addition the metrics way will bring, there are still some very *human* issues the team has to address at the outset and on an ongoing basis. Some of these can be tackled by training, mentoring, and fostering an open and dynamic work environment, but there are others that need more conscious and concentrated attention.

5.3. BABBAGE'S CONSTERNATION

A quote attributed to Charles Babbage — one of the pioneering minds behind the computer — goes: "On two occasions I have been asked [by members of Parliament], 'Pray, Mr. Babbage, if you put into the machine wrong figures, will the right answers come out?' I am not able rightly to apprehend the kind of confusion of ideas that could provoke such a question."

Such "confusion of ideas" can be seen at two levels. On one hand, this points to a lack of understanding of the whole idea of computation, a lacuna which may not have been fully filled even today. One of the reasons why software engineers have such a hard time eliciting requirements from users is that users have very little idea what a software system can and cannot do for them. When a house or a bridge is commissioned, the users are clearer in their expectations. Houses and bridges have been in human consciousness (and consumption) for many centuries now. Software systems should breed such familiarity when they have been around for that long a time. But the confusion of Babbage's hecklers was also whether the machine could transmute wrong numbers to right answers. Numbers are strange things; they are stark in their objectivity but allow no conclusions until the context is known. A height of six feet for a man may be considered average in the United States, but in India it is certainly tall. Metrics are ultimately numbers, and we share the parliamentarians' craving for something like Babbage's analytical engine to give us right answers even on wrong inputs. There is no such consummate machinery. Metrics are just numbers; there are no absolute right or eternal wrong answers about them. Whatever does not fit into the absolute-eternal mode — especially when parliamentarians have entered into it — commonly gets called politics. At the organizational and team levels, metrics and politics often go hand in hand.

5.4. METRICS AND POLITICS

In Chapter 4, we observed that it takes sufficient political will to take action on metrics findings. Political will is something one hears about whenever there is a lack of it. Politics is a word with powerful overtones. In interpersonal situations, politics has a negative connotation; it hints at dissembling, duplicity, deceit, or just plain doublespeak. But politics is also about communicating ideas, mobilizing people, spreading the gospel, and getting things done. In short, politics helps the polity help itself. In enterprise software development, metrics occupy the cusp of these two types of politics, and this is what makes them so interesting.

There is politics in every human enterprise that involves two or more individuals. Industry feels that academe is free from the politics of market share and outwitting the competition. Academe believes industry is blissfully devoid of the politics of securing grants and publication pressures. Politics in industry and academe comes in very different flavors, but both can be as pernicious or productive depending on how one plays the cards. Davis (2004) in his *Great Software Debates* reflected on the inward and outward nature of politics in these arenas.

As the most ready view of metrics is numbers, and numbers are easily held against people, metrics may quickly become instruments of vendetta. In the hit parade of metrics credos in Chapter 3, it was said that using metrics to measure people was an absolute "no-no." DeMarco and Lister (1987) in their enduring *Peopleware* talk about how only "sanitized averages" should be made available to the boss, to avoid individual reprisals. In spite of all this wisdom, metrics get called upon in fixing blame. A friend of mine related an incident when a root cause analysis session using a fishbone diagram (always contentious, these bones!) almost led to a free-for-all fistfight. In many cases, out-of-context metrics data are shared with customers to "jack" particular individuals.

In the foreword to the very first book on software metrics, *Software Metrics* by Gilb (1977), Weinberg says: "To some readers, measurement is a method of squeezing the last gram of humanity out of the computing business." He then asks what can be done to prevent this kind of "dehumanizing application of metric ideas." These reflections from thirty years ago remain apt even today. Much of the politics about metrics is about this dehumanizing of software development (note how it was called "computing business" then). Metrics should help tap the richness of the human qualities software development needs to succeed — communication, intuition, experience, understanding, improvisation, and much more. For the software industry to gravitate toward a metrics culture, the political perception of metrics has to change. Metrics must be seen less in isolation as numbers and more in connection as facilitators of change.

This is a book about how simple, intuitive metrics can help enterprise software development. Reams have been written about corporate politics; I believe it is an area of active research. We will not delve into the political ramifications of every new metric presented in this book, although certain observations will be made on the sly, which may help you see things in a political light. Enterprise software development almost always takes place in a corporate milieu, and politics is very much there in corporate milieus. The above discussion should make you aware (if you are not already) that politics plays an important role in making metrics make a difference in enterprise software development. There is a school to teach you how politics can help you make a difference: the school of hard knocks. Some call it *life*.

Working with metrics becomes somewhat easy if some declarations are made at the outset. The instrument of declaration can be called the *metrics charter*.

5.5. A METRICS CHARTER FOR YOUR PROJECT

Connoisseurs of test-driven development often talk about building test cases before building the software. Analogously, in metrics-driven development, we should clarify what we want the metrics to do for us before we start doing anything with the metrics. A metrics charter for a project should address at least (but not only) the following questions: What is to be measured? What are the metrics to be used? What new insight are the metrics expected to provide (that could not be had without the metrics)? What kind of action can be taken on the insights provided by the metrics? What is the time period for the metrics initiative? Which stakeholders would be directly affected (for better or for worse) by the metrics initiative? What is the mechanism for collecting, calculating, and compiling metrics data? Will any automated tools be used for the metrics initiative?

The questions need to be answered as precisely as possible. This precision depends on a lot of things, most notably whether the metrics initiative will have any impact or not. A pathetic answer to the first question would be: We want to measure how well this system satisfies our customers. A far better one: We want to measure the number of defects identified by users in the first week after each release.

Regarding the new insights expected from the metrics, a reasonable quest would be the percent of development hours lost due to network outage. Without the metrics, customers always see these kinds of environmental issues as one-off. Only when you have clear numbers collected over time can you make a strong pitch for adjusting schedule and budget.

It is important to have some idea of the corrective action that may (or may not) be taken. Although the nature and extent of the action may depend on what the metrics tell you, it is crucial to test the waters about the political will to act on the metrics. If the metrics check how much a set of requirements is changing (like the *Mutation Score* introduced in Chapter 7) and the level turns out to be unacceptably high, is talking to the customer about it an option? Or is management too insecure to "backchat" with the customer?

The time period for the metrics initiative is also very important; anything that is not time-boxed does not get done. Clear starting and finishing lines have to be set for the results from the time in between to be scrutinized and acted upon.

The mechanism mentioned in the charter is the process, if you will, for how the practitioners will go about collecting data for the metrics and recording them. As stated in Chapter 4, automation can go a long way in making a metrics initiative work for the better. The charter also mentions stakeholders. All of the stakeholders whose lives will be affected by the metrics initiative need to read the charter, give input to it, and be listed on it.

But the charter is not a legal document and it should not read like one. It stops short of identifying individuals and their responsibilities in the metrics

Table 5.1. Sample metrics charter

Name of the project	MAGIC 2.0
Start date	July 1, 2006
End date	January 1, 2007
What is to be measured	Design change across iterations
Metric(s) to be used	*Morphing Index*
Automated tools for metrics data collection, if any	None at this time
Measuring cycle	Four months
Stakeholders participating in the metrics initiative	Technical lead, application developers, project manager
Expected insight from metrics data	Quantitative measure of design change
Action plan on metrics data	Root cause analysis of design change
Customer concurrence on metrics initiative	Yes

initiative. If this is done, the responsible individuals may see to it that there are enough caveats and extenuations included to make the charter a full proof document and that's about it. Once again, a metrics initiative should not appear to be one person's or one group's agenda; it is a self-regulating mechanism for the whole team.

The best way to explain often is by example; Table 5.1 gives a metrics charter for a fictional project, although the questions and answers are nonfictional!

5.6. SUMMARY

This chapter brought to light some of the practical issues in taking a project the metrics way. Metrics are always powerful political ammunition, to be used for better or worse. Practitioners need to remain mindful of this angle and use it to their and their project's best benefit. A first step toward taking a project the metrics way is a metrics charter. It lists the major concerns, expectations, and strategies about the metrics initiative. An example of a metrics charter was given.

We next move on to Part 2 of the book — where we get more specific and build our own metrics in light of the discussions in Part 1.

REFERENCES

Davis, A. M. (2004). *Great Software Debates.* IEEE/Wiley-Interscience.

DeMarco, T. and Lister, T. (1987). *Peopleware: Productive Projects and Teams.* Dorset House.

Gilb, T. (1977). *Software Metrics.* Winthrop Publishers.

Grady, R. B. and Caswell, D. L. (1987). *Software Metrics: Establishing a Company-Wide Program.* Prentice Hall.

Humphrey, W. S. (1996). Using a defined and measured personal software process. *IEEE Softw.,* 13(3):77–88.

Humphrey, W. S. (2005). *PSP: A Self-Improvement Process for Software Engineers.* Addison-Wesley.

PART 2.
CONSTRUCTS

ITERATIVE AND INCREMENTAL DEVELOPMENT: A BRIEF BACKGROUND

6.1. OVERVIEW

In this chapter, the genesis of software engineering methodologies is briefly reviewed. The power and the beauty of an iterative and incremental approach are underscored, with emphases on the Unified Software Development Process. The chapter concludes with directions on how we seek to harvest our metrics from the software development process.

6.2. MARCH OF THE METHODOLOGIES

When "writing" software came to be acknowledged as not merely computer programming, software engineering's journey to maturity began. Software's place in the pantheon of engineering disciplines and what sets it apart in its own peculiar niche were discussed at some length in Chapter 3. The following discussion provides a quick survey of the different methods that at various times appeared as recipes for software-building *nirvana*.

"In the beginning there was the waterfall" (Beck 1999). This technique prescribed that software be built in a succession of clearly defined and demarcated sets of activities: requirement specification, analysis, design, implementation, and testing (Tilley et al. 2003). The implicit assumption was that everyone knew whatever they needed to know *a priori*; customers knew what system they wanted and what the system wanted from them, analysts knew that what they heard from the customers was what the customers wanted to tell them, designers knew they could get the design right the first time, implementers knew all they had to do was translate the design into code, and testers knew what to test. In the waterfall model, projects progressed in a unidirectional path, like the truth of water flowing downhill. In spite of all the inadequacy ascribed to the waterfall model later — often justifiably, its value lies in the first semblance of order it brought to the hitherto free-form software development.

The Unified Software Development Process (aka Unified Process or UP) took the best idea of the waterfall model and made it better. Software Development Life Cycle (SDLC) was now a two-dimensional matrix (Schach 2005) of *phases* (inception, construction, elaboration, transition) and *workflows* (requirements, analysis, design, implementation, test). The UP is use-case driven, architecture centric, iterative, and incremental (Jacobson et al. 1999). In essence, UP places great emphasis on understanding the scenarios of user interaction with the system, culturing an architectural framework that supports reusability and extensibility, and building software iteratively and incrementally. It recognizes that getting it right the first time is absurd for anything other than trivial systems and seeks to absorb effects of changing user needs through awareness and coordination.

Extreme Programming (XP), almost eponymously, takes one more radical step in the building of enterprise software. It is one — perhaps the most promising — among a gamut of "agile" methods that "…attempt to offer once again an answer to the eager business community asking for lighter weight along with faster and nimbler software development processes" (Abrahamsson et al. 2003). XP repositions the conventional software process sideways. "Rather than planning, analyzing, and designing for the far-flung future, XP programmers do all of these activities — a little at a time — throughout development" (Beck 1999). The XP major practices, called the "circle of life" (Newkirk 2002), such as *planning game, small releases, metaphor, simple design, tests, refactoring, pair programming, continuous integration, collective ownership, on-site customer, 40-hour weeks, open workspace, just rules,* etc., are exciting new perceptions in software building in the large.

Project teams are often confused as to the best choice of methodology among the above for their project; Datta (2006) derives a metric, the *Agility Measurement Index,* to help such decisions.

6.3. ONE BEGETS THE OTHER

It is important to recognize the element of *evolution* in one methodology making way for another. A methodology seldom expires, to be replaced by another. Usually a methodology serves for some time and for some kinds of software projects. Then some of its bottlenecks are exposed in the grind of building and supporting production-level systems. A new methodology, probably long in gestation, is then born, addressing specific lacunae of its predecessor.

The waterfall and the UP models testify to this organic progression. Waterfall — many of its frailties notwithstanding — remains an important milestone in enterprise software development. Every software engineer knows that the waterfall approach can and does deliver quality software in suitable contexts (Brooks's contrary view notwithstanding; see Section 2.3.7), where risk is low, unknown factors are negligible, and the problem domain is well understood. But the model has been proved to be largely inadequate in situations which were never meant to be *waterfalled* (one beauty of the English language is its great plasticity; almost any noun can be *verbed*!) — and here is where the UP steps in.

Although hardly ever viewed in this way, deploying the UP involves several waterfall cycles — mini-waterfalls, if you will — in a carefully controlled manner. UP introduces an effective wrapper around the basic activity sets defined in the waterfall model and adds a touch of dynamism to it. In a rather naive but illuminating sense, UP may be thought of as waterfall contained in a "for" loop, with clever manipulations of the loop invariants, the iteration index, and other global variable(s) which each pass through the loop may update. Waterfall represents a sort of special case for the more general circumstances UP deals with. It is not uncommon in studies of the "hard sciences" to stumble upon the special case of a particular theory, often empirically, and then build up the general theoretical framework. The evolutions of the waterfall model and UP can be seen in an analogous light.

As mentioned earlier, the slew of agile methods — most visibly XP — embodies another generational stride in software methodologies. (I deliberately do not say *paradigm* shift or *seismic* shift; science and engineering seldom care for such jargon.) While there is much that is fresh and effective in these approaches, some of the precepts surely need more refinement. For example, *pair programming* is very good if two very good programmers converge; any other combination might not be that felicitous. Similarly, not every software developer may be comfortable with the idea of on-site customers.

The hunt for enduring themes in the march of the methodologies leads us to the concepts of *ceremony* and *agility*. In the next section, we discuss the direction of each and how their interplay leads to guiding principles of present-day software development.

6.4. CEREMONY AND AGILITY: TWIN CONCERNS

Ceremony in the context of software development has come to be associated with a strict observance of formalities in the process of software development. (Some authors prefer the word "discipline" [Boehm and Turner 2003] to mean something similar. I feel "discipline" should not be overloaded; we readily associate the word with efficiency and economy. Moreover, discipline is inherent in any methodology; without it, a methodology should hardly be called so.) The detailed documentation, weekly meetings, design reviews, test scripts — all the "concrete" paperwork related to a project contribute to ceremony. A certain degree of ceremony is necessary — indeed, vital — for the success of a project; requirements need to be elicited unambiguously, analysis and design artifacts clearly communicated, users and developers have to agree on the acceptance criteria, and test results should be shared for quality audit. But ceremony comes with an overhead. It often calls for deploying project resources in activities which are at best *peripheral* to actual software development. How much ceremony a project needs is a call that needs to be made early and made correctly if the project is to succeed. Software engineering folklore is dotted with stories of projects that only generated documents or of razor-edge systems delivered but never used, because the users did not really need or want them.

Agility in a software development methodology is its facility in absorbing change and its effects. Change in what? Change principally in requirements and the ripple effect downstream. Every new model of software development seeks to better understand, evaluate, and manage change which inevitably occurs while software is designed and built. It is a fact of life that requirements will undergo change, customers will change their minds, their perception of the role of the software will change, the environment in which the software operates will change, and so will the technology with which the software is being built. As Fowler (2005) says: "In building business software requirements changes are the norm, the question is what we do about it." The most important aspect of a successful software process is its ability to coordinate and control the effects of such change. The word "agility," though co-opted only recently by software methodologists, reflects a lasting objective of software processes: the capacity to adapt to, and deliver in spite of, change.

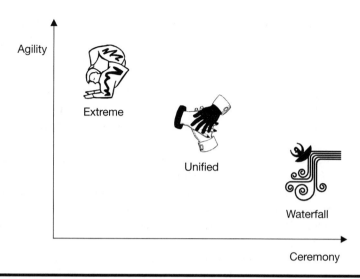

Figure 6.1. Methodologies in the ceremony-agility space

While ceremony and agility are not explicitly at cross-purposes, it is difficult to trace their interconnections in a live project. Every software project seeks to make some sort of peace — maybe merely a truce — between the pulls of ceremony and agility. The waterfall, UP, and agile method each have their own devices to resolve these demands of ceremony and agility. Figure 6.1 shows some of the methodologies in the ceremony-agility space.

One of the most lasting ideas to have emerged from software engineering so far is the effectiveness of iteration and incrementation in building software in the face of inevitable, and ineluctable, change.

6.5. RECURRENT THEMES: ITERATION AND INCREMENTATION

An iterative approach toward *building* things both appeals to and militates against our subconscious notions of how things should be built. For painters, composers, writers, and filmmakers, iteration is the cornerstone of the creative process. What starts as a tentative brush stroke, a few bars of music, scribbled notes, or a "rush print" is chiseled with infinite care, over endless revisits — iterations really — into a finished piece to be shared with the world. (Of course, there are exceptions to this general *modus operandi*. Mozart is said to never have revised his work; he seemed to compose by divine dictation!) Engineers (civil, mechanical, electrical, etc.), on the other hand, hardly build in this vein. It is absurd to start constructing a bridge or a road or a home, build a bit, have users test whatever is built, and use their feedback to modify or build further. Such a bridge or road or home never gets built. The very fact that the iterative approach works so well for software points to the quirks of software and software engineering that were discussed in detail in Chapter 3. But the iterative approach is also evocative of a style of programming all of us use when we first program (and some still do). CABTAB (Code A Bit, Test A Bit), though well suited to small and trivial systems, amounts to unmitigated hacking when applied to anything that is neither small nor trivial. The idea of *incrementation* brings in the vital element of control that makes iteration such a powerful way to build software.

Incrementation makes sure the development activities undertaken iteratively are actually *converging* — after each iterative cycle there is a tangible and testable addition to the body of functionality the software system delivers to the user. Being tangible confirms that the end user can perceive an incremental change in the system's behavior over a past datum (as opposed to mere managerial glib talk: "You can't see it, but the underlying design is pretty neat now; that's what we did in this iteration."). Being testable is qualifying in a set of user-defined tests (as opposed to self-testing by the developers, who are instinctively easy on the parts of the system most likely to break). Often, the idea of a *release* is closely associated with incrementation. To release part of a system is to deploy it in the actual production environment, where real users (or their designates or a subset of real users, as in the case of increasingly popular beta releases) are free to run amok with it and report all problems. The combination of iteration and incrementation — in addition to its alliterative value —embodies a simple, powerful, and controllable strategy for developing enterprise software. Iterative and incremental development (refer to Section 2.3.7 for related discussion) works best in increasingly common milieus where rigid up-front planning is impossible due to a variety of factors.

Every software methodology since waterfall has tried to resolve its limitations. Iterative and incremental development is not a radical new idea; it has been around under other aliases for a long time (Fowler 2005). (A long time by software engineering standards, that is. There are long times and there are long times. My wife, a budding geologist, regards everything less than ten million years as not long enough.) In the next section, salient features of the UP are outlined.

6.6. THE UNIFIED SOFTWARE DEVELOPMENT PROCESS: A FRAMEWORK

Genesis of the UP offers great insights into the collaborative nature of software engineering. It also shows how methodologies attain wide relevance through intermingling of varied ideas. The "three amigos" —what Jacobson, Booch, and Rumbaugh came to be called after joining hands — have given a durable and extensible schema of organized software development in UP. In their words, "...the Unified Process is more than a single process; it is a generic process framework that can be specialized for a very large class of software systems, for different application areas, different types of organizations, different project sizes" (Jacobson et al. 1999). The key characteristics of the UP are highlighted as being use-case driven, architecture centric, iterative, and incremental (Jacobson et al. 1999).

The high-level view (in fact, *very* high-level view, thirty thousand feet perhaps) of the UP given above brings out its contours well. First and foremost, the UP, more than being just a process, is also a process *framework*. It is sort of a template to create processes, given a broad objective. One such *instantiation* (the choice of the word is deliberate, reflecting the similarity to class-object relationship) of the UP is the RUP or the Rational Unified Process. (RUP in turn is also called a process framework [Kruchten 2004].)

An issue worth examining in passing here is what the UP, or for that matter any development methodology, promises. Is it a *potion* that the prince (development team) needs to fell the monster (project vicissitudes) and win the princess (customer satisfaction)? Is it a *panacea* that delivers a terminally ill project to eternal health? Or is it a *prescription,* which, like every prescription a doctor writes, is given on the assumptions that: (1) the patient must take the medication when and as advised and (2) the patient must not indulge in activities which, though not explicitly proscribed, will clearly prevent him or her from getting better (e.g., climbing a mountain while being treated for a sprained ankle). A prescription gives directions for regaining and maintaining health, but there is a lot it does not say, gaps which are expected to be filled by the experience and common sense of the patient or caregivers. Similarly, software development methodologies contain prescriptions for building systems that offer best returns on their investment. To be general and widely applicable, they need to have many ellipses and innuendos. Indeed, in reading between these lines lie the challenge and charm of building software. Interpreting process prescriptions is helped by wisdom and experience, and by heuristics (refer to Section 2.3.5) when wisdom and experience need to be bridged. As discussed earlier in Chapter 2, the following chapters explore metrics to help practitioners act in situations where a methodology offers no mantra.

6.6.1. Unified Process: Salient Features

Among the UP's foundational principles of being use-case driven, architecture centric, and iterative and incremental, the first two relate closely to how software is designed, while the latter concerns the way software is built. The UP is a matrix of *phases* and *workflows.*

The workflows correspond to the activities that are readily associated with software development — *requirements, analysis, design, implementation,* and *test.* The phases *inception, elaboration, construction,* and *transition* embody the monitoring and control mechanism. The four major milestones — Life Cycle Objectives, Life Cycle Architecture, Initial Operational Capability, and Product Release — calibrate the outcome from the phases in their respective order. However, end users can and should see results independent of the completion of phases. The system grows incrementally over iterations. Each increment leads to, as stated earlier, tangible and testable results. As the project moves forward, the iteration window may be thought to move across the spectrum of phases. It may be noted, in a clear departure from the waterfall way, that each phase of this model has components of all workflows (that is, every type of development activity, from understanding requirements to testing). The extent to which a workflow is addressed in a phase varies from one iteration window to another.

The iterative and incremental approach offers a powerful and elegant abstraction. However, like most powerful and elegant abstractions, it comes with some baggage. What slice of the problem domain (more specifically, which particular requirements) should be addressed in an iteration? What constitutes an increment that is neither too trivial (testing and feedback becomes fatuous) nor too involved (becoming a project by itself)? How to manage the inevitable changes in requirements that will arrive out of showing parts of the functioning system to users? (*IKIWISI* — I Know It When I See It — syndrome is endemic; a working feature of the system usually inspires users to realize that is *not* what they wanted!) How to plan time, budget, and resources for an iterative and incremental strategy? And most significantly, how to ensure that iterations and increments are leading the system to grow into a cohesive whole, integrated in function and purpose and not just a potpourri of modules? In other words, how to make the development effort converge into something useful for the end user? There are no ready answers to these questions. In the next few chapters, we will develop mechanisms to search for and find these answers, and when answers remain elusive, to suggest workarounds.

The next section lays out the road map for how and where we seek to introduce metrics orientation in an iterative and incremental software development approach.

6.7. THE ESSENCE OF OUR APPROACH

The preceding sections established the centrality of an iterative and incremental strategy in constructing software systems. The following chapters introduce the role and relevance of metrics in the workflows — *requirements, analysis, design, implementation,* and *test* — and develop a suite of metrics for practitioners' use.

A note on notation: In our discussion, *analysis* refers to the analysis workflow, whereas analysis means the various broadly analytical activities associated with software development. Any other usage of the word should be clear from the context. Other words like requirements, design, implementation, and test have been used similarly.

In the next chapters, we will briefly discuss the intent and desiderata of development activities and then devise metrics to better perform, monitor, and coordinate them. While developing the metrics, we will have occasion to examine and reflect upon the many tensions that underpin enterprise software development. These observations will help us place the utility of metrics in its context.

What is presented from now on is not confined to a particular process or methodology. Iterative and incremental development allows for feedback (refer to Section 2.3.6), and feedback allows information gleaned from metrics to influence the development process for the better. Our focus on iterative and incremental development in this chapter set up a background for applying the metrics. We briefly touched upon UP as an iterative-and-incremental-based methodology. The metrics and general ideas presented in this book are applicable in any iterative and incremental approach. There is no endorsement, stated or implied, of a particular process or product.

Kruchten (2001) captures the essence of iterative and incremental development as "...continuous discovery, invention, and implementation, with each iteration forcing the development team to drive to closure the project's artifacts in a predictable and repeatable way." Driving the project's artifacts to closure in a predictable and repeatable way remains one of the greatest challenges of software engineering. The metrics presented in this book seek to facilitate this closure.

6.8. SUMMARY

This chapter laid the foundation for the following chapters in Part 2, where we will develop metrics for enterprise software development. To summarize:

- Waterfall, UP, and agile methodologies represent three major approaches to software development, each drawing ideas from its predecessors.
- Ceremony and agility remain two pulls that software development methodologies must successfully counterbalance.
- An iterative and incremental approach is an effective way of building large-scale enterprise software. As feedback mechanisms are built into iterative and incremental development, metrics can readily aid the development process.

In the next chapter, we derive the *Correlation Matrix* and the *Mutation Score* to help practitioners better connect requirements with other downstream activities and artifacts of the software development life cycle.

REFERENCES

Abrahamsson, P., Warsta, J., Siponen, M. T., and Ronkainen, J. (2003). New directions on agile methods: A comparative analysis. In *ICSE '03: Proceedings of the 25th International Conference on Software Engineering,* pp. 244–254. IEEE Computer Society.

Beck, K. (1999). Embracing change with extreme programming. *Computer,* 32(10): 70–77.

Boehm, B. and Turner, R. (2003). Observations on balancing discipline and agility. In *ADC '03: Proceedings of the Conference on Agile Development,* p. 32. IEEE Computer Society.

Datta, S. (2006). Agility measurement index — A metric for the crossroads of software development methodologies. In Proceedings of the 44th ACM Southeast Conference (ACMSE 2006), pp. 271–273.

Fowler, M. (2005). The New Methodology. http://www.martinfowler.com/articles/newMethodology.html.

Jacobson, I., Booch, G., and Rumbaugh, J. (1999). *The Unified Software Development Process.* Addison-Wesley.

Kruchten, P. (2001). From Waterfall to Iterative Development — A Challenging Transition for Project Managers. http://www-128.ibm.com/developerworks/rational/library/content/RationalEdge/dec00/FromWaterfalltoIterativeDevelopmentDec00.pdf.

Kruchten, P. (2004). *The Rational Unified Process: An Introduction,* 3rd ed. Addison-Wesley.

Newkirk, J. (2002). Introduction to agile processes and extreme programming. In *ICSE '02: Proceedings of the 24th International Conference on Software Engineering*, pp. 695–696. ACM Press.

Schach, S. (2005). *Object-Oriented and Classical Software Development*, 6th ed. McGraw-Hill.

Tilley, T., Cole, R., Becker, P., and Eklund, P. (2003). A survey of formal concept analysis support for software engineering activities. In Stumme, G., editor, *Proceedings of the First International Conference on Formal Concept Analysis — ICFCA '03*. Springer-Verlag.

REQUIREMENTS: THE DRIVERS OF SOFTWARE DEVELOPMENT

7.1. OVERVIEW

Requirements are the *raison d'être* of enterprise software systems. Although the whole business of software building is driven by requirements, practitioners often rue the lack of clear guidelines for going about understanding, structuring, and documenting requirements. This chapter explores some of these challenges. In addition, the *Correlation Matrix* and the *Mutation Score* are presented; the former aids traceability of development artifacts with requirements, while the latter keeps track of the extent to which requirements change over iterations.

7.2. THE REQUIREMENTS REALM

I was once discussing with a friend, a doctor of medicine, the lasting challenges in her profession. (My interest in medicine stems partly from the moving account by Maugham [1992] of his medical internship in *The Summing Up*. Added to it is a belief that doctors make more money than engineers.) My friend agreed that technology has made some of a doctor's tasks easier, both in diagnosis and therapy, but she believed the most basic of a physician's duty, addressing a patient's symptoms, remains nearly the same as it was since Hippocrates' time. The whole line of treatment depends on how the doctor *elicits* and interprets a patient's true difficulties from other related or unrelated complaints.

Understanding requirements from software users (or would-be users) is an exercise not entirely unlike the patient-doctor interaction. Software systems are usually commissioned to ease up specific "pain points" for an organization or its clientele. The systems are meant to enhance performance, simplify operations, and ensure higher customer satisfaction by orders of magnitude. But seldom, if ever, do users know, or are they able to express, what the software actually needs to do to deliver these benefits. This is the crux of the requirements problem.

The activities related to the understanding and documentation of requirements have been variously described as "elicitation," "gathering," "specification," or simply "requirements capture." This wide swath of jargon points to the confusion surrounding the task. Indeed, success with requirements calls for a spectrum of skills: engineering judgment, communication, understanding of human psychology, and, last but not least, political acumen. The study and practice of these dynamics are often referred to as *requirements engineering.* Davis (2004) illuminates some of the major challenges with requirements in his book. A unified framework for requirements management is developed by Leffingwell and Widrig (2000).

Requirements are important because they are what the end users can directly associate with and will measure the final software product against. The software development process at every juncture needs to ensure clear traceability exists between every artifact that is being modified and the *parent* requirement that called for its creation in the first place. This is one of those shibboleths software engineers find very easy to agree to and very hard to implement.

7.3. REQUIREMENTS TO USE CASES: AN UNEASY TRANSITION

The idea of use cases (Jacobson 1992) brought a generational shift in the perception of enterprise software. It was notably different from the *feature-*oriented view in vogue earlier, where customers provided a laundry list of their demands from the system and developers ticked them off one by one as the system was built. Use cases underscore a transactional relationship between software and its users; a software system is used for a set of related purposes, and the use is manifested in a series of user-system interactions, each providing some value to the user.

Rumbaugh et al. (2005) call use case "the specification of sequences of actions, including variant sequences and error sequences, that a system, subsystem, or class can perform by interacting with outside objects to provide a service of value." A set of use cases for a system serves as a *contract* between the builders and users of a system to specify the utility the system is expected to deliver to the users. The greatest gift to a software engineering practitioner is a set of clear and concise use cases, written in simple, natural prose, carefully avoiding equivocation or ambiguity. And this is also the rarest gift.

It is inane to expect users to come up with their own use cases. Often, software projects originate with a one-liner (flatteringly called the "project vision") resulting from a conversation at the coffee machine ("Our online reporting system sucks. Can your team fix it?") or a short e-mail. Users (or business partners, that is, those who commission a software project on behalf of the actual users) have "kind of an idea" what they want. And often that is all they have. Asking them to produce a requirements document or a set of use cases will most likely result in preferences in font or color and the image at the top left corner of the main page, but little, if any, direction on how fast the application should respond or how soon the application must adapt to a radically new line of business. Does this mean the latter issues are less important to the users than the former? On the contrary, it means requirements are best understood and specified by those who will actually build the system. And understanding requirements is the first step toward discovering and refining use cases.

Requirements, when written out by system analysts in close consultation with the system's users, usually result in a set of statement clusters, each cluster uniquely identifying and describing a service the users require the system to fulfill. (For example, "The system shall allow the user to enter his or her user ID and password. Upon entry, the system shall verify the credentials, and on successful verification present a page listing his or her account details.") The bulk of the requirements are straightforward demands of some functionality from the system; they are usually called *functional* requirements. These have to be translated into use cases. The analyst's finesse lies in reorganizing the requirements statements in a *serve-and-volley* format, as a series of user-system interactions. There are many formats for writing use cases, such as tabular, block text, with placeholders for peripheral information such as preconditions and postconditions, etc. The choice of format depends on a number of factors, most notably the project's level of ceremony (refer to Section 6.4). Anything that brings the users and developers to a consensus regarding the system's functionality and is recorded in a durable medium for future reference (there will be many occasions to refer to this information as the project moves forward) is fair game for specifying use cases.

But beyond the mere functional, users do have more subtle desires. What if the system takes ten minutes to authenticate a user when the user is done supplying his or her credentials in ten seconds? Is there a guarantee a server crash will not wipe out all the financial data for a user? These are hardly something the system *explicitly* does for the user, but every user *implicitly* expects the system to ensure these are taken care of. Such requirements — rather negatively — are called *nonfunctional*, and there is no intuitive way to match nonfunctional requirements with use cases. Datta (2005) presents a mechanism for integrating use cases with the nonfunctional requirements. Fulfilling nonfunctional requirements plays a vital role in successful software, when success is defined as delivering a system users will use. (Refer to the sidebar in Chapter 8 titled "Requirements and Use Cases: A Marriage of Convenience" for related discussion on requirements and use cases.)

7.4. REQUIREMENTS INTERACTION

When users start to voice requirements and developers to hear and understand them, both parties assume each requirement is stand-alone or each exists by and for itself. This is far from the truth, but it is important not to muddy the waters at this point by considering how requirements might and do interact. We will examine this aspect in analysis and design, when we start worrying about how everything should finally fit together. However, practitioners need to keep in mind that what appear as separate chunks of functionality ultimately will be delivered by closely collaborating components. It is usual for customers to think development time and functionality are exchangeable: Can we take this particular requirement out and deliver the product a month earlier than planned? This speaks to a common confusion about how enterprise systems are designed and built. A metaphor might clear the air.

When planning a dinner for guests, one plans a menu, shops for the groceries, and then gets down to the actual cooking. While the menu may offer a fare of great variety, it always helps if ingredients used in one dish can be used in other dishes too. Salt and sugar are used across many items, while chicken may be used in the soup as well as the entrée. Optimization of shopping and cooking efforts is closely linked with how much the ingredients are used across the different menu items. Very broadly, something similar goes on in software building. Starting from requirements, the best solution in terms of labor and cost is the one that allows components to work as closely together

as possible. But an added layer of complexity comes from changing requirements. This has no parallel in the dinner metaphor — one hardly expects guests
to give a list of what they want (and do not want) to eat and keep changing
their choices until dinner is served.

7.5. CHANGING REQUIREMENTS

The birds and bees of software engineering can be said to be awaking to
requirements change. Requirements change with amazing certainty, in every
software system other than term projects in school. Changing requirements and
their effects on the evolution of software methodologies were briefly touched
upon in Chapter 6. Like the warning on a pack of cigarettes or a liquor bottle,
requirements should carry a disclaimer that they are liable to change, without
notice or apparent reason! I know of a project whose manager made it a rule
for customers to sign off on requirements — real ink signatures on real paper,
and no e-mailed acquiescence. The manager made much noise about how this
was going to save the team's collective posterior in the long run. The system
was built and delivered based on the needs signed off on. Meanwhile, every
attempt to foist new or changed requirements was thwarted. Several months
later, a satisfaction survey revealed that the system had not even clocked 10%
of its projected usage. Customer satisfaction, not unexpectedly, was nothing to
write home about.

The essence of software engineering — more so for enterprise systems,
where the stakes are critically high — is to design and deliver software that
adapts to changing requirements. Doing this is not black magic, but it requires
forethought and discipline.

Changing requirements may well be considered the most important factor
in building durable and usable enterprise software. The fact that requirements
can and do change reflects a strange facet of software (discussed in Section
1.2.3): a software system is never complete in the sense a house or a car is. The
apparent plasticity of the software medium provokes users to ask for more, upon
realizing what they asked for is not what they wanted. Successfully catering to
such demands creates big challenges as well as great satisfaction for software
engineering practitioners.

Based on the above discussion, the following highlights the most important
attitudes that need to be brought to the requirements culture:

- Every downstream artifact must trace back to at least one requirement.
- Change in requirements must be accepted as organic to the software
  development process and must be monitored and documented.

7.6. GROWING OUR METRICS

Growing our metrics is a theme central to this book. To be successful, software metrics need to be devised along with developing software. Metrics are not something invented in laboratories and then distributed to be applied. "Growing" also underscores that software metrics indeed *grow* from one version to the other; applying them leads to new insights, which in turn helps improve them.

In the last section, two major areas of importance when looking at requirements were identified. These ideas are now developed further.

7.6.1. Correlation Matrix

Correlation Matrix is a tabular representation that maps each artifact of the software development process to specific requirement(s). We are in the business of software building because users have certain requirements. Everything we create in the building process needs to be traceable to a particular requirement. The link from an artifact to a requirement may not be direct, but it should not be so obscure as to prevent the connection from being understood and documented.

Table 7.1 gives the *Correlation Matrix* for a hypothetical system with four requirements and six artifacts. In Chapter 13, the use of the *Correlation Matrix* is illustrated in the case study.

As new artifacts are created, the *Correlation Matrix* is kept updated. At any point in the development life cycle, the *Correlation Matrix* offers a snapshot of all the artifacts the project efforts have created so far and which specific requirement(s) each of these entities helps fulfill. When requirements change, the *Correlation Matrix* gives a quick idea of which artifacts stand to be affected by the change. This information is vital in systems that involve many require-

Table 7.1. Sample *Correlation Matrix*

	Requirements			
Artifacts	**1**	**2**	**3**	**4**
Use case 4: Register	X			
Supplementary specification		X		X
Analysis class: Accounts			X	
Sequence diagram: Withdraw Money			X	
Code component: UserInputVerifier.java	X		X	
Test case: Transfer Funds				X

ments and artifacts, where change in any of the former may potentially start a ripple effect in the latter.

7.6.2. Mutation Score

Concrete and documented user requirements are the foremost wish software engineers would ask if Aladdin's genie made a guest appearance. If the wish was granted, software engineering would be a piece of cake.

Requirements are never concrete; even when documented, there is no guarantee they represent what the users mean them to mean. This is a fact of life software engineers must live with and live in spite of.

To make matters easier to handle, we devise a measure. *Mutation Score* is a measure of the number of times requirements change over the number of iterations the software system undergoes.

Let the *Mutation Score* for requirement R_n be denoted by MS(R_n). Let m be the number of iterations for a project.

1. At iteration 1, set MS(R_n) = 0.
2. For iteration 2 to m, if R_n has changed, MS(R_n) = MS(R_n) + 1.

Repeat steps 1 and 2 for all requirements $R_1, R_2, \ldots$

How do we determine change in a requirement? We define change in this context to be any modification of the written description of a requirement perceptible when one version of a document is compared with another. The reasonable assumption is made that requirement descriptions change only when some of the described functionality changes.

What does the *Mutation Score* buy us? Among a set of requirements, those with high *Mutation Scores* across a series of iterations may indicate any or a combination of the following:

- Mere whimsicality on the part of users
- Analysts are revising their earlier understanding of these requirements
- The environment in which the software is meant to operate is undergoing unforeseen changes
- Incremental release of the software is giving the users new perspectives on its use

We will take up dealing with these issues in later chapters. For the time being, the *Mutation Score* helps keep tabs on the more capricious requirements; their changes will affect corresponding artifacts listed in the *Correlation Matrix.*

7.7. SUMMARY

This chapter briefly reviewed the role of requirements and presented the *Correlation Matrix* and the *Mutation Score*. To summarize:

- Requirements drive the software development process.
- Functional requirements can be directly mapped to use cases. However, nonfunctional requirements also play an important role in ensuring customer satisfaction.
- Requirements undergo frequent changes; enterprise software systems have to be delivered in spite of changing requirements.
- *Correlation Matrix* helps connect each artifact generated during development to specific requirement(s).
- *Mutation Score* measures the extent to which requirements change over iterations.

The case study in Part 3 demonstrates the use of the *Correlation Matrix* and the *Mutation Score*. In the next chapter, we explore analysis and design and how metrics can help perform these better.

REFERENCES

Datta, S. (2005). Integrating the FURPS+ model with use cases — A metrics driven approach. In Supplementary Proceedings of the 16th IEEE International Symposium on Software Reliability Engineering (ISSRE 2005), Chicago, November 7–11, pp. 4-51–4-52.

Davis, A. M. (2004). *Great Software Debates.* IEEE/Wiley-Interscience.

Jacobson, I. (1992). *Object-Oriented Software Engineering: A Use Case Driven Approach.* Addison-Wesley.

Leffingwell, D. and Widrig, D. (2000). *Managing Software Requirements: A Unified Approach.* Addison-Wesley.

Maugham, W. S. (1992). *The Summing Up.* Penguin Classics.

Rumbaugh, J., Jacobson, I., and Booch, G. (2005). *The Unified Modeling Language Reference Manual,* 2nd ed. Addison-Wesley.

ANALYSIS AND DESIGN: ON UNDERSTANDING, DECIDING, AND MEASURING

8.1. OVERVIEW

This chapter examines the closely related activities of analysis and design in enterprise software development. The metrics *Meshing Ratio, AEI Score,* and *Morphing Index* are presented to facilitate analysis and design. The derivation of the *Morphing Index* brings out two aspects. On one hand, it shows how metrics making itself is iterative, while on the other it reflects the formulation of a metric out of a development scenario. This also sets the stage for the case study we delve more deeply into in Part 3.

8.2. ANALYSIS AND DESIGN OR ANALYSIS-DESIGN?

Analysis and design are like day and night — easy to tell the difference, but hard to decide where one ends and the other begins. Just as day and night together make up the diurnal cycle, analysis and design represent a continuum of two diverse but closely related activities in the software development life cycle. Analysis and design have very different foci and objectives, but they can and should segue seamlessly into one another. Much of the confusion about analysis and design results from the closely interactive nature of their activities. In discussing analysis and design together, this chapter will highlight their differences but — more importantly — reflect on their synergy.

During enterprise software development, trying to do analysis and design together often ends up doing neither and instead doing something seemingly more concrete — coding. The results of such coding are usually disastrous, with few chances of recovery. What makes analysis and design so exciting — and difficult — is their inherent subjectivity. There are no equations, formulas, or prescriptions to guide you; it is all about bringing into play your own intuition, experience, and nameless "gut feelings." True, there have been efforts to *codify* some of the wisdom of analysis and design. *Analysis patterns* (Fowler 1996) and *design patterns* (Gamma et al. 1995) are now supposed to be parts of the software engineer's tool kit, but knowing when to apply these ideas requires the maturity of a practitioner with several years of hands-on experience. After several years of hands-on experience, a practitioner has his or her own set of heuristics (refer to Section 2.3.5) to fall back on, techniques that have stood him or her in good stead in the knottiest of problems. Patterns are as good as the aptness of situations where they are applied; their inappropriate use causes more harm than good, and their inappropriate use is far from uncommon. I have seen designs where misplaced fealty to the *singleton* pattern gave a component needless and inefficient solitude or the *facade* pattern create layer after layer of redundant code. Patterns known only by hearsay, when applied, can cause problems which even raw ineptitude cannot match. Software engineering is full of egos and alter egos: thus it is not surprising there is also an active *antipatterns* lobby that warns against the stereotypes of a patterned outlook (Brown et al. 2001).

In sum, there are no sure-shot recipes for success with analysis and design; neither are there quick "numbers" to guide our path. The next few sections discuss the desiderata of the analysis and design activities, devise metrics to give us some insights on how we may go about them, and finally fit the parts into the bigger puzzle. For a software engineering project to be successful, sound analysis and design are a necessary condition.

8.3. ANALYSIS: THE WHAT

From thirty thousand feet, analysis is about understanding the problem and design is about deciding how to solve it. Such sweeping comments are mostly treacherous; this one is no exception. What is the *problem*? How do we ensure *understanding*? What is *decision* all about? And what exactly is a *solution*? These are difficult questions, and they must be tackled.

Any software system (outside of the classroom) exists to fulfill the needs of some group or individuals (called stakeholders in Section 2.3.2) who have some material interest in the system. Requirements capture these needs in writing; analysis is the next step in making sense of these needs. A common problem with analysis is addressing the task with too much baggage.

8.3.1. Leaving the Baggage Out of Analysis

Baggage in analysis is about thinking too much like the customer, too much like the designer, or worse still, too much like the implementer or tester. In explaining basic mechanics, the construct of "free-body diagrams" is often used. The strategy is to consider a physical object as a "free body" — bereft of its position, orientation, or motion — and just focus on the mechanical forces impinging on it. Something similar is helpful in analysis. At this stage, it is best to concentrate only on understanding the user's need fully and unambiguously, without worrying about how a particular feature is to be designed, built, or tested. Understanding fully and unambiguously calls for not only reading the lines but, more importantly, reading between them.

Analysis starts with reading the requirements description. Analysis also starts with a key assumption: for the time being, each requirement is taken to exist by itself. Considerations of how system components will interact to fulfill the requirements are firmly kept at bay.

This is also a good time to underscore the delicate interplay between requirements and use cases. Refer to the sidebar titled "Requirements and Use Cases: A Marriage of Convenience." For reasons highlighted in the sidebar, requirements were chosen to indicate the primary artifact for user needs.

8.3.2. The Act of Analysis

What is analysis about? What do we mean when we say "let's get down to analysis"?

In many projects, analysis is a part of the initial "slack" period in the development life cycle, when teams are staffed, infrastructure readied, and the users given time to make up their minds about what exactly they want. In these projects, real work is taken to be "coding," which starts when the deadline looks distinctly near. These projects usually get into trouble.

Analysis must start early, but it is not just an arrangement to keep the time sheets rolling until the project gains momentum. Analysis is about scrutinizing

REQUIREMENTS AND USE CASES:
A MARRIAGE OF CONVENIENCE

I have often wondered whether "marriage of convenience" or "strange bedfellows" better describes the combination of requirements and use cases. Not wishing to be prurient, I leaned toward the former in naming this sidebar. Requirements have been around for as long as human beings have had needs. For software systems, requirements came to be studied and managed ever since people started paying other people to build software for them. Use cases, alas, do not have such atavistic associations. They came about very much in memorial times; even so, they have their share of legends. Jacobson is reputed to have written the first use cases in the mid-1980s; he coined the Swedish term *anvendningsfall,* which literally translates to "situation of usage" or "usage case." These probably sounded a bit gauche, so the sweeter "use case" was settled upon (Cockburn 2002).

The real point about requirements and use cases does not, however, relate to their roots. There is no formula to go from requirements to use cases or vice versa. But every project that follows a modern development methodology needs to make this transition — not once, but continually as requirements change. This is the key angle. Requirements change, and use cases, like all the other downstream artifacts, must respond to this change. Thus, use cases, in spite of being so useful, are derived artifacts. Real users connect more quickly and directly to requirements, and requirements drive development, via the use cases. Like a happy marriage (convenience surely a part thereof), requirements and use cases complement one another. In this book, I chose to use requirements as the main artifact for capturing and monitoring user needs.

---

requirements and clarifying them to the point they have no ambiguities. Analysis is about reading the user's mind. But analysis is more than that. Analysis, finally, is about identifying the *players.*

We define *players* to be software entities which interact to deliver the functionality of the system. Why not just call them *components*? Players and components differ in a subtle but significant way. According to Larman (1997), assigning responsibilities is the most precious talent software development needs to harness. Players can be viewed as the first cut at identifying entities that will *do* specific things. Players are creatures of analysis; in design, they incarnate as concrete components, with data members and operations. *Analysis classes* may be one way of describing players, but I believe the term is misleading. During analysis, the last thing one should do is worry about "classiness"; it gives a gratuitous object-oriented slant to the artifact. Object orientation is predominantly a design and implementation paradigm. It does not hurt to think in terms of objects from early on, but it certainly hurts to color analysis too much in those terms. A "player" in our discussion is an initial placeholder for the *doers* of our system. In design, a player may be represented as a class or several classes, depending on the level of granularity preferred, but let us not worry about that for now.

Noun analysis, verb analysis, etc. are several standard techniques for analyzing. Each has its backers, usually intense, often rabid. I have known practitioners to split hairs over whether nouns are to be underlined in red and verbs in blue or vice versa. ("You know, nouns are the key, so they should be red." "But verbs are what need to be done, so they must be red.") These approaches boil down to reading descriptions of functionality and picking out what needs to be done and who it seems is the best person to do it. Often, what needs to be done goes far deeper than what the users have said they want to be done. This happens due to many factors, but most notably due to the expected (and sometimes blissful) ignorance of users about what actually goes on behind the facade of any engineering artifact. Braking a moving car and expecting it to stop reasonably quickly is a basic user need. But what occurs between pressing the brake pedal and the car's ultimate state of rest is typical engineering magic unbeknownst to the driver who braked. In analysis, we are still navigating the problem space; it is better not to worry too much about how to get things done. Instead, we concern ourselves more with finding potential candidates that can *do* the work — the players. Each requirement is examined, and one or more players are assigned to it. The assignment should be based on the letter as well as the spirit of the requirement. This is an especially good time to address the latter, as users are still easily accessible and their understanding of their problem is still being facilitated by the analysts. And it is early enough for the initial goodwill among stakeholders to prevent charges of oscillation. (There always comes a time in the life of a project when developers and users trade allegations of "going back and forth" in finalizing requirements or becoming fixated on the finality. The iterative and incremental approach ensures the project lives to fight another day; the waterfall model does not.)

Let us consider a fragment of a requirement description:

> The system shall accept user ID and password from the user. Upon successful verification, the system shall present the Account Sum-

mary Page to the user. If the user ID and password are not successfully verified, the system shall present the Error Page to the user, with the error message "The user ID/password entered does not match our records."

Who are the players here? Evidently, the system ultimately caters to all the needs and is certainly a player, but that does not help us much. System is too general an idea, too black a box; engineering is all about peeping inside black boxes. Let us regard "system" as some super-player, benign and indulgent, under whose auspices the real players get on with their game. The description talks about "presenting" pages to users (we assume Account Summary Page and Error Page are Web pages displayed on a browser). One player can be Page_Presenter, which dishes out a page to the user, knowing the right one in each circumstance through some trick. Then there can be another: User_Credential_Verifier, a player that decides, given an ID and password, whether a bona fide user seeks access. We do not consider the Account Summary Page or Error Page as players for our purpose; they are clearly not *doing* anything other than just being presented for the users' perusal. (Web pages can do and do many things without the help of the deeper layers. It used to be with JavaScript earlier; now AJAX seems to have opened the floodgates of what can be done with Web pages or even parts thereof. But I remain skeptical how much functionality should spill over from the middle layers to the presentation layers. These transgressions question the whole logic of multilayered architecture. In this example, we take Web pages to be just vehicles for data exhibition.) We are not done with picking players yet.

Reading between the lines was mentioned earlier. The requirement excursus given above does not mention anything about how quickly the system needs to verify the user ID/password to decide whether the user may be welcomed or thrown out. But just because it does not does not mean the users will endure a ten-minute verification period kindly. It might be a good idea to have a player, Performance_Checker, to oversee these timing issues. This is a covert player — an *undercover agent,* if you will — which the analyst stumbles upon while fishing around the requirements. As stated in Chapter 7, these concerns are often lumped together as nonfunctional requirements and dumped to be taken up later, when the seemingly paramount functional requirements have been fixed. The effects are distressing. For more on this, see the sidebar titled "Requirements: Nonfunctionals Need to Be Functional Too!"

To reiterate an earlier view, a key point about identifying players is to consider them, *for the time being,* as playing the game all by themselves. We do not yet account for other players and the laws governing the interaction

---

REQUIREMENTS: NONFUNCTIONALS NEED TO BE FUNCTIONAL TOO!

Years ago, new in the industry, I had a hard time figuring out why nonfunctional requirements had to be factored into the functioning of an enterprise software system. They have to be because the software system under advisement is *enterprise*. Enterprise software systems are not just about delivering functionality to the users. They are also about developing a system that is easy to build, use, maintain, and modify. Parameters such as usability, reliability, performance, scalability — grouped together as the nonfunctional requirements — ensure the development effort leads to a *sustainable* software system. The major difficulty is that nonfunctional requirements are not readily reflected in use cases and are prone to being swept under the carpet, only to pop up later, uncomfortably close to the deadline. Datta (2005) makes an attempt to connect use cases with nonfunctional requirements. The bottom line remains: functional requirements come out of reading the lines and nonfunctional ones from reading *between* them.

---

amongst the players, that is, rules of the game. That is the realm of design, which we will get into in the latter part of this chapter. However, enterprise software is about interaction, so it does not pay to be totally blind to other players. We will next derive the metric *Meshing Ratio* to give us a quantitative idea of how much the players we have picked are already interacting, without consciously knowing it.

In passing, this is a good time to reflect upon some characteristics of analysis and design. There are no blacks and whites in this game, no absolute do's and don'ts. It is all about ascribing relative importance at certain times, if only to revise priorities at a later stage. In managing this duality lie the beauty and finesse of building superior software. A quick way to tell a good design book from a bad one (or a good design guru from one of contrasting talents) is to check whether absolute commandments are being doled out. There can be none in this game. It is only through deep understanding and experience that practitioners come up with rules of thumb and remain very aware of their limitations. Later in this chapter we will discuss how *abstraction, elision,* and *indirection* help foster some discernment that aids design and analysis.

Before moving to the derivation of the *Meshing Ratio,* let us review some major pitfalls of analysis.

8.3.3. Analysis Paralysis

I first came across the phrase *analysis paralysis* in a book by one of the "three amigos." Of late, it seems to have gained much currency, as even the online encyclopedia *Wikipedia* gives it an honorable mention: "Analysis paralysis is an informal phrase applied to when the opportunity cost of decision analysis exceeds the benefits....In software development, analysis paralysis manifests itself through exceedingly long phases of project planning, requirements gathering, program design and modeling, with little or no extra value created by those steps." In short, analysis paralysis is getting caught in the quagmires of analysis and not going any further. (Taking the hint, we will not get caught in the nuances of "opportunity cost" and "decision analysis" in the above lines and will focus on moving ahead.)

Analysis is a fascinating activity; at every reread of the requirements, at every discussion with the users, at every review of existing artifacts, new insights are unearthed. It is easy to get carried away, and it happens often. Over-analysis is as bad as overdesign, and both are as prodigal as overkill. Engineering is all about getting the most done with the fewest resources, and overdoing is as much to be avoided as underdoing. Overanalyzing leaves one tired, frustrated, and increasingly convinced the problem is too hard to crack. Below is a list of the major causes of analysis paralysis and some workarounds:

- **There is no correct analysis** — Analysis is all about understanding the problem domain; there is no "right" or "wrong" understanding, just different ways of understanding. The central interest in analysis is clearly knowing what the user wants to get done through the software system the user is commissioning. This knowledge is acquired slowly, in an onion-like manner, by peeling away layers of wishes and expectations. There is nothing the user should or should not want; the analyst needs to honor whatever is wanted. Lack of prejudice, openness, and not letting memories of past projects (failures as well as successes) interfere too much are essential traits for analyzing well.

- **Forget about coding or even detailed design** — There are schools of thought that are pretty hung up on *roles* in the software development life cycle. They prescribe tasks for Designers, Testers, and such other upper-cased entities and proscribe any other actions for these individuals. Roles are important as long as they prevent different phases of software development from influencing one another. It is in the best interest of a project for analysts and designers to be well versed in the totality of the development life cycle, yet have the maturity to see analysis, design, coding, and testing as different activities, with very different goals. While analyzing, a common tendency is to do a bit of phantom design or phantom coding and take quick, surreptitious dives into thinking ahead and try to reason out how the analysis artifacts would incarnate in the downstream phases. A high-level design view does help during analysis, but it needs to remain strictly high level; low-level design issues should never rear their heads. I know of a project where the lead analyst, in a requirement elicitation session, mentioned inner classes, vectors, and hash tables by the dozen, in a glib display of his grasp of Java technology. The customers put up with it for some time. Then one of them quipped that everything was fine, as long as the development team did not make a "hash" of things. The moral of the story is not to get too much ahead of oneself during analysis; it will not help analyzing and may even put off the customer. The best analysis artifacts are the ones that are specific enough to capture every detail worth knowing and general enough to serve any design or implementation paradigm. Ideally, the same analysis artifacts should be able to support procedural or object-oriented technologies. As almost all enterprise systems are now built by object-oriented techniques, it does not hurt to think of the players as potential classes. Any deeper preoccupation with their implementation in code should, however, be avoided.

■ **Document your artifacts, don't get hooked onto them** — A popular way to make short work of analysis is to think that thinking about analysis is analysis. I have been shown the nouns and verbs in requirement descriptions underlined in red or blue as proof that analysis was done. With the high attrition, burnout, and turnaround rates typical of software projects, here today, gone tomorrow is a fact of life. The only way to guard against this is to have every activity documented in standard notation. Indeed, documentation, in spite of the derision it generates in some software engineers (usually bad ones), has an important role to play in engineering, and software engineering is no exception. I have used the sidebar titled "Software Engineering and Documentation" to vent some strongly held views. Document analysis artifacts in whatever form the team decides is best for the project, but document them. Often a spreadsheet will suffice; at other times, diagrams linking requirements with the players are all that is needed. Projects with much ceremony may also call for a full-blown "analysis model." In sum, there must be a set of electronic or paper documents which contains the results of analysis that can be referred to later, but strongly guard against efforts to perfect the analysis documents. They will never be exhibited as trophies of the project's success (if they are, the project did or will

SOFTWARE ENGINEERING AND DOCUMENTATION

Software engineers do not like writing. They believe their design and code are *self-documenting* and leave it at that. There is even widespread derision about documentation in the community; it is not unusual to find young software engineers complain *all* they have been assigned to do is documentation, implying the task poses no intellectual challenge. Interestingly, I have come to believe writing plays a vital role in software engineering.

I will not go into the usual justifications for documenting things — people leave, projects go on, new people need to get up to speed, etc. While true, it sounds rather trite. As reflected earlier in the book, there is still a significant cognitive gap between software and users of software. We know almost instinctively what a house or a car can (and cannot) do for us, but the utility of software systems is yet to breed this level of understanding. And the best way to understand and be understood is to write. Nothing helps more in building enterprise software than clear, concise writing of user expectations, design idioms, implementation choices, and testing directions. Every software engineer, to be good at his or her game, needs to devote time and discipline to writing. Raymond (2001), in his essay "How to Become a Hacker," calls for the honing of writing skills and "appreciation of puns and word play." Incidentally, "hacker" to Raymond is, in his words, a "true and original sense of an enthusiast, an artist, a tinkerer, a problem solver, an expert."

not succeed). Analysis documents are fuel for the subsequent design activity; they need just that much attention and no more.

- **Iterate, iterate, and iterate** — Iteration takes practice to do well, and the best time to get into the iterative mode is during analysis. The essence of analysis — understanding the problem domain — calls for going back and forth a number of times. In the first pass, understanding will be sketchy, but just enough to get started; the next round will increase depth and focus, and so on and so forth. The worst thing during analysis is to feel pressured to get it right in one go. No such thing can happen; if it does, whatever was gotten right needs a serious relook. The key is to believe there is always scope for revisiting and refinement; there is always another chance.

- **Proof of the pie is in the eating** — Analysis by itself will get a project nowhere. It is a means to an end, a very important means, but only a means. A common problem ascribed to the waterfall model, though it can afflict any model, is generating documents instead of working software. Analysis is especially susceptible to this malaise. It is easy to build castles in the air, but all this concerns the users very little; they are least interested in studying interpretations of their problem in the developer's idiom. How good or bad analysis has been will become manifest only at the time of the first release, when the users see for themselves what the software is up to and are able to play with it and try to break it. The biggest deterrent to overanalysis is to remember that analysis is tested better in design and best in coding.

Remaining mindful of these common analysis paralysis causes and effects will help practitioners do a better job of analysis, which will in turn aid better design and implementation.

8.4. MESHING RATIO

We have been talking about how analysis is about identifying players — entities that would deliver, by collaboration, what the users want from the system. We have not discussed how the players interact — what the rules of the game are. That is the domain of design. It is time now for a quick measure of how analysis has been going, an indicator metric which at the end of iteration tells us something about the way analysis has examined the requirements. Enter the *Meshing Ratio.*

Meshing Ratio gives the extent to which the players identified during analysis link with the requirements of a system. "Meshing" underscores the connectedness between the players fulfilling a set of requirements.

Let the system have n requirements, and at the end of an iteration of analysis, we have identified m players. Write down the identifiers of the requirements and the names of the players in two columns on a piece of paper. A line joining a requirement with a player indicates that the player has a role to play in delivering some parts of the requirement's functionality. The act of analysis should have already identified player(s) for each requirement, and drawing the line makes the connection concrete. What we are doing here is very much like the "match the following" questions we were asked in school. After all the lines have been drawn, maximally there can be mn (m times n) links between the two columns. We define the *Meshing Ratio* for the ith iteration, MR(i), as:

$$\text{MR}(i) = (\text{Actual number of links})/(\text{Maximal number of links})$$

Actual number of links is the total count of links in our diagram, say x. Thus,

$$\text{MR}(i) = x/mn$$

Let us look at the boundary conditions. When $x = mn$,

$$\text{MR}(i) = mn/mn = 1$$

When $x = 0$, it is the proverbial "trivial" case; there are no links and thus no correlations between the players and the requirements. Thus, in this case:

$$\text{MR}(i) = 0/mn = 0$$

If there are as many links as players or vice versa, that is, $x = m$ or $x = n$:

$$\text{MR}(i) = m/mn = 1/n$$

or

$$\text{MR}(i) = n/mn = 1/m$$

The first and third cases, $\text{MR}(i) = 1$ and $\text{MR}(i) = 1/n$ or $1/m$, respectively, are especially interesting; the former is called a *spider web* and the latter an *island*. In a spider web scenario, every player has a finger in every requirement. This is as good (or bad) as one player doing every chore. Software development is about delegating responsibility, and a spider web goes against that grain. In island scenarios, either each requirement is serviced by a single player or each player is associated with a single requirement. Both these suggest that either requirements are too fine-grained or players have too narrow a scope. An example of a requirement that is too fine-grained would be: *The system allows users to enter the date range for generating the transaction report.* Like use cases, requirements also need to be of a granularity which delivers some business value to the user and not just end up as atomic transactions. A value of $\text{MR}(i)$ between 1 and $1/m$ (or $1/n$) indicates there is some amount of interaction between the players already as they fulfill the requirements. Design will further refine and lay down the rules for this interaction. If each requirements addresses one core functionality, it is likely initial analysis will bring out players whose number is close to that of the requirements, that is, $m = n$. The value of the *Meshing Ratio* can quickly tell us which way analysis is leaning, toward the spider web or the island. Such back-of-the-envelope insights go a long way in engineering and a longer way in software engineering, where there are no mathematical formulas to guide you.

But isn't all this in the name of analysis a sly infiltration of design? It is, and that is the whole point.

8.5. SEGUEING INTO DESIGN

Toward the end of analysis, we need to start thinking about design. Such thoughts best appear unconscious and unbidden, because we are still doing analysis and do not want to get ahead of ourselves.

As stated earlier, analysis is about identifying the players; design is about making the rules of the game. Making the rules of the game sounds rather free-form. In reality, rules are bound by realities, *constraints* as they are often called. The biggest constraints are user expectations and the willingness of the users to pay for what they want. Other constraints may be technological (e.g., the customer is stuck with twenty licenses for a server bought for another project that was scrapped and wants to put the money to some use by deploying your project on that server), related to schedule (e.g., the marketing team got the contract with the usual promise of delivery yesterday), or political (e.g., the new boss wants to prove to his boss that he was right after all). Design is about reaching a tenuous and ephemeral balance between various tugs and pulls, usually divergent.

Design, like many other worthwhile things, is best understood by example. An igloo, a wigwam, and a mud hut conjure pictures of these typical dwellings in our minds. Which one has a better design? The very question betrays a common confusion about design. Design is about creating or contriving for a particular purpose; an igloo, a wigwam, and a mud hut are best suited to the specific sheltering need of their inhabitants. It is inane to compare designs; each design is driven by the requirements. Analysis bridges requirements with design.

Deciding the rules of the game, in the context of design, is about specifying how components interact amongst themselves (that is, *synergize*) to deliver the overall functionality of the system. A software system is like a beehive, a Brownian motion of messages flying back and forth amongst components, as each entity fulfills its role in a master plan. Why have so many components? Why not just have a few hulks do all the work? The arguments have been repeated to the point of cliché, but still they are true: monolithic components soon become unmanageable code clumps, maintenance turns into a nightmare, and enhancements are impossible. Delegation of responsibilities helps get out of this quagmire, and object-oriented programming promises an especially in-tuitive way of deciding who should do what. In my opinion, this promise is sound, but it has gotten too much hype. Getting the promise to work is far from easy.

Object orientation offers the powerful abstraction of viewing software components in the light of real-life entities, which have identities as well as behavior. This is supposed to make the modeling of the problem domain easier or at least more intuitive. But object orientation is not merely about naming classes after real-life ideas. (Almost all object-orientation books I have read have examples with a class called *Animal* and of course with subclasses *Dog* and *Cat*, or for the more geometric, *Shapes* with offspring *Square* and *Circle*.) The crux lies in deciding *who does what* or giving a job to one who can do it best. And this takes a lot of experience, practice — and mistakes — to master.

Software design, indeed a sizable part of software development, is about combining three interrelated but distinct points of view, discussed in the next section.

8.6. ABSTRACTION, ELISION, AND INDIRECTION

Software design is a mind game. One hardly ever deals with anything concrete in the sense cogs and wheels are, buildings are, or even hardware circuitry is. Design is not the diagrams it begets, nor the language in which the artifacts are expressed. In fact, design is one of those things which can seldom be taught, but is always open to being learned. (See the sidebar titled "Design Is Not UML!" for some rumination on the state of software design instruction.)

Every practitioner who has thought about design and has had to do it for a living has strong views about design. This is good, because weak views never take a discipline anywhere. What follows is my take on three enduring themes in design: *abstraction, elision*, and *indirection*.

In common sense, abstraction is often associated with generalization. There is indeed an element of generalization in abstraction. A part of abstraction is about making conjectures about larger issues from small observations. But abstraction is more than just generalization. Abstraction is a way of looking at circumstances so that essential ideas are highlighted and inessential details are not. In our lives, we are abstracting all the time, about nearly everything. Abstraction is built into the human mind to see coherent patterns and make sense of the constant bombardment of information through the senses. Abstraction is especially useful when making decisions. When I shop online for flight tickets, my concern about the price is paramount. At the airline counter, I am usually focused on getting an aisle seat. At the gate, just before boarding, my

DESIGN IS NOT UML!

For me, one of the charms of teaching is talking to students about things beyond what is being taught. I am subjected to many an interesting question, observation, or entreaty for advice, from what will be asked on the test to the morality of outsourcing to how to install a cable modem for a home computer. One student was trying to talk me into postponing a homework submission because he had an object-oriented design test coming up in two days. By way of negotiation, I asked what he was learning in design. "Oh, UML and stuff," the answer came, expected and distressing.

The reason we teach our students design is UML is because we hardly know any better. It is not unusual in the industry to be shown sheaves of diagrams when the design is asked for. What *is* design? There is no one answer, even if we are just talking about software design. Throughout this book, in many different contexts, we explore the theme of design. But design is certainly not the language used to express it: design is not UML. Design is a way of seeing, making connections, discerning similarities when none seem to exist and differences when all appears the same, making the best of given constraints, and much more. It is indeed difficult to teach these through conventional mores of instruction. Even then, when we teach design — which we must — we must wake to the distinction between grammar and literature, between Mozart's music and its score sheets. Software engineering needs this attitude, in its instructors and practitioners, and needs it now.

main worry is whether the airplane has four engines, which I think is the minimum safeguard for a trans- or intercontinental flight. At each stage of this process, my primary focus shifts; some details blur to give some other factor main clarity. Abstraction is about this shifting focus of our attention as we tackle a situation in steps. It also involves training and tuning our perception so that we can sift the meat from the minutiae, without even thinking about the process.

Before moving on to the relevance of abstraction in software design, I will mention a book whose title is an elegant example of abstraction. In *The Moon and Sixpence,* Maugham (1993) explores the mercurial genius of Charles Strickland, a thinly veiled personification of the Postimpressionist painter Paul Gaugin. "The moon and sixpence" brackets two very diverse objects — diverse in their celestial and terrestrial stations, diverse in romantic and mercenary connotations, diverse in eminence and insignificance — in a breathtaking leap of abstraction, based perhaps on the mystery of their shinning facades. Abstraction is about seeing similarities when none seem to exist.

Abstraction plays a powerful role in software design. It involves seeing in layers, addressing the issues of a particular layer, and then moving on to another set of issues in the next layer. It involves not worrying about performance tuning before the software performs anything; it includes not splitting hairs over sorting algorithms before knowing fully what needs to be sorted. Abstraction sounds so much like plain vanilla common sense that you may wonder why I am making such heavy weather of it. It has been my experience that many of the ills of software design come from bad abstraction, that is, crossing our bridges before we come to them or, worse, building bridges over hypothetical chasms. Common sense, alas, is less common than it appears.

Once players have been identified in analysis, it is for design to abstract how functionalities may be fulfilled by the interacting players. What is essential? Look for "showstopper" chunks of functionality and decide — based on current understanding — how best it is best delivered. A caveat is due here. Initial user interaction will likely suggest every bit of functionality can be a showstopper, but requirement elicitation should also ensure prioritization of requirements which are agreed upon by all stakeholders. I have often employed the widely used VED scheme, and it works well. Based on business importance, each requirement is marked vital (V), essential (E), or desirable (D); this gives a clear idea which has to be taken up first and makes the task of abstraction easier. Thus abstraction is a key element in conceiving a durable design idiom for a set of requirements.

We now turn to the next member of the triumvirate: elision. To go from place A to place B, even if A is my home and B is a friend's home on the next street, I get directions from an online oracle. The driving directions come with a map, and the map comes with a "zoom" button, which lets me switch back and forth between views with more and less detail. Elision is at play here, hiding details that are not germane to my query and highlighting landmarks that are. Elision guides us in the way we express software design.

Elision is concerned with highlighting the important, but more importantly hiding the unimportant. In all software engineering artifacts, elision plays a pivotal role. Without it, too much clutter would cloud our thought and expression. But the level of elision is varied to suit different depths of focus, at different stages of development. Class diagrams start off being just a rectangle and end with every data member, method signatures, and their access modifiers. Sequence or collaboration diagrams show only relevant messages for a given scenario. In activity diagrams, only the important decision points are shown. At every step, we show just the extent of detail that is necessary for that step: this is elision at play.

Elision is not just about the aesthetics of making our diagrams cleaner. UML has provided the much-needed notation for expressing and documenting the thinking behind the building of software. Indeed, notation plays a very important role in the conceptualization of a problem and its solution. Leibniz even philosophized about a system of notation so powerful and sweeping that solving a problem would be reduced to mere manipulations of notations (Davis 2000). The power of elision not only ensures design has a better chance of being implemented in its true *spirit,* but also lessens the chances of misunderstanding and misinterpretation. Elision, as applied to software engineering, is a technique for clear *expression* of design ideas.

Among the trinity, indirection is perhaps the most difficult to explain. That is not unexpected, as the very word conveys a hint of the ambiguous. I first encountered the idea of indirection in a brilliantly written book by Eckel (2002), *Thinking in Java.* Eckel endows the reader with a new perception of object orientation. He recognizes the salient object-oriented programming theme as being able to separate *what changes* from *what does not change.* A strategy toward this end is to cleverly segregate *interface* from *implementation*; languages such as Java support and strongly encourage this style of programming. At the programming level, indirection can be realized in many ways. The simplest form may be manipulating a value through its memory address. Design patterns such as *Proxy, Proxy Server,* and *Delegation* offer mechanisms for introducing indirection in design. David Wheeler is once said to have remarked: "There is no problem in computer science that cannot be solved by an extra level of indirection" (Dennis and Seater 2006). From a designer's point of view, indirection is important as it helps keep the focus on the broad nature of the problem rather than get carried away with the nuts and bolts of the solution. Indirection, like all other powerful and sublime strategies, has to be used with care. Otherwise, there is every chance of increasing complexity through the very efforts to reduce it.

The idea of indirection is closest to the *execution* of design in code. Thus, abstraction, elision, and indirection cater to the three related but distinctly different levels of conception, expression, and execution of design ideas.

It is easy to rhapsodize about abstraction, elision, and indirection at an idea level; gauging whether or how well they have been harnessed is the difficult part. We next derive the *AEI Score* to reflect these aspects of a design. Once again, what is meant by design in the current discussion is what often is called "high-level design." This mainly concerns the collaboration of components, vis-à-vis "low-level design," which is mainly about implementation details.

ABSTRACTION, ELISION, INDIRECTION:
A TOUCH OF *MAHABHARATA*

The Indian epic *Mahabharata* ranks alongside the *Iliad* and the *Odyssey* (perhaps exceeding them) in breadth and grandeur. At the surface, there is the usual interplay of good and evil and, after a cataclysmic conflict, triumph of the former. But what makes *Mahabharata* so interesting is that, beyond black and white, there is an infinite variety of colors. Passion, patriotism, love, perfidy, lust, valor, intrigue, faith, faithlessness — you name it; all this is there. Some of the characters are gods, some demigods, some merely mortal, and some switch back and forth between these leagues. The following is a watered-down version of three *Mahabharata* episodes to highlight elision, indirection, and abstraction. (The watering down is to shorten the stories and filter some aspects not suited to a book on enterprise software!)

All of these stories involve Arjuna, the ace warrior and third of the protagonist brothers, the *pandavas*. From an early age, Arjuna's archery skills were legendary; impressed, the gods later granted him weapons of total annihilation (of course, with advice never to use them; something of a nuclear deterrence formula, one gathers). When Arjuna was still a trainee, he and his peers gathered in a field to show off their skills. Their trainer put a statue of a bird on a bough and asked each of his pupils to take aim. But before they shot the arrow, they had to tell him what they saw. Some said they saw the sky, the fields, the tree, its branches, and the bird. Each was asked to move aside, until Arjuna stepped in. What Arjuna said he saw was the bird's eye, only the bird's eye, and nothing but the bird's eye. This is elision in play. The sky, the fields, the tree, the branches, and the bird are all there, but in this circumstance, all but the bird's eye needs to be elided.

With this kind of a beginning, no wonder Arjuna made it big. In search of a commensurate bride, he came to the *swayamvar* of Draupadi. Now

An epic context has been chosen to summarize our discussion of abstraction, elision, and indirection. See the sidebar titled "Abstraction, Elision, Indirection: A Touch of *Mahabharata*."

The preceding discussion highlights some of the desiderata of design, underlying principles and techniques that serve as basic guidelines. It is important to remember that software design is ultimately about fulfilling user requirements by the most optimal use of resources and within given constraints. In the next two sections, we will derive the *AEI Score* and the *Morphing Index*.

Draupadi is something of the Helen of *Mahabharata* — for whom strong men go to war and weak ones die. In those days, the likes of Draupadi called the shots when it came to marrying. The *swayamvar* was the occasion where nubile women chose their husbands from an assembly of suitors. Draupadi went a step further: not satisfied with their reputations, she wanted each suitor to perform an act of great expertise in her presence. Each suitor was asked to shoot the figure of a fish revolving above his head by looking down at its image in a pool of water on the floor. After all competitors had embarrassed themselves (and a very strong one was disqualified on an issue of pedigree), Arjuna took aim, and Draupadi was his. He was too consummate an archer to be fooled by the additional layer of indirection brought in by the image on water.

After all this competition and romance, the plots heats up. The *pandavas* are in bloody battle with their blood brothers, the *kauravas.* With fighting about to start, Arjuna has second thoughts; he finds it meaningless to kill his kin for a kingdom. Then Krishna, Arjuna's charioteer, gives him a pep talk. Krishna in fact pulls an ace from his sleeve, saying he is the creator, preserver, and arbiter of the universe, and it is in his design that Arjuna must fight and win. Arjuna has so far been rather pally with Krishna but remains somewhat skeptical about the talents Krishna now says he has. In verisimilitude, Krishna gives Arjuna the *viswaroopdarshan* (literally, a view of all creation), which abstracts the origin and destiny of all beings and all circumstances and shows all to be within Krishna's power and knowledge. Krishna also gives Arjuna advice on a way of life, the topic of much philosophical discourse since. Needless to say, Arjuna was enthused enough to get into the war and fight to win. But the way Krishna addresses Arjuna's qualms on life and living — common to all ages and cultures — shows abstraction in play, at its most powerful.

These metrics help practitioners understand the direction in which design is heading.

8.7. AEI SCORE

AEI Score measures the extent to which a particular design utilizes the ideas of abstraction (A), elision (E), and indirection (I).

Table 8.1. Sample questionnaire for *AEI Score* calculation

ID	Question	Yes	No	Some/ sometimes
1	Can users readily relate to the tasks of every player identified during analysis?	3	1	2
2	Do the analysis artifacts mention any design detail?	1	5	2.5
3	Do the design artifacts depend on any specific implementation detail, such as algorithm or data structure?	1	10	5
4	Does analysis or design build on ideas specific to a particular language, platform, or technology?	1	3	2

Sanity check is peculiarly popular among software engineers. Many software engineering books make it look like some abstruse art, and by mastering it one is assured of success. Sanity check may mean anything from running through a checklist to see if one is too adrift from one's goal or to check for variable values or invariants as code runs to catch exceptions early. This is a powerful technique, equally applicable to the human activities of analysis and design as to the mechanical execution of code. The *AEI Score* calculated after design iterations helps a sanity check on the state of the design. A questionnaire is used, which the designer has to answer; based on the responses, a score is generated, which reflects how much the design is aligned to the principles of abstraction, elision, and indirection. The questionnaire needs to be *customized,* that is, questions added and removed or weights given to the answers changed, for each project. A sample questionnaire is given in Table 8.1.

How is the questionnaire completed? It is best done in parts; some of the questions would need input from users, while others can be answered by the analysts and designers. Each question's possible answers are assigned a weight based on their relative importance, with highest weight given to the most preferred answer.

The *AEI Score* is the ratio of the sum of scores for the actual answers to each question to the sum of scores for the most preferred answer to each question, based on whether the answer was yes, no, or some/sometimes. If in a hypothetical case the responses to the questions in Table 8.1 were

1 = Yes   2 = No   3 = Some/sometimes   4 = Some/sometimes

Total score = 3 + 5 + 5 + 2 = 15

the most preferred answers for each question would have been

$$1 = \text{Yes} \quad 2 = \text{No} \quad 3 = \text{No} \quad 4 = \text{No}$$

$$\text{Total score} = 3 + 5 + 10 + 3 = 21$$

So, for ith iteration, the *AEI Score* is

$$\text{AEIS}(i) = 15/21 = 0.71$$

Consistency needs to be maintained in framing the questions for different projects. Variation of the *AEI Score* values across iterations of a project points to changes in design direction. The questions in the *AEI Score* questionnaire should be broadly relevant to the notions of abstraction, elision, and indirection.

After each iteration of design, the *AEI Score* offers an opportunity to stand back and see how much the design conforms to the three canons of software building. Design remains very much a subjective pursuit. By asking some questions, and weighing their answers, calculation of the *AEI Score* brings in some objectivity in examining the state of design.

However, the state of design may change, principally due change in requirements. Change in design affects all downstream artifacts. Our next metric, the *Morphing Index,* measures the extent of change in design.

8.8. MORPHING INDEX

Through the *Morphing Index,* we seek to measure how much the design of a software system changes, or *morphs,* over iterations. This is a tall order. Even if we do not worry at this time about the drivers of design change, such as changing requirements, we need to delve into some of the dynamics of design to be able to devise this metric. Metrics used by practitioners are often born in the helter-skelter of delivery deadlines and project vicissitudes. In developing the *Morphing Index,* some of that atmosphere is created. This will also set us up nicely for Part 3 of this book, where a case study is presented to show how the metrics can be applied in an enterprise software project.

8.8.1. Setting the Stage

In Part 3, the "characters" in the case study as well as the context are developed. For the time being, Tina, our protagonist, is introduced. Tina works for an organization which builds enterprise software systems for its clients. She works as a technical lead, one of the roles to which this book is directed, as stated in Chapter 1. There will be much to say about Tina's project and the people with whom she is working, but all that can wait until Part 3. For the present, let us follow Tina as she finds it necessary to build the *Morphing Index* metric.

Tina joined the development team as a technical lead several months into the project. Officially, requirements gathering and analysis were over, design was nearing the end, and implementation about to start. There was a general feeling that "things would straighten out" once code begun to be cut. During the first few meetings with the developers and the system analyst, Tina found herself staring at reams of documentation. There were several versions of each document, often contradictory and always more complicated than the previous. It seemed even the basic direction of the design was undergoing too many changes. Without sounding impolite or impolitic, Tina asked the members of her team why they thought things were changing so much. The analyst said customers could not make up their minds, adding "as usual" with a deprecating smile; the developers said they went by the analyst's word. The project manager, whom Tina briefed "offline," seemed to believe this was what iterative and incremental development was meant to be. Wasn't it all about letting customers change their minds? He generously added that he was of course no expert in these new technologies (in his coding days, real programmers wrote in assembly language), and he deferred to the tech lead's judgment. But how much was the design changing anyway?

Tina had no answer to how much. But without that answer, she knew she could never convince the manager that flags must be raised to bring the customer and the development team to the same page. Perhaps we can help her with the answer to "how much" change. With a touch of lyricism (which Tina will probably not be in the mood for), let us first call the situation the shifting sands of design.

8.8.2. Shifting Sands of Design

Tina's plight should be familiar to anyone who has been in the trenches of software development. Software is perhaps the only industrial artifact that has to absorb change in its purpose, environment, circumstance of use, etc. and yet deliver the originally envisaged value at the same or increased level (refer to Section 3.2.3). To absorb this change, design must also change, inevitably and during development.

Our objective is to derive a metric that will quantify the change in design from one iteration to another. In the following sections, we develop the *Morphing Index* iteratively, a plain vanilla version first, to see what it can give us, and then refine further to make it more useful.

8.8.3. Making of the Metric

Morphing Index tries to capture the extent to which a particular design is changing between predefined baselines. Before presenting the metric, it is important to settle the question of context.

Software design tries to devise the optimal collaboration of system components so that user needs are best met. As discussed earlier in Chapter 6, use cases play a major role in specifying user-system interaction. A scenario is a specific sequence of actions that illustrates an aspect of this interaction. Scenarios are to use cases as objects are to classes: a scenario is basically one instance of a use case (Booch et al. 2005). Scenarios are starting points for design artifacts such as sequence diagrams. The *Morphing Index* will reflect the change in design for a particular scenario between two iterations.

8.8.4. Derivation: First Pass

To specify a metric, we often need to streamline the understanding of a familiar term. For this discussion, let us regard "design" as the interplay of components and their collaborations toward fulfilling a system's requirements. This agrees with intuitive ideas of object-oriented design; objects or class instances communicate amongst themselves via messages to get things done. Changes in the number of classes and messages are a sure symptom of design change. (For the remainder of this chapter, "class" and "component" will be used interchangeably.) Based on this observation, let us define the *Morphing Index* for the ith iteration, RI(k), as follows.

Let m = total number of components and n = total number of messages. Then

$$\text{RI}(k) = \frac{\sum_{i=1}^{m} C_i}{\sum_{j=1}^{n} M_j}$$

Evidently, C_i and M_j denote the ith component and the jth message, respectively. $C_i = 1$ if the component C_i exists, $M_j = 1$ if the message M_j exists, $C_i = 0$ if the component C_i does not exist, and $M_j = 0$ if the message M_j does not exist. Thus the *Morphing Ratio* for the kth iteration is the ratio of the total number of components to the total number of messages.

With due deference to rigorists and carpers ("So simple a ratio can hardly capture the subtleties of design." "Some classes are more equal than others; just counting classes does not help." "Not all messages do useful things."), let us reflect on what the *Morphing Index* does deliver. If the fraction has a value much greater than 1, there are many more classes than messages. This indicates something like what we earlier called the island syndrome, where classes are trying to do things pretty much by themselves. This certainly clamors for better delegation of responsibilities. A very low value points to a gaggle of classes chatting back and forth through many messages. This is usually a case of too high coupling. As classes interact in new ways, variation in RI(i) values gives an inkling how the design has changed relative to a previous iteration.

The *Morphing Index* in its present form is rather naïve, but it tells us something, and something is better than nothing. Still, we need to nose around for inadequacies: When would a flat head count of the number of classes and messages not suffice or, worse, give a misleading view of things? It is quite possible that the number of classes and/or messages changes without the intent of the underlying design changing notably. In the initial stages, this is rather common; going back and forth, trying out different combinations, is inherent to the process of designing. In fact, iterative and incremental development supports and encourages it. Let us see how we can make the *Morphing Index* more "intelligent."

As per the current definition, the *Morphing Index* would change each time a class/message is added or removed. All classes and messages do not do equally important things. Based on what they do, an element of differentiation should be introduced into the calculation of the *Morphing Index*. It is time for a second pass through the derivation.

8.8.5. Derivation: Second Pass

To differentiate between classes and messages, it is important to understand how and why they differ. Not all components fulfill equally important responsibilities; not all collaborations facilitate equally vital tasks.

In enterprise software systems, fulfilling business functions is of primary importance. Business logic may be varied and not always very logical. (As pointed out earlier, Fowler [2003] has gone so far as to call it "business il-logic"!) As examples, it may include deciding whether a customer is eligible for a discount (based on the retailer's policies and the customer's purchase history) or calculating the interest rate (depending on an account holder's ac-count balance). Other essential functionality, such as logging, exception han-dling, instrumentation, and database access, crosscuts these business concerns and may be handled by aspect-oriented programming in conjunction with ob-ject-oriented programming. (In an earlier paper, I suggested a metric, the *Cross-*

cutting Score, to help decide whether functionality is best delivered via a class or an aspect [Datta 2006].) Other activities used in implementing business logic are usually encapsulated in helper or utility classes. Based on this difference in their functions, we can segregate classes into the following categories:

- **Primary** — Business objects
- **Secondary** — Components that encapsulate crosscutting functionality
- **Tertiary** — Utility, helpers, etc.

What are the different kinds of things messages do? During implementation, messages translate to method calls, the services offered by one object when invoked by another object. Any message can serve one of the following purposes:

- **Creational** — Creating class instances (e.g., invoking a constructor in C++/Java)
- **Computational** — Manipulating available data based on business logic (e.g., calculating the total price of a purchase)
- **Transmissional** — Fetching or sending information from one component to another (e.g., database calls)

Let us now attach weights to the different types of classes and messages. For components, the weights are:

$$\text{Primary} = 3 \qquad \text{Secondary} = 2 \qquad \text{Tertiary} = 1$$

Evidently, highest importance is ascribed to primary components, least to tertiary, and the secondary ones are in between. We assume each component has one clearly defined responsibility.

For messages, the weights are:

$$\text{Creational} = 2 \qquad \text{Computational} = 3 \qquad \text{Transmissional} = 1$$

We take computation as being most important and transmission the least in the tasks messages carry out. Assigning weight is a simple but effective way to determine the relative contributions of the factors contributing to a metric. A particular assignment of weights can always be called "arbitrary" and often is. In such situations, I usually invite the detractor to suggest an alternate scheme, and it works. There is nothing sacred about these weights for the classes and messages. If in an application the tertiary components are far more complex than the primary ones, or transmissional messages serve a more meaningful purpose than computational ones, feel free to flip the weights around. The key idea is that classes and messages vary in their importance in a particular scheme of design, and weights bring out that difference.

We now redefine the *Morphing Index* for the *k*th iteration:

$$\text{RI}(k) = \frac{\sum_{i=1}^{m} w(C_i)}{\sum_{j=1}^{n} w(M_j)}$$

Evidently, C_i and M_j are the *i*th component and the *j*th message, respectively. $w(X_a)$ is the weight assigned to the *a*th component or message. Thus the *Morphing Index* for the *k*th iteration is the ratio of the weighted sum of components to messages.

What does this refined *Morphing Index* buy us?

■ There is now more "granularity" in the measure. Variation in the number of components and messages, together with their relative importance, affects the value of the metric.

■ *Morphing Index* values over iterations can serve as a heuristic to gauge whether the system's functionality is evenly distributed across components or cluttered in a few.

■ Changing values of the *Morphing Index* show the extent of design change over iterations.

We now return to Tina for a moment and examine some issues in applying the *Morphing Index*.

8.8.6. Back to Tina

With the *Morphing Index,* Tina hopes to convince her manager of the reigning chaos in the project and its fallout. After hours of sifting through UML diagrams to identify classes and messages between them, Tina came up with her spreadsheet. It showed the *Morphing Index* values versus each use-case scenario for the four design iterations already made. The graphs were expectedly jagged. Tina presented the metrics data to her manager.

The project manager commended what he called Tina's "spunk" and came up with more questions. Tina was asked to find out why the numbers spoke the way they did and what the underlying causes and probable cures might be. It was time some of the timeless metrics wisdom hit home for Tina. This was covered in greater detail in Chapter 4, but it does not hurt to repeat a bit.

- **One single metric, by itself, is hardly ever helpful** — The *Morphing Index* gives some insight, but raises more questions than it answers. If the design has gone back and forth so much, without converging, has there been some problem with the analysis? Were the requirements elicited, understood, specified, and documented correctly? Did the users have a clear idea of the system they want? Would plunging headlong into coding have helped? Tina needed a set of metrics covering the development process, each revealing a facet and together giving a sense of what is and what needs to be done.
- **Metrics seldom, if ever, work as afterthoughts** — The jagged graphs on Tina's spreadsheet could not recoup the time already lost on the project. More disturbingly, when presented to the team, they were taken to insinuate incompetence and raised rancor. There are major political and interpersonal implications for any metrics initiative, and these must be addressed up front (refer to Chapter 5).
- **To be most effective, metrics need to be a part of the development process** — The software development life cycle is deeply interconnected; every artifact stands to be affected by, and affects, upstream and downstream artifacts, respectively. Only when metrics align with this continuum can they possibly make a difference.

We will pick up with our protagonist again in Part 3. We now take a look at a metric which examines an idea very similar to the "morphing" we have been dealing with so far.

8.9. AN ALLIED METRIC: WHITMIRE'S VOLATILITY INDEX

Whitmire (1997) says "volatility is the likelihood or probability that a change will occur. It is an important characteristic of applications, domains, and design components and must be watched — carefully." He then derives a measure of volatility based on earlier discussion in the book. As mentioned in Chapter 6, Whitmire combines measurement theory and the theory of objects to build up a rigorous foundation for object-oriented metrics.

Seeing the *Morphing Index* and Whitmire's measure in the light of one another gives a key insight: there are always different ways to formulate metrics of similar scope and focus. Each has its pros and cons, and the choice of one in a particular scenario is influenced by experience and perspective.

8.10. SUMMARY

This has been a long and involved chapter — and that is no surprise. Analysis and design represent the most subtle and influential aspects of software development. To summarize:

- Analysis is about understanding user requirements and identifying players that will fulfill the requirements.
- Design decides the rules by which the players play; it is the collaboration of components to deliver a piece of functionality in the most optimal way.
- The *Meshing Ratio* measures how closely the players identified during analysis mesh or connect with one another.
- The *AEI Score* reflects on the state of a design's adherence to the canons of abstraction, elision, and indirection.
- The *Morphing Index* helps in understanding the extent of design change.
- All of these metrics are calculated per iteration of analysis and design. In the case study in Part 3, their application and interpretation are illustrated.

In the next chapter, we tackle implementation. By viewing implementation merely as code cutting, many of its nuances are overlooked, often with harmful effects. We will see how metrics can help us understand and "do" implementation better.

REFERENCES

Booch, G., Rumbaugh, J., and Jacobson, I. (2005). *The Unified Modeling Language User Guide,* 2nd ed. Addison-Wesley.

Brown, W. J., Malveau, R. C., McCormick, H. W. S., and Mowbray, T. J. (2001). *AntiPatterns: Refactoring Software, Architectures, and Projects in Crisis.* John Wiley and Sons.

Cockburn, A. (2002). Use Cases, Ten Years Later. http://alistair.cockburn.us/index.php/ Use_cases,_ten_years_later.

Datta, S. (2005). Integrating the FURPS+ model with use cases — A metrics driven approach. In Supplementary Proceedings of the 16th IEEE International Symposium on Software Reliability Engineering (ISSRE 2005), Chicago, November 7–11, pp. 4-51–4-52.

Datta, S. (2006). Crosscutting score — An indicator metric for aspect orientation. In Proceedings of the 44th ACM Southeast Conference (ACMSE 2006), pp. 204–208.

Davis, M. (2000). *The Universal Computer: The Road from Leibniz to Turing.* W. W. Norton and Company.

Dennis, G. and Seater, R. (2006). Alloy Tutorial Session 1: Intro and Logic. http://alloy.mit.edu/fm06/s1_logic.pdf.

Eckel, B. (2002). *Thinking in Java,* 3rd ed. Prentice Hall.

Fowler, M. (1996). *Analysis Patterns: Reusable Object Models.* Addison-Wesley.

Fowler, M. (2003). *Patterns of Enterprise Application Architecture.* Addison-Wesley.

Gamma, E., Helm, R., Johnson, R., and Vlissides, J. (1995). *Design Patterns: Elements of Reusable Object-Oriented Software.* Addison-Wesley.

Larman, C. (1997). *Applying UML and Patterns.* Prentice Hall.

Maugham, W. S. (1993). *The Moon and Sixpence.* Penguin Classics.

Raymond, E. S. (2001). *The Cathedral and the Bazaar: Musings on Linux and Open Source by an Accidental Revolutionary.* O'Reilly.

Whitmire, S. A. (1997). *Object-Oriented Design Measurement.* Wiley Computer.

IMPLEMENTATION: IT TAKES SOME DOING

9.1. OVERVIEW

There is one school of thought which says software development is all about implementation. There is another school which calls implementation a minor cog in the wheel. Both schools have something to them, but implementation goes beyond either. Implementation is more than coding, but how much more and more in what way are not widely understood.

This chapter briefly discusses the idea of implementation. *Specific Convergence* and the *Interface Map* are then presented to help practitioners implement better.

9.2. PROOF OF THE PIE

In some circles, "show me the code" — spoken with some zip and authority — can and does send shivers down the spine of the tyro practitioner. Code (that is, lines of symbolic instructions) seems to embody the software product in its most tangible form. You can count lines of code; the kilo lines of code metric was referred to earlier (Chapter 3), though somewhat unflatteringly.

Code can do many things. You can run the code. You can hope code has the power to make the customer happy, but the customer does not care about code. To put it another way, the customer cares about code as much as we care about the bricks that go into making our homes. All engineering products, software included, have something of the *gestalt* in them: "...a structure, configuration, or pattern of physical, biological, or psychological phenomena so integrated as to constitute a functional unit with properties not derivable by summation of its parts" (Merriam-Webster 2006). In essence, code, though an integral part of software that delivers user needs, is not the software. Implementation is about making software out of code, guided by the blueprints of design and streamlined by the checks of testing.

Implementation and testing go very much hand in hand. There are methodologies which advocate that tests be planned and written before implementation. The JUnit (2006) framework greatly helps writing "tester" code by establishing checkpoints in the development of actual application code. However, we must be mindful that implementation and testing have very different intents, and it does not help to confuse the objectives of one with the other. In this book, their connections will be pointed out, but they will be treated separately and differently.

Simply put, implementation is translating design into a working software product. At its most detailed, design prescribes all the features of every code component, along with their interfaces and interactions. This is sometimes called "low-level design." Implementation is creating code constructs in any programming language as specified by this design. Often, *pseudo-code* serves as the intermediary between low-level design and implementation — natural language sentence fragments that describe code in detail. The finesse of implementation lies in interpreting design. There will always be decisions the implementer has to make on the fly. Design cannot and should not decide everything. Design that tries to decide everything usually gets mired in minutiae; it misses the forest for the trees.

Implementation is seldom simple. Design is seldom complete in the sense that every bottleneck is identified and resolved, every performance hog removed, and every contingency planned for. Exception handling is one among many issues implementers have to handle pretty much on their own, often without directions from designers. A litmus test of good design is how error management is addressed. Even if a sincere effort has been made, the task is never complete without wading into code. The reason is straightforward; unless the errors start hitting you, you do not start fixing them in earnest. The more they hit you one at a time, the greater the need for a common fixing strategy hits home. If errors do not start hitting you pretty early in implementation, there is certainly not enough testing going on. And this is bad news. Thinking about exceptions and about graceful ways to handle them marks the threshold between design and implementation. It is the crucial point where the ideation of software building starts turning inward into execution. One passing tip in exception handling (from one whose memory of being a foot soldier in the software trade is quite fresh): no matter what smart stuff you "catch" or "throw," always remember to have an intelligible error message print on the screen or have an error log. These messages are often the only sense one can make from a nasty exception stack.

In spite of the best efforts of analysts and designers, implementation will uncover some holes in the architectural framework. If these are mere cracks, local attention might help, but for anything more menacing, it is in the interest of the project's long-term health not to cover it up. Iterative and incremental development allows for, indeed encourages, failing early, to ensure we do not fail later and fail finally. Finding and fixing design errors during implementation also has a human angle to it. As the human angle in software engineering is usually neglected in books about software engineering, let us devote some attention to it.

I joined the industry in the heady nineties, one of a bunch of fresh graduates entering into our first "real" jobs, tentative and excited. It was generally held in our circle that design was the place to be in software development. The quicker one cut through the drudgery of implementation and into design's higher echelons, the better. None of us knew how we got that view, but it seemed rather sublime and we held onto it. This caused some ribald attitudes. As implementers (usually the first role new entrants to the industry get), we were ever eager to catch designers on the wrong foot. Any design flaw that happened to be uncovered during implementation was gleefully sent back to the designer and followed up with smirking remarks — often in an e-mail — about "inconsistency" and "flawed design." It speaks well of the organization that such free and frank exchanges were allowed and not stifled based on "juniority" or insubordination. The fact remained, though, that for us the design defects were always someone else's problem. Many from that group went on to play the designer's role in a few years time and lived to feel sobered. It then dawned on us that design is an ongoing process. It starts with design workflow but does not end with it. Quite a bit — and important bits — carries over to implementation workflow as well. One of the biggest lessons in the practice of software engineering is the absolute fluidity of roles. There is scope — indeed need — for every practitioner to do analysis, design, implementation, and testing and even specify requirements in every phase of the project. If implementers and testers (usually the youngest and most energetic members of a project team) are given a voice, design will improve during implementation and testing. Translating design into code needs a new look at the design by fresh eyes at every iteration. The fresher the eyes are, the more errors and inconsistencies will be found and fixed, before it is too late.

Performance tuning is not a primary concern during implementation. The aim is to get the system up and running and then deal with those issues. But if performance issues start cropping up, it is foolish to ignore them just because implementation is not yet done. In one project, a simple database query was found to take more than a minute pretty early on. Developers were instructed not to get "bogged down" in such "details" and keep up the coding. The project failed the user acceptance test for the system because it was too slow. Large-scale rework was called for, causing management heartburn and resulting in customer gripes. The diagnosis was a highly expensive join of database tables, dumped as "design oversight." If early symptoms had been heeded, matters would not have come to such a point. Performance, along with usability, reliability, etc., is one of those covert user expectations that frequently makes or breaks a project. And it is during implementation that these telltale signs start showing up. They need to be noticed and acted upon. It is never too late to improve design, but the earlier the better.

9.3. THE ESSENCE OF IMPLEMENTATION

Requirements, analysis, and design are all on paper. Implementation is the first step toward what a software system ultimately needs to be, a working engineering product. Implementation may start with a "quick-and-dirty" prototype that helps improve requirements elicitation or may begin formally when design has matured. Whenever and however it is set afoot, the implementation must create code that satisfies predefined test cases. The indicator of success for implementation is passing tests, preferably carried out by those who were not a part of the implementation.

In the waterfall model, implementation was more cut-and-dried. It started when design ended and ended when testing started. Implementation followed predefined design, which came out of frozen requirements. This worked, and still works, for projects of limited scope, but for enterprise software systems, implementation is a whole new animal. Like an animal species, it has to adapt to changing situations, to stay current and relevant.

9.4. ITERATIONS, INCREMENTS, AND IMPLEMENTATION

In iterative and incremental development, implementation is revisited in every iteration, and the system grows by increments. The power of iteration hits home strongly in implementation as in no other workflow. What does it mean to iterate over the code? Throw away already written code and write afresh? Somehow hack the existing code and implement the new functionality? Refactor (Fowler 2006) existing code to improve its design? There are no easy answers. These questions confuse and confront practitioners, especially those new to the trade. The iterative and incremental model looks smart on paper; it also calls for additional thought to put into practice.

These doubts are somewhat cleared by understanding the model, starting with its name. It is worth noting that "iterative" and "incremental" always seem to go hand in hand. What does that mean? It means iterations are bound by the reality of increments. Tangible progression of the software system occurs through increments — functionality added over iterations. Iteration and increment, in a way, snugly fit the metaphor of means and end. Iteration is how you go and increment is where you go. Both are equally important; one without the other makes little sense. It cannot be overemphasized that every increment should preferably lead to a new release in the production system, free to be reviewed, played with, broken — that is, tested most wantonly — by real users. There is no sense in an "internal" release, to be pussyfooted around with by those who built the code or their cohorts. Every increment must give something real to real users (those who will finally use the software or foot the bill). The users may not like parts of an incremental release or may realize there are things in it they did not know they did not want and come back with some new or modified needs. All this is good; it embodies the very spirit of iterative and incremental development: the earlier you hear back from real users, the better.

But who decides on the extent of a particular increment or what will be included in an iteration? The biggest problem with iterative and incremental development — seldom pointed out — is ensuring the process converges, that is, all the pieces of the jigsaw puzzle finally come together to give a cohesive system and not just a bunch of incremental releases strewn together. Let us call this the challenge of convergence.

9.5. THE CHALLENGE OF CONVERGENCE

Convergence is about coming together, usually from different directions. In math, to converge is also to reach a limit, such as the sum of a series of numbers. Here we will take convergence to mean the successful fitting together of functionality, developed over iterations and released as increments, to give the software system defined by the project's scope. Why is this challenging? As with all knotty questions, anecdotal evidence illumines.

There was a project where both the developers and the customer were very gung ho about iterative and incremental development. For both groups, this was their first brush with the new way of software building. From what they had read and picked up from industry buzz, iterative and incremental development seemed to promise customers they could change their minds about requirements all the time and still have the project done on time and within budget. More insidiously, developers had the idea they were not bound by any development plan. Ad hoc building and testing, a little bit here and a little bit there, was expected to bring home the bacon. Many months, much burned budget, and commensurate recriminations later, the customer scrapped the project because one software project had been commissioned as opposed to a number of little modules which seemed to do their bit "somewhat adequately" but were just not working in harmony.

It was a bitter lesson for all. In addition to the dent in their professional pride, the developers had been spending many, many hours on the project — at the cost of health and home, and it bitterly hurt to feel everything came to naught. (In hindsight, those many, many hours should have been a hint that something was seriously wrong with the project. Of course, everyone was too overwhelmed for such subtleties.) The lesson was a lasting one. The very power of the iterative and incremental model lies in its gravest pitfalls; it is much easier to make a mess of things with this model than with other approaches. And when the mess does happen, if things had been "frozen" and "signed off" on beforehand a la the waterfall model, at least there would be some refuge in documents (not that it helps in the long run), which is never the case with iterative and incremental development.

One important step in preventing this sort of misfortune is setting the right customer expectations. It has to be made clear that changes in requirements can be absorbed, but only when properly coordinated. The changes will be tracked, implemented over iterations, and released for validation in increments. Within an iteration, there can be no addition or modification to the requirements being implemented. But customers are customers, so whimsicality with requirements will exist to some extent.

The real issue is ensuring increments do not end up becoming separate projects but rather contribute to the *organic growth* of one project from conception to completion. The challenge lies in understanding how much a particular increment contributes to the overall project's progress or how far it will take the project down the life cycle. The *Specific Convergence* focuses on these concerns, by giving a measure of how (and where) implementation is going.

9.6. SPECIFIC CONVERGENCE

What drives iterative and incremental software development? It is not easy to pinpoint one driver, but by far the most important is *risk*. We are all familiar with risk in our lives; it can range from the life threatening (venturing into the Pacific in a paddle boat) to just inconveniencing (leaving behind your umbrella in heavy rain). Krutchen (2004) defines risk in software development as a "variable that, within its normal distribution, can take a value that endangers or eliminates success for a project." Two points come out strongly in this succinct definition of risk. The so-called risk variable may have a value even within its "normal" distribution that can cause problems for the project. Thus, to a certain extent, risks can be seen up front. They are not wholly unforeseen exigencies, like earthquakes or terrorist attacks. Since risks can be identified beforehand, there is scope for successful risk management. Risks, if not managed, will ultimately jeopardize project success, defined as fulfillment of project objectives, on time and within budget and any other conditions that have been agreed upon.

The "three amigos" put it pithily: "It is one thing to know in a vague sort of a way that software development involves risks. It is another thing to get them out in the open where everybody can see them, be guided by them, and do something about them" (Jacobson et al. 1999). They suggest maintaining a risk list that includes risk description, priority, potential impact, monitoring responsibility, and contingency plans. Kruchten (2004) talks about direct and indirect risks, depending on the extent to which the project has a handle on managing a particular risk. He also highlights two important risk attributes: the likelihood of the risk occurring and its potential to affect the project when it does. It is essential to differentiate risks based on these factors; all risks are not equally ominous: the project architect defecting to a competitor is more of a headache than an absconding junior developer would be!

A key theme in iterative software development is attacking the highest risks first. For some types of risks, especially technical ones, it is easy to get started in this direction. If some aspect of development has a high element of "unknowns," such as the use of a new language, a third-party product never used before, or people new on the job, it is best to tackle it as early as possible. As stated before, the mantra of iterative and incremental development is if you must fail, fail early. The unspoken caveat adds that if it is early enough, you can live to fight another day.

We will not go into the nitty-gritty of risk management here; tomes have been devoted to it in the software engineering literature. As one experiences more and more battles, one develops a *nose* for risks, and that is the best equipment a project can have to smell risks early. Such olfactory wisdom always helps, as we will find when we derive the *Specific Convergence*. But first, we need to discuss some more notions relating to implementation.

9.6.1. Deliverable Unit

The idea of a *Deliverable Unit* (DU) isolates a unit of work that an individual or team is expected to complete within a specified time, that is, *deliver* as a part of the overall development plan. The scope and extent of a DU will evidently vary from project to project, team to team, and iteration to iteration. Finally, however, all DUs must *fit* together into a cohesive whole — the product to be delivered to the end user. A jigsaw puzzle simile was used earlier; DUs can be seen as pieces of the puzzle.

How is a DU determined? Here we venture into deeper waters. Let us first decide when a DU can be called complete. A DU is complete when and only when it has satisfied predefined tests. This is not to say a DU has to conform to unit tests; that would make it indistinguishable from a program module. A DU is more than just a program or a group of programs; it is all the code it takes to deliver a unit of functionality *of value*. The last sentence sounds close enough to the definition of a use case, and that is deliberate. Broadly, a DU corresponds to something which can thus be tested from a functional point of view. A DU may correspond to a sequence of actions and reactions through which something meaningful gets done by the system or all or part of any end-user functionality.

Inter- and intra-team allocation of tasks in software development often happens along DUs intuitively. Suppose we are building a very large online financial application. Based on user inputs on the Web tier, data have to be fetched from or persisted in databases through middle-tier components. Instead of delegating work by "layers" of user interface, business logic, or database access, it will be much more useful to make each team member or subteam responsible for a "link" on the main menu. They will need to implement the round-trip functionality an end user expects when the hyperlink is clicked. This will certainly make integration and testing much easier. Also, as a link is completed, users can easily verify and give feedback. This is, in essence, developing by DU.

DU is also a smart way to measure progress. Lines of code has diminished further in meaning as much code is now generated in integrated development environments. Therefore, measuring the lines of code written in unit time makes little sense. Keeping track of the DUs helps trace the progression of a project in terms of its deliverables. The *Specific Convergence* will use the idea of a DU in its derivation. But before that, we need to specify *Risk Factor* and *Effort Factor.*

9.6.2. Risk Factor

Every DU has risks associated with it. Risks may be a function of many issues: design complexity, technology bottlenecks, capricious customers, or simply developer ineptitude. The *Risk Factor* is a ranking of the overall risk in terms of severity, on a scale of 1 to 5 (or 1 to 10 if the differentiation needs to be more fine grained); a lower value indicates lower risk. A particular scale, once adopted, has to be followed consistently for a project. With sufficient experience (that is, living through as many successes as failures to neither let it go to your head or take to heart), assignment of a *Risk Factor* to a DU becomes intuitive. Inexpedient choice of *Risk Factor* and paying the price is part of the experience process, so there is no reason to despair! Whenever a DU is decided upon and delegated to an individual or team, its *Risk Factor* is also to be agreed upon by all stakeholders. The best way to work around risks is to accept that they exist and identify and track them. Deciding on a *Risk Factor* is a way of quantifying the level of hazard a DU is likely to encounter in its life cycle.

9.6.3. Effort Factor

Estimating the effort of software development remains one of those "twilight zones," often called a "gray area." Many estimation techniques have been formalized, such as function point analysis (CMU-SEI 2007). The industry also abounds with "seat-of-the-pants" methods of "sizing" which work well in some scenarios. Large organizations usually train their personnel in sublime estimation tactics. Then they ensure real estimation is done on some *template* (usually a spreadsheet with lurking formulas), which is tweaked according to concerns not always aligned to the canons of sound software. It is common to "pad" the initial estimation based on the haggling history of the customer manager who must finally approve it. This, though mischievous, is sometimes a necessary prophylactic for the development team. The effort estimate leads directly to the projected cost, and customers believe the easiest way cost can be brought down is to squeeze the estimate.

But the real difficulty with effort estimate lies at a far deeper level, one which has been touched upon in a surprisingly (maybe not that surprising, given who the author is) early classic of software engineering by Brooks

(1995), *The Mythical Man-Month.* In the eponymous essay, Brooks establishes the folly of assuming the interchangeability of man and months (now read as person and months) in the effort unit man-month. The essay highlights the strongly human elements of software development, which remain as relevant decades later. What makes effort estimation so hard is capturing the delicate dynamics between people who develop software and the time they spend developing it. Here, we assume *Effort Factor* is the estimated effort, in appropriate units such as person-hours, person-weeks, or person-months, for a given DU. We make no assumptions about how the *Effort Factor* is arrived at. *Effort Factor* may be decided through any standard technique, ad hoc intuition, empirical data, or whatever the organization and the practitioners deem fit for a project.

Now the stage is set to unveil *Specific Convergence.*

9.6.4. Deriving Specific Convergence

Specific Convergence seeks to measure how much the implementation activities of a particular iteration contribute toward *convergence,* that is, fulfillment of the implementation objectives for the whole system across all iterations. The metric, as defined below, is a positive fraction. As each iteration completes a larger portion of implementation activities, the value of *Specific Convergence* tends toward unity. The variation of the *Specific Convergence* values across iterations offers insight into how implementation is progressing.

We assume, at the beginning of implementation, that the total functionality to be implemented is divided into *n* number of DUs. This partitioning can be made based on several considerations, primary among which is the incremental release plan. For each of the *n* DUs, a corresponding *Risk Factor* and *Effort Factor* is ascertained.

An important task in iterative development is *iteration planning,* that is, deciding what parts of functionality are to be addressed in a particular iteration. As discussed earlier, risk plays an important role in these decisions. For a given iteration, let *m* be the sum of the number of DUs already implemented, including the ones in the past as well as the current iteration(s).

We define the *Specific Convergence* for the *k*th iteration, SC(*k*), as:

$$SC(k) = \frac{\sum_{i=1}^{m} RF(DU_i) * EF(DU_i)}{\sum_{j=1}^{n} RF(DU_j) * EF(DU_j)}$$

where m = total number of DUs implemented until and including the kth iteration, n = total number of DUs to be implemented across all iterations, and $RF(DU_i)$ and $EF(DU_i)$ are the *Risk Factor* and *Effort Factor*, respectively, of DU_i.

Specific Convergence is thus a ratio of the products of the *Risk Factor* and *Effort Factor* for the DUs implemented up to and inclusive of the kth iteration to the product of the *Risk Factor* and *Effort Factor* for the entire set of DUs that need to be implemented across all iterations.

It is important to note that the denominator (as well as the numerator) of the *Specific Convergence* fraction may change from one iteration to another. It is unlikely all DUs will be identified when implementation begins: new DUs will be spawned as older DUs are found to be more complex or bulky than expected or users come up with new or modified requirements. However, with later iterations in the life cycle (that is, with increasing k), the value of $SC(k)$ must get closer to 1. If it reaches 1, all implementation activities come to an end.

Let us play with some numbers to see what light *Specific Convergence* can shed. For a hypothetical project with five DUs, Table 9.1 gives the DUs and the corresponding *Risk Factor* and *Effort Factor*. The rows for Plan A and Plan B show two different implementation paths in the sequence of DUs addressed in the iterations. For example, in Plan A, DU_1 and DU_2 would be included in iteration 3, DU_3 in iteration 1, DU_5 in iteration 2, and DU_4 in iteration 4.

Table 9.2 gives the values for *Specific Convergence* from iterations 1 through 4. SC(4) for Plan A and Plan B is 1, which is expected, as all the DUs must be completed by the time all iterations end. But the paths Plan A and Plan B took toward convergence are different across the iterations. Plot of the *Specific Convergence* values versus the iteration is an interesting study. This is shown by plotting the *Specific Convergence* values against the iterations for Plan A and Plan B in Figure 9.1.

Table 9.1. *Risk Factor, Effort Factor,* and iteration plans for a project with five *Deliverable Units*

	DU$_1$	DU$_2$	DU$_3$	DU$_4$	DU$_5$
RF	3	1	4	2	5
EF	100	250	500	50	300
RF * EF	300	250	2000	100	1500
Plan A	3	3	1	4	2
Plan B	2	2	4	1	3

Table 9.2. *Specific Convergence* values for **Plan A** and **Plan B**

	SC(1)	SC(2)	SC(3)	SC(4)
Plan A	0.48	0.84	0.97	1
Plan B	0.02	0.16	0.52	1

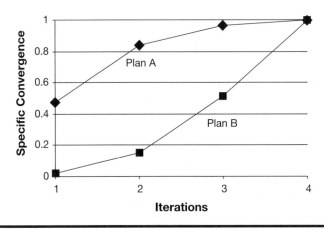

Figure 9.1. *Specific Convergence* versus iterations: **Plan A** and **Plan B**

Evidently, the curve for Plan A has a higher slope for earlier iterations and becomes flatter for the later ones. The curve for Plan B shows the opposite trend. For Plan A, much of the heavy work has been done earlier, and later iterations are an easy saunter; Plan B, on the other hand, saves much of the uphill climb for later. Which, then, is the preferred approach?

In Plan A, the choice of DUs for the iteration sequence shows that those with higher values of *Risk Factor* * *Effort Factor* are tackled earlier, while Plan B chooses to defer these DUs until later. The spirit of iterative and incremental development is to tackle the most difficult parts earliest, so in this example, Plan A is the way to go.

Specific Convergence gives us important direction in iteration planning. The value of SC(k) is a quantitative measure of the amount of implementation done so far, not just in terms of the total functionality to be implemented but also taking into account risk and effort projections. Based on the *Specific Convergence* value for a particular iteration, implementation plans for subsequent iterations can be modified if necessary. The case study in Part 3 shows how the *Specific Convergence* helps a development team.

9.7. INTERFACE MAP: AN ARTIFACT FOR THE FOOT SOLDIER

So far, we have taken a general view of implementation. *Specific Convergence* focuses on the implementation workflow per iteration, giving us an idea how far implementation is from completion.

Those who have spent time in the trenches of software development know the plight of the foot soldier. A foot soldier goes by different names, including "developer," "application programmer," and "software engineer" among other epithets, some more honorific, some less. Whatever the name, the demands from a foot soldier are very similar. (The sidebar titled "From Programmer to Engineer: What's in a Name?" is a tongue-in-cheek take on how names have evolved in the business of software making.) The foot soldier is in charge of coding, the actual *writing,* line by line, of the instructions which will be compiled (or interpreted as per the language) and then run as executables. The foot soldier's lot, though gravid with learning opportunities, is seldom one of much authority or even comfort. In rare cases, coding is guided by clear design guidelines; often, the rigor of analysis and design is wished away with "we'll fix it all in code." And when code is not equal to such consummate fixing,

---

FROM PROGRAMMER TO ENGINEER: WHAT'S IN A NAME?

There was a time when programmers called themselves programmers and were proud of it. Then came the age of software engineers. To be called just a programmer was not honorific enough; all sorts of epithets cropped up: *application programmer, software developer, coder* — you *name* it! Out of all these naming issues, if one thing stands out it is how a software engineer's charter differs from that of a programmer. Programming is indeed a very important concern in software engineering, but certainly not the only concern, not even the central concern at every stage of software development. It is time software engineers become more sensitive to the far-reaching influences of analysis and design on a system's long-term health and act accordingly. In the meanwhile, software and other information-technology-enabled industries can go on spawning names; I recently came across a business card with the designation *customer service specialist executive.* I am sure the designate has unique and sweeping powers.

the foot soldier has to answer. In short, the buck stops with the foot soldier. Talk about metrics to the foot soldier — metrics which capture the "essence" of the "development process" from a "holistic" point of view (I have both been talked to and have talked in such a vein) — and you will surely get a grunt and maybe a few colorful comments. Foot soldiers hardly have the latitude for metrics.

Like other processes of interest, software development differs widely when viewed at the macro and micro levels (refer to Section 3.2.4). The study and practice of software metrics, conventionally, address the macro level. Macro views offer broader generalizations: it is easier to say how hot or cold a cup of coffee is than to specify the motion of molecules in the liquid, even though the latter has a strong bearing on the coffee's temperature.

In this section, the *Interface Map* is presented; its scope is at the micro level of software development. It helps foot soldiers clarify how factors beyond their control affect their tasks. The *Interface Map* should allow foot soldiers to hold their ground when the buck comes tumbling down the ladder and stops at their feet.

As a young system analyst working for the first time at a customer location, I learned a very important lesson. Like all important lessons, it was pithily put. It is relevant to all group activities, but most relevant to organized software development. One morning as we were preparing for one of those make-or-break meetings with the business partners, my manager said she wanted me to follow the CYA principle, which she always did. Looking at my bemused face, she explained that CYA stood for "Cover Your X" (X stands for the posterior, so the relevance of the "A" in CYA is not that remote!). CYA boils down to this: assuming you will be blamed at one time or another, always have alibis ready. I have since made CYA an abiding principle. The *Interface Map* will facilitate the practice of CYA among those who need it most, the foot soldiers.

Before defining the *Interface Map,* the *Implementation Unit* is introduced.

9.7.1. Implementation Unit

Implementation Unit (IU) is the smallest unit of software production. We are all familiar with IUs; they are usually stored in a single computer file, such as a class, an Active Server Page, or a stored procedure. Implementing an IU is most often the onus of one practitioner; if the task is too much for a single person, the IU may be broken up into smaller IUs. IU is where the rubber meets the road — an individual gets down to making software, one instruction at a time.

How do we relate IU with DU? A DU can be thought to consist of several IUs, each of which contributes to the functionality the DU delivers to the end user. One IU can be part of more than one DU; indeed, this is how the interaction of software components is reflected. But those IUs which belong to multiple DUs have to be carefully implemented — their flaws can affect several different lines of functionality.

Both DUs and IUs are constructs for delegating responsibility. Identifying, allocating, and keeping track of who does what is a major concern in any enterprise and more so in software development, as this is a young discipline. In light of the earlier discussion about components and their collaborations, every IU will need to interact with other IUs to deliver their collective functionality. Interact here means exchanging and modifying information between and by the IUs. This kind of interaction may be done through method calls, passing parameters and receiving return values, or an instance of one class may be used as a data member of another class in a less explicit way of interaction. It finally boils down to close cooperation between the IUs for any of their work to be done.

The most common problem the foot soldier faces while building an IU is other IUs not fulfilling their obligations to it. Many of us have reasons to remember this. In one of a friend's first major projects as a developer, code was being written to allow users to enroll their credit cards for online statement reporting. My friend was handling several of what we just now learned to call IUs. One of them had to fetch data for a user from the back end only if a particular flag was set. This flag indicated a user's eligibility to view electronic statements. Whether or not a user was eligible was decided deep inside another part of the application. This vital piece of information was supposed to be conveyed via an IU someone else was developing. When coding started, the mechanism for getting the flag was not yet in place, and my friend was told by her team lead to "hard code" the flag value and code on from there. Once again, this was her first major project, so the advice was taken at face value. Two days before the deadline, she had to pull an all-nighter to fix her code to accept the flag in a format she had no idea her IU was expected to accept. The IU obligated to give her the flag had changed its interface several times (she was assured there were pressing reasons for this!) in between. My friend was supposed to have kept track. Many of us have learned the strategies of team play in similar ways: make it clear what you expect to be given and how you expect it to be given, and make as much noise about it as possible.

The *Interface Map* specifies how dependent a particular IU is on other IUs to fulfill its task. "Interface" points to contracts IUs must agree upon before interaction can begin, that is, the agreement on give and take that defines collaboration for software components. Interface is a deep and subtle idea in software development. As an everyday example, a car's interface to its driver includes its steering wheel, brake and gas pedals, and gear stick. Internal machinery may vary on different cars, but as long as the interface stays the same, drivers can drive any of them. The interface is also meant to serve and respond to certain user actions: the steering wheel has to be guided by the fingers and palm and not pounded by a hammer, the pedals have to be worked by pushing down and not pulling up, and so on. For interactions to go smoothly, interfaces need to be honored. One way of describing interfacial relations between IUs is through the *Interface Map*.

9.7.2. Presenting the Interface Map

For a given IU, the *Interface Map* is a two-dimensional matrix. Along the vertical axis are listed all the other IUs with which the IU needs to interact. Along the horizontal axis is noted all that is required from the other IUs. Check marks in the grid indicate what is required from whom. Table 9.3 shows the *Interface Map* for some hypothetical IU_1, $IM(IU_1)$. If there are n IUs for a project, there will be n *Interface Maps*, one for each IU.

Let us look at an example to see what a "real" *Interface Map* would look like. The DU of interest in our system allows the user to enter an amount in U.S. dollars and displays back the equivalent amount in euros, using the current conversion rate. Let the following IUs contribute to the DU:

■ **EnterAmount.jsp** — A JavaServer Page (JSP) to accept input from the user
■ **ShowResult.jsp** — A JSP to display the result to the user
■ **CurrencyController.java** — A controller class to coordinate the acceptance of input and calculation of output

Table 9.3. Sample *Interface Map*

	Flag A	Return value x	Data member z	Stored procedure B	...	Utility component W
IU_2			X			
IU_3	X					
...						
IU_m				X		
...				X		
IU_n		X				X

**Table 9.4. The *Interface Map* for *Implementation Unit*
CurrencyController.java**

	Error checking of input data	Formatting of input data	Conversion rate	Converted value of currency amount
EnterAmount.jsp	X	X		
Rates table			X	
Calculator.java				X

- **Rates table** — A database table to store the latest conversion rates between currencies
- **Calculator.java** — A utility class to calculate the conversion

Table 9.4 shows the *Interface Map* for the IU CurrencyController.java. It should be noted that ShowResult.jsp does not appear in *Interface Map* CurrencyController.java; this is because the IU CurrencyController.java does not need to interface with ShowResult.jsp to carry out its tasks. But the favor may not be returned; in that case, CurrencyController.java will appear in *Interface Map* ShowResult.jsp. Also, CurrencyController.java has two distinct needs from EnterAmount.jsp; it requires error checking (such as catching nonnumeric characters in the amount value, etc.) and formatting (such as stripping off white space, etc.) of input data.

The *Interface Map*, in one snapshot, gives the nature and extent of the interfacing between the IUs. Because the artifact will change over iterations, it is in the best interests of the practitioner in charge of an IU to keep its *Interface Map* updated.

9.8. SUMMARY

This chapter discussed implementation. To summarize:

- Implementation has to converge; that is, pieces of functionality developed over iterations and released incrementally must finally fit together to make one cohesive software system.
- Risk and effort are important considerations in implementation.
- *Specific Convergence* expresses the extent to which implementation in an iteration measures up in the total implementation effort.
- Ultimately, implementation is about software making at the individual practitioner level. Those entrusted with the actual writing of code —

foot soldiers of the software trade — have to resolve many dependencies amongst code components.

■ The *Interface Map* helps the foot soldiers clarify, document, and disseminate these dependencies.

In the next chapter, we take up testing, perhaps *the* most spoken about and *the* least understood activity of software development. The *Exception Estimation Score* is presented to help make a difference.

REFERENCES

Brooks, F. P. (1995). *The Mythical Man-Month: Essays on Software Engineering, 20th Anniversary Edition.* Addison-Wesley.

CMU-SEI (2007). Function Point Analysis. http://www.sei.cmu.edu/str/descriptions/fpa_body.html.

Fowler, M. (2006). Refactoring home page. http://www.refactoring.com/.

Jacobson, I., Booch, G., and Rumbaugh, J. (1999). *The Unified Software Development Process.* Addison-Wesley.

JUnit (2006). JUnit, Testing Resources for Extreme Programming. http://www.junit.org.

Kruchten, P. (2004). *The Rational Unified Process: An Introduction,* 3rd ed. Addison-Wesley.

Merriam-Webster (2006). *Merriam-Webster Online Dictionary.* http://www.m-w.com.

10

TESTING: HUNT FOR A LITMUS PAPER FOR SOFTWARE

10.1. OVERVIEW

Software testing can be easy or difficult, depending on when you are doing it or, for that matter, what you call testing. If testing for you is one big bang at the end of analysis, design, and implementation, you may practically rebuild the system during testing. But if testing has been a part of implementation — every artifact released after unit testing, and major chunks of functionality tested by users — a "judgment day" may not arrive at all. Testing can be seen and done at various levels; no other life cycle activity depends so much on how it is pitched. In this chapter, the common confusion about testing is briefly reviewed and the *Exception Estimation Score* is proposed to help navigate the testing space.

10.2. THE ISSUE WITH TESTING

Irrespective of the timing, scope, ease, or difficulty of the testing process, there is abundant confusion about what exactly constitutes testing. In colloquial use, a *test* either corroborates or refutes certain presuppositions about a product, process, or people. The problem with software lies in finding or agreeing upon these presuppositions. Testing software is about testing software's behavior under conditions of interest, but it is no easy task to simulate or even conceive of all those conditions of interest. For all nontrivial software systems, testing every execution path is practically impossible under project constraints, simply because there are so many such paths (Schach 2005). Therefore, real-life testing can only cover some selected scenarios. Circumstances which *seem* most prone to failure are selected most readily. Thus, the decision to test a particular scenario is ultimately a subjective one, contingent upon — you guessed it — experience and intuition! The aim of this chapter is to arrive at a metric which will help arrive at a more objective choice of what to test.

I find it especially confusing that there are so many names for testing. In a project, everyone sticks to their own terminology, seldom with a clear idea of what it might mean. Once, at quarter past midnight, with delivery due the next morning, we were grappling with an avalanche of bugs. Many of them were supposed to have been fixed. Crisis management ideas flew fast and furiously. Advanced fatigue and the advanced hour ensured they were more original than useful. Someone asked, without a hint of the humorous, whether *white-box* testing instead of *black-box* testing might bring the bug count down; we had been doing the latter with commensurately dark results. There is a moral to this story, and it is not the need to tell black from white!

Testing comes down to tackling two levels of concerns: in the nomenclature from the last chapter, whether an *Implementation Unit* is functioning as it is supposed to (which is often whether it fulfills the obligations to other *Implementation Units* with which it interfaces) and whether end users get the functionality they expect from a *Deliverable Unit*. Unit testing and functional testing should take care of these two levels, respectively. Developers are encouraged to write unit testing code before they write the code to be tested, but this advice can be heeded only if stakeholders value *quality* code and are ready to pay the price in the form of the time and effort it takes to ensure quality. Some customers take umbrage at being told their money is being spent on writing test cases first: "But where is the code to test?"

When to start and stop testing are questions that assail every project. It would be in the best interest of software development if we could say testing is always being done and never stops, but that is impractical. The earlier testing starts, the better, with unit tests for each *Implementation Unit,* then expanding to the functionalities of *Deliverable Units,* and finally stopping in the hope residual bugs will not pop up at inappropriate times. Bugs are always there in code; it is just a question of whether a critical concatenation of circumstances will occur to unravel them. In one project I know of, the customer manager was very sensitive to the development team's morale; at the drop of a hat, there was pizza and other goodies in honor of the "great work being done." Once a large poster was put up that screamed out in purple letters: "100 days since production launch, and still no bugs!!!" A manager from an adjacent department, known for his acidic humor, passed by the placard and, with a customary smirk, said: "They are all in there, waiting to hit." Though the forecast did not come so crushingly true (at least as far as I know), he had a point. Bugs are design features that prove to be infelicitous to system behavior under some situations.

Interestingly, some studies make many fine distinctions between what we broadly lump together as bugs (Schach 2005). Schach (2005) relates an anecdote about how the word "bug" came to be used in the computer context. It seems that on September 9, 1945, a moth flew into the Mark II computer Rear Admiral Grace Murray Hopper (one of the designers of COBOL) and her colleagues were using at Harvard and got stuck in the relays. Hopper canonized the creature by taping it into her logbook and noting: "First actual case of bug being found." Apparently, "bugs" were used to denote causes of malfunction long before, since the time of Thomas Alva Edison, who commented on them in 1878.

We will use "bug" to mean any *unintentional* feature of a software system that leads to an *unacceptable* behavior of the system. Unintentional means something that did not come from deliberate design. Unacceptable is defined as anything the end users are not willing to accept. The word "bug" has a direct — almost visceral — appeal, which its sanitized cousins like "defect," "fault," etc. lack. I like the word "bug."

10.3. TESTING METRICS

Testing may be said to be the most *metricized* of all software development activities. Defect densities, bugs per lines of code, and bug resolution rates abound in all organizations that swear by processes. These metrics are good by themselves, they make better spreadsheets and graphs, and they are best in instilling a "feel-good factor" about past projects. They are essentially at the macro level, *a posteriori,* and take a predominantly statistical view of matters. Statements like the above are best backed up by anecdotes, and I give one below.

The tech lead in one project was very quality conscious. This is a good thing, because quality is, after all, *the* thing. As the team was coming together in the first few weeks of the project, he gave a diktat that the number of bugs found in each round of testing was to be recorded and graphs drawn plotting bugs versus time. Then came the clincher — the graphs should point down. One spirited team member put his thumb over the microphone on the speaker phone (the meeting was an onsite-offshore call) and asked the other team members: "Isn't this fudging?" They apprised him of the unsuitability of such "f" words. The tech lead, to drive home the point further, said the graphs would send a strong message to the higher-ups. That project generated many graphs (pie charts, bar charts, scatter plots, you name it). It also left the spirited member with a lasting abhorrence to metrics.

Anecdotes apart, the main problem with many of the conventional testing metrics lies in the fact that they are good on large collections of data but offer little help in testing a particular piece of software. How is one helped in the task of testing in one's own project by something like "on average 80% of the total number of bugs were reported during user acceptance testing for the projects done in the past two years"? We wish to explore relationships that will guide practitioners in fixing the testing priority for different parts of a system. There is no litmus test for software, and it is unlikely there ever will be. The challenge is to test what needs to be tested most.

10.4. THE CHALLENGE OF TESTING

The message of the oft-cited quote about war beginning in the minds of men seems to be that the act of warfare is just the culmination of a process that started much earlier, in the very thinking of those who will ultimately wage it. (Waging war is, of course, metaphorical; those who *really* wage it make sure they stay out of harm's way.) Along the same lines, we can just as well say the grounds for software bugs exist before the software is even built. True, bugs do sometimes occur due to inadvertent oversights, but more and more smart compilers and integrated development environments go a long way in weeding out these errors.

The most treacherous bugs often are those called "logical errors," a problem with the way the solution was *thought out.* These "way-of-thinking" bugs can vary from the trivial to the fatal. For example, an error many beginning programmers commit is to assume array indexing in a language such as Java starts from 1 instead of 0. The compiler does not complain, and it is only while running the code that one gets a nasty exception stack. A fellow software engineer learned the hard way to appreciate — amid significant pain — how more subtle errors cause havoc. In the dead of night, everyone on the development team at a customer location was awakened by a "level 1 alert." A level 1 alert — as implied by the primacy of "1" — was a serious thing in their terms of engagement with the customer. It meant something was badly broken with the application that they had built and were now supporting. Every half hour it remained broken, the issue would automatically get escalated to the next higher authority in the chain of command. Level 1 alerts in the dead of the night were even worse; experience showed that the chain of command was more implacable than usual at such times. The issue was a showstopper: it was an e-banking application. One account holder had logged into her account and was shown someone else's account information. She was livid, thinking someone else might jolly well be soaking up her details. As the development team members sped down the freeway from their apartments to the office, someone dryly said that people who logged into accounts at that time of night were probably looking for someone else's data. It was meant to be a joke, but it went ignored; everyone was saving their strength for the bitter things ahead. Over the next few days of soul-searching, and searching close to a million lines of code (amid constant reminders from customers that "this was really bad for business" and innuendos to "review the ongoing contract"), the bug was unearthed. In one of the data objects, variables were declared at the class level instead of the method level, which led to a classic data corruption scenario that first lessons on object-oriented programming talk about. Maybe a momentary lapse on the part of the developer or losing sight of the bigger picture where the class was to be used caused the error (it is very easy to lose sight of the bigger picture; in applications with hundreds of classes, worrying too much about the bigger picture is considered a distraction for foot soldiers). The moral of this story is that bugs originate from a chemistry of actions and circumstances; often, root causes are very hard to find. We will now see what can be done about this difficulty.

Before we derive the next metric, the *Exception Estimation Score,* it will help to explain what is meant by "exception." "Exception handling" is a phrase popularized by languages such as Java, and it is a nice phrase. The word *exception* here carries the sense of "taking exception to" remarks or situations. Taking exception is a way of reacting to unexpected circumstances, especially ones which dismay or inconvenience us. "Exception" brings a certain dignity to the business of bugs. When we take exception to something (say an indelicate comment), effort is usually made to take it in stride and move on, always preferable to a full-blown *faux pas.* We now shift our jargon from bugs to exceptions, because we want to home in more on what we can do in spite of the bugs.

10.5. EXCEPTION ESTIMATION SCORE

The *Exception Estimation Score* is a measure of how likely it is for a *Deliverable Unit* to have serious, showstopping exceptions. The word "likely" is often used to denote probability, but that is not its meaning here. Probability is always useful for collections of events, but we are trying to make informed decisions about individual *Deliverable Units* here. We aim to arrive at a score for each *Deliverable Unit* which will tell us whether it has a higher testing need than other ones.

Every *Deliverable Unit* needs to be tested. Rolling out untested code into production is one of the cardinal sins of software development; never do it. However, because everything cannot be tested with the same intensity, testing resources need to be deployed with discretion. Simpler parts of the system should not be overtested at the cost of neglecting more complex ones.

10.5.1. Testing Dimensions

Testing dimensions are different fronts which can adversely affect testing success for a *Deliverable Unit*. We will consider four dimensions.

Technical — Certain factors, such as the use of a new technology or involved algorithms, are more likely to create exceptions. When I first started using Java Message Service (the "wrapper" Application Programming Interface [API] for middleware messaging platforms), we spent a lot of time and went through several rounds of bug fixing to fully understand the "message time-out" mechanism. Even when we thought it was all done, the Java Message Service components and components interacting with them gave us the most trouble in production. Every new or complex mechanism has some nuances which one learns only by trial and error. The fewer the trials, the more exceptions should be expected.

Another facet of the technical dimension is code reuse. Reuse is sometimes a glorious name for cut-and-paste. The Shakespearean gag about a rose smelling as sweet when called by any other name settles the issue of names. When one yanks chunks of code out of their context and transplants them elsewhere, it pays to be careful. Even after a few compilation cycles have corrected the egregious mismatches (names of variables, etc.), the *intent* of the code's original use must align reasonably with the new scenario. For example, if the original context of the code did not worry much about performance, it may have used a Java container class such as the hash table. If this code is now used blindly in a place where the overhead of fetching elements through their hash keys is too much, reuse will create a sorry state.

The technical dimension covers all the technology- and technique-related origins of exceptions. Like the other dimensions discussed next, decisions have to be made for a project regarding specific concerns in the technical dimension.

Behavioral — User behavior stands to influence software behavior in an important way. Inputs from users serve as the *excitation* to which the software system must *respond* (other than timer-initiated batch processing programs, sometimes called "chron jobs"); the excitation-response model is apparent in interactive systems such as Web-based ones. Users can request anything they want irrespective of what the system might be expecting.

A simple example is entering alphanumeric data in a numeric field (such as telephone number) of an online form. If unexpected inputs go too deep inside the system, they cause unexpected difficulties. A useful strategy is to verify user inputs immediately as they are entered, either through client-side scripting or the outermost server layer. A *Deliverable Unit* which has processing based to a large extent on user inputs has a higher likelihood of generating exceptions in the behavioral dimension. Thus, the behavioral dimension is concerned with how user behavior can cause exceptions in the system.

Political — We discussed at some length how metrics mesh with politics (refer to Section 5.4). It is a fascinating topic. We have been treating metrics as decision facilitators, and whenever decisions are made, there is politics. The political dimension focuses on some specific politics.

In a project meant to overhaul the customer service infrastructure of a large financial company, the development team was asked to build a system to automate the recording, tracking, and resolution of customer complaints. The new system was to be radically different from the one in place for many years. The transition was planned in phases. Feelers were sent out to the department where the customer service executives (individuals who took customer calls) worked, and the plan was agreed upon by all stakeholders. The first few releases of the system received very negative feedback, such as response times were slow, the system "hung" frequently, and the GUI "sucked." In sum, the old system was "so much" better. It slowly dawned on members of the development team, and fortunately also on their business partners who were interfacing with the customer service department, that they were up against issues that had little to do with how the new system performed. There was a perception among the service executives (maybe planted by unseen vested interests) that commissioning the new system would be a step toward redundancy — many of them could lose their jobs if the new system successfully replaced the old one. How their concerns were addressed and the project delivered to reasonable satisfaction is a different story, but this is a typical case of the politics of end-user testing.

Environmental — The environment for a software application is a complex framework where hardware, software, and communication media must work together to give the system a platform to function. Enterprise software needs to be deployed on application servers which provide environmental support such as transaction handling, load balancing, etc.

Servers have varying degrees of tolerance for load levels and transactional volume. Anecdotal evidence points to how important these factors may turn out to be. Thanksgiving and Christmas were nail-biting time for one online shopping portal. Even though the development team hoped more and more buyers would flock to the customer's Web site (which would mean greater budget allocation and more work for the team in the next year), there were worries whether the servers would withstand the load. Sometimes an organization purchases a license for a certain type of application server without correctly estimating future business growth. In one such situation, the customer pleaded that "something be done" with the code so that it could run on servers meant to handle far less load and performance demands because the customer was stuck with a license for that server. Thus testing of software systems stands to be affected significantly due to such environmental factors.

10.5.2. Deriving the Exception Estimation Score

The various *testing dimensions* were described in the preceding section. The idea is to identify and analyze some factors that can have a major influence on the outcome of testing. The start of an iteration, when the *Deliverable Units* (DUs) are identified and delegated to teams or individuals, is a good time to determine the testing intensity to which each DU needs to be subjected.

On a scale of 1 to 5, let each DU be assigned a *testing score* for each *testing dimension*. A score of 1 for a dimension means it is least likely to affect the DU's testing outcome, while a score of 5 means it is most likely. The scores for each dimension are added up to give the *Total Testing Score* for a DU. *Exception Estimation Score* for a DU is defined as the ratio of its *Total Testing Score* to sum of the *Total Testing Scores* for all the DUs addressed in a particular iteration. Thus, taking $TTS(DU_n)$ as the *Total Testing Score* for DU_n, the *Exception Estimation Score* for DU_i, that is, $EES(DU_i)$, is given by:

$$EES(DU_i) = \frac{TTS(DU_i)}{\sum_{j=1}^{n} TTS(DU_j)}$$

where n = total number of DUs in an iteration.

10.5.3. Acting on the Exception Estimation Score

Once the *Exception Estimation Score* has been calculated for each DU in an iteration, the DUs are ranked accordingly. Those with higher scores need more rigorous testing. Even if the development team does not have much of a handle on the political or even the behavioral and environmental dimensions, calculating the *Exception Estimation Score* will help in understanding and documenting the factors of influence in the testing process. An application of the *Exception Estimation Score* will be demonstrated in the case study in Part 3.

Some DUs may appear to be more equal than others in their testing needs. To allocate project resources effectively, there needs to be a way to distinguish which DUs need higher testing attention. The *Exception Estimation Score* helps development teams decide the relative importance of DUs in terms of their testing needs.

10.6. SUMMARY

This chapter talked about testing. Testing is by far the most discussed activity in software development, probably because it has little of the mysticism of analysis and design or the intensity of implementation. Testing is never complete; not finding faults to date is no guarantee faults will not be found in the future. A key point about testing is deciding which parts of the system need closer testing attention than others. Toward that end, the *Exception Estimation Score* was presented.

In the last few chapters, we traversed the software development life cycle through requirements, analysis and design, implementation, and testing. Along the way, a set of metrics and artifacts was presented to help practitioners make decisions within these activities. In the next chapter, we will put the discussions of Part 2 in perspective.

REFERENCE

Schach, S. (2005). *Object-Oriented and Classical Software Development,* 6th ed. McGraw-Hill.

PUTTING IT
ALL TOGETHER

11.1. OVERVIEW

In the last few chapters of Part 2, we reviewed the main activities of the software development life cycle. We also developed metrics and artifacts for each activity. Even as our constructs are varied in nature and scope, they come together in a coherent strategy for the whole life cycle. In this chapter, their interrelations are explained by considering a hypothetical project *flow,* and we also get ready to delve into the case study in Part 3.

11.2. GETTING A "FEEL" FOR THE METRICS

The previous chapters dealt with the nitty-gritty of software development. Each major activity was dissected, from understanding requirements to analysis, design, implementation, and testing. Metrics and artifacts were presented for each activity. Table 11.1 gives a snapshot.

Each construct, in its own context, serves a purpose. Each helps us understand and capture the key theme about the activity in focus. However, as underscored in Section 4.3.2, metrics work best when they work together. Metrics can synergize in a variety of ways, depending mainly on where a project is in the development life cycle. Before illustrating such a scenario, this is a good time to reiterate the attitude of this book.

Table 11.1. Metrics and artifacts: A snapshot

Metric	Use
Correlation Matrix	To map each artifact of the software development process with a specific requirement
Mutation Score	To measure the number of times a requirement has changed over a given number of iterations
Meshing Ratio	To measure how closely analysis components relate with requirements
AEI Score	To measure the levels of abstraction, elision, and indirection in design
Morphing Index	To measure the extent of design change across iterations
Specific Convergence	To measure how much the implementation activities of one iteration contribute toward completing implementation for the system
Interface Map	To specify the dependencies of a unit of implementation
Exception Estimation Score	To measure the relative testing attention a unit of delivery needs

A remark in passing: I recognize that some of the constructs presented earlier (such as the *Interface Map*) do not strictly qualify as metrics in the sense we do not get numbers out of them, but others (such as *Specific Convergence*) do give us numbers. Being a bit lax with names (like abusing the notation, as they say in math), from now on "metrics" will be used to mean both the constructs which lead to numbers and those that do not.

11.3. THE WHOLE POINT — REVISITED

Chapter 3 explored different perspectives on software engineering metrics. The chapters following it discussed the use of metrics to monitor and control software development activities. The metrics in this book help practitioners do their tasks more effectively and with more insight. Iterative and incremental development offers a platform for applying the approach.

In his profound and poetic book *The Timeless Way of Building*, Alexander (1979) reflects how the most natural and the most powerful way of *making* something is to *grow* it. The usefulness of iterative and incremental development comes from the fact that it offers an almost organic way of growing the software system. However, as with all systems that grow, an important principle is at play: feedback.

As discussed in Section 2.3.6, feedback is harnessed to great effect across many engineering disciplines. The success of iterative and incremental software development depends on how well feedback is utilized. In a way, feedback is built into this development model, but it takes some thinking and doing to use it successfully, and that is where metrics come in.

Metrics help evaluate the inputs and outputs of a development activity. Based on this, the activity can be regulated toward faster and closer convergence of its goals. How the metrics described in the past few chapters can help us do this is illustrated next.

11.4. A MECHANISM FOR THE METRICS

Each metric by itself gives us some idea on a particular aspect of development. Some idea is infinitely more than no idea, so metrics by themselves are good. However, to influence the development process significantly for the better, metrics must mesh. Meshing means a set of metrics which are interpreted in the light of one another, each illumining part of the whole and together giving insight into end-to-end development. This is best explained by a picture. The following discussion refers to Figure 11.1 in examining what goes on inside a particular iteration in the development life cycle.

On either side of Figure 11.1 are vertical rectangles representing the software product at iteration $n - 1$ and iteration n. The incremental release from the nth iteration is marked; this is the outcome users can see, feel, and test. The space between the rectangles is the scope of the iteration where requirements elicitation and understanding, analysis, design, and implementation take place. It needs to be noted that activities within an iteration may not be temporally sequenced. There is much overlap in roles and activities, and development often proceeds with analysis, design, implementation, and testing done together, by the same practitioners. In Figure 11.1, time flows from bottom to top as the software system gets built over increments.

Each development activity generates artifacts. The artifacts of one activity feed other activities. Whether an activity has been done well, or done at all, can be determined only from the artifacts it produces. Example artifacts for *requirements* workflow are the requirement documents, minutes of meetings with users, etc.; for *analysis* workflow, they are the list of probable components, players as they have been identified, and their interactions; for *design* workflow, they are the detailed class and sequence diagrams; for *implementation* workflow, running code; and for *test* workflow, test cases, scripts, and results. The degree of ceremony (refer to Chapter 6) varies from project to project and is reflected in how artifacts are made and maintained. Managers,

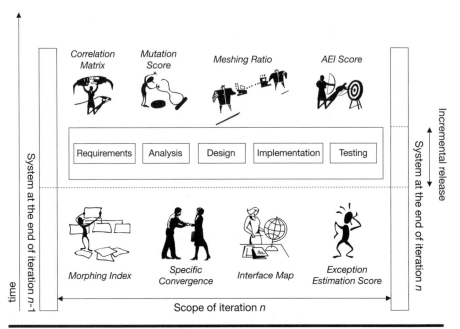

Figure 11.1. Iteration, increment, and the metrics

developers, and customers need to agree at the outset how much ceremony is needed and stick to it.

Metrics and artifacts share a curious relationship. On one hand, metrics work on information, and information is contained in the artifacts. On the other, metrics and their interpretations are artifacts themselves.

We now discuss the scope of each metric as shown in Figure 11.1, going form left to right. *Correlation Matrix* relates every project artifact to one or more parent requirements. Its scope is thus across all the development activities. *Mutation Score* captures how many times each requirement has changed over a number of iterations. *Meshing Ratio* maps the relations between the players identified during analysis and the requirements. *AEI Score* reflects how closely a design aligns with the canons of abstraction, elision, and indirection. *Morphing Index* quantifies design in terms of components and messages exchanged between them; it can be used to measure how much design changes between iterations. *Specific Convergence* measures how much the incremental release from one iteration goes toward convergence, that is, delivery of the entire system's functionality. *Interface Map* captures the dependencies between *Implementation Units,* the atomic deliverables in the charge of an individual or small groups of practitioners. The *Exception Estimation Score* helps decide which *Deliverable Units* (chunks of functionality of value to end users) need higher testing attention. The case study in Part 3 shows how these metrics are calculated and interpreted in a project life cycle.

11.5. NUMBERS AND THEIR MEANINGS

What finally is the take-away from a metric? Is it a magic number which somehow catches and cures all evils? How do metrics help us build better enterprise software? Some of these philosophical issues were dealt with in Chapters 1 and 2 and in Part 1.

I was once in charge of ensuring a certain process was being followed consistently by several teams that were working on a suite of projects. This was essentially policing, the kind of work which makes one disliked by all. We came up with a couple of metrics which reflected how closely each team was fulfilling its process tasks. Every Friday, each team was given a score, and it was circulated to all the teams and their managers. The metrics showed an interesting trend over the three-month life cycle. In the first couple of weeks, most of the teams were sloppy (some deliberately so) about the process tasks; they seemed to be cynical about the whole metrics approach and cared little about what score they got. Then some of the managers began to notice that their teams had a poor showing in some numerical measure compared to others. Suddenly the teams were galvanized. There was even some healthy competition between them; when the scores were read at weekly meetings, the highest scoring team was applauded. Then something really interesting happened. Nearing delivery time, when all the teams were getting ready with their releases, some team members asked for an appointment with me in the cafeteria. They insisted on the cafeteria, so I knew a heart-to-heart talk was in the offing. The long and short of their litany was that the numbers were driving them crazy; they were being pushed hard to get better weekly scores. Ironically, this was the time when the number side of metrics should have mattered the least. The metric scores were just instruments to inspire better process habit. The process habit should have taken hold by then. It was time to shift focus from the process to the product and ensure delivery schedule and quality were met. A metric is always a means toward an end. Incidentally, all the projects met the delivery deadline.

A mechanism for using metrics should be ready to tune its scope and significance to different points in the life cycle. The real finesse in making metrics work is to know when to apply what and when to attach what level of importance to a metric's values. As an example, the *Exception Estimation Score* will be less relevant at the beginning of an iteration than it should toward the end, close to incremental release. Toward the start of an iteration, however, the *Mutation Score* gives a picture of how much requirements have changed from the last iteration. This information is not that useful toward the end of an iteration.

Just defining the metrics is not enough. Metrics need to be integrated within the dynamics of software development. Dynamics is a word of wide reach. We take dynamics to mean the relationships between diverse causes and their effects in the software development enterprise. Each metric has its place in this cosmos. To get the best out of the metrics, that place needs to be shown. This is what Part 3 gets into.

11.6. THE ROAD AHEAD

Jacobson et al. (1999) describe the phases of software as inception, elaboration, construction, and transition. The names sound explanatory, but these ideas are far from trivial. The metrics presented in the last few chapters need to be positioned amongst these phases.

To pique your interest in the road ahead, Figure 11.2 gives an impression of how the metrics may vary in importance across the phases. You should not to take the curves too literally — they give an *impressionist* view and are *not* based on empirical data. Part 3 will explain some of the intuition behind this figure.

11.7. SUMMARY

This chapter took a perspective view of metrics and their role in the development process. Figure 11.1 explained how the metrics fit into the iteration-increment scheme. Figure 11.2 gave an idea of how the metrics vary in their importance across the phases.

We next move on to Part 3 of this book. Through a case study, we will see how the constructs in Part 2 can be used to guide enterprise software development.

REFERENCES

Alexander, C. (1979). *The Timeless Way of Building*. Oxford University Press.
Jacobson, I., Booch, G., and Rumbaugh, J. (1999). *The Unified Software Development Process*. Addison-Wesley.

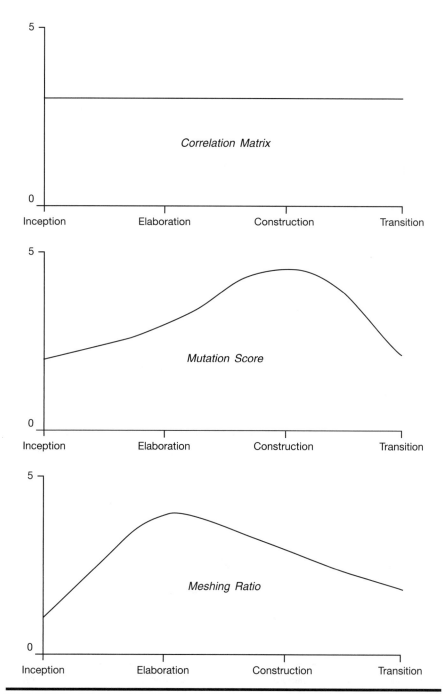

Figure 11.2. Varying importance of the metrics across phases on a scale of 0 to 5

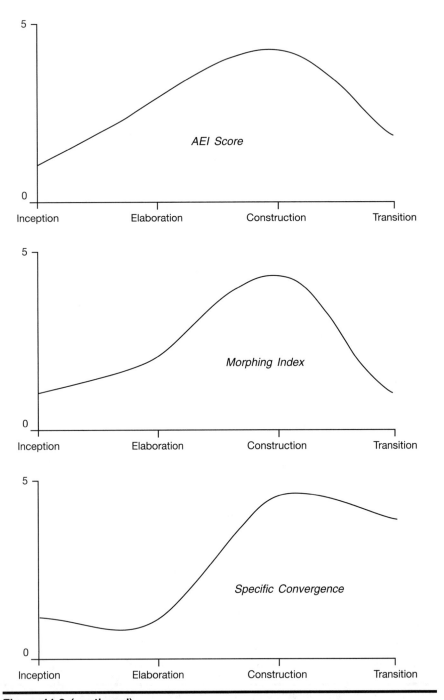

Figure 11.2 (continued).

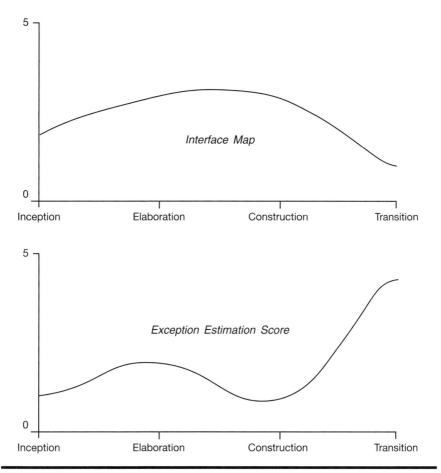

Figure 11.2 (continued).

PART 3.
CASE STUDY

THE PLOT THICKENS

12.1. OVERVIEW

Part 3 of this book illustrates the constructs introduced in Part 2 and contexts discussed in Part 1. As doing is the best way of showing, a case study is used. This chapter provides a road map for Part 3 by giving the background for the case study, acquainting the reader with individuals (*characters*, if you will) who make the case study so interesting, and discussing what can be taken away from the case study.

12.2. BACKGROUND

Programming computers is fun. But building software — especially enterprise software systems that involve other people's money, security, or well-being — is serious business. Lives and livings depend on it, and it can cause both sorrow and happiness. Thus, to drive home the gravity, we will talk about it in a light vein.

The chapters in this section of the book are best read with a *fictional* frame of mind; do not be overly concerned about the real-life links of the people and circumstances, but be awake to the overall *sense* of the story. This is not the same as saying the people and circumstances are *fictitious*; I expect the discerning reader to find many similarities to the real world of software development. The similarities may be too many and too close at times, so it is best to take all of this as a story. I offer the usual disclaimer: all of the following characters and situations are creatures of my own imagination, and any resemblance to reality is purely coincidental.

SymphSoft Tech began as a start-up in an era when starting up was fashionable and fun; even companies which were a decade old at the time called themselves start-ups. To go anywhere in the software business, you had to have a short, pithy name or, better yet, just an acronym. Therefore, *SymphSoft Tech* in time became SST. Fortunately, unlike many start-ups, SST went way beyond starting up and lived to see many more stable days. As we pick up the story, SST is headquartered in Santa Clara, California, and has development centers in Bangalore and Pune in India. It employs close to three thousand *techies* — mostly young, and has close to fifty clients, a few of which are Fortune 500 companies. Surviving the dot-com bust, when many peers perished, has given the honchos at SST the confidence to make it really big.

SST recently hired Tina in a tech lead role (the tech lead role was discussed in Chapter 1 and we met Tina briefly in Section 8.8). Tina joined the software industry in the late 1990s, when Y2K threatened exponential problems. She started as a programmer, graduated to a software engineer and later a senior software engineer, but then found her organization (one of the big names in the industry) to be too bureaucratic. Then she was lapped up by SST, which promised her "challenge, responsibility, and the power to make a *difference*."

SST has a group of projects (called an account) with a large financial organization. This client company, *Money Matters* (MM), has been in business over a hundred years. It is into retail banking, travel, and credit cards, with a few other lines of business in the works. MM has hired SST to "develop, enhance, and maintain" its suite of Web-based applications. MM's own technology department had been doing these things to date. Officially, SST has been contracted to "supplement the services" of the technology department. The company grapevine at MM has been hinting at more ominous things, most notably the "O" word.

SST did not, however, get the whole of MM's technology pie. Three other organizations were awarded similar contracts. All of the contractors, including SST, were asked if they had any issues "working in conjunction with other independent entities toward the furtherance of MM's business interests." All four believed one-fourth pie was better than no pie and agreed to the terms. SST's principal client manager put it more complaisantly: "Why not?"

12.3. TINA'S PROJECT

Two days after joining SST's Pune office, Tina was summoned to Rajiv's cubicle. Rajiv was a senior project manager in charge of the MM account, simply called the account manager at times. SST believed in egalitarianism, so employees even with Rajiv's seniority and clout sat in cubicles. Rajiv welcomed Tina into the SST family and said good things about her skills and experience and how honored SST was when she accepted the offer. To lend his remarks some verisimilitude, Rajiv asked Tina to take up the MAGIC project.

In less than a week, Tina was in Tampa, Florida, at the client location. She was in charge of design, implementation, and delivery of MAGIC. Additionally, Rajiv commented that SST also expected her to build relationships with key customer personnel and get more business. "In this role, you also get to do some business development, which I believe is something you would want to do in the long run. And feel free to call me for any help. All the best!" Rajiv had said when Tina last spoke to him in Pune, plane ticket in hand. Tina felt rather pleased about the expanse of her role and sent an SMS to friends from the airport's departure lounge: "SST cool. Off to US."

This was not the first time Tina had been in the United States. She had two previous stints, a couple of months apiece, in New York City and Denver, Colorado. Upon arriving in Tampa, she quickly went into the functioning mode. SST had several other "resources" working on other MM projects in Tampa, so Tina was among friends.

Monday morning, Tina was at SST's office in downtown Tampa. Samar introduced himself as the portfolio manager for SST's Tampa projects with MM and started to introduce Tina to the MAGIC team. Roger, MAGIC's project manager, told Tina he was very delighted to have her on his team, inquired whether the flight was smooth and commented that it was always his dream to visit India, and said, "Things should really start to move now that you are here." Tracy, MAGIC's system analyst, shook Tina's hand warmly and added that Tina should come to her if she needed any help settling in. Samar suavely remarked that Tina was one of the best and brightest, and Roger seemed to agree. Roger fished out his palmtop and invited Tina to join the next "weekly alignment meeting," at 9:00 A.M. the next morning. Then Samar took Tina to a conference room to brief her on MAGIC.

MAGIC, it seems, is an acronym that stuck as the project's name due to its, well, magicality. Merchant Account Generation & Information Collection, sweetly shortened to MAGIC, was one of the first Web-based applications launched by MM's Cards and Personal Finance Group (CPFG). Simply put, it was planned to be an online credit-card application system for MM's corporate customers. That was more than five years ago, when offering that kind of service was a major edge over the competition. The system was developed in-house by MM's technology team, which has also enhanced and maintained it. A year ago, MM's board made a major policy decision. MM's main line of business was financial services, and it made far better sense to outsource technology activities on a contractual basis to a software shop, possibly in India. The technology department was to be gradually downsized, until there were just enough personnel to oversee the granting and monitoring of contracts and interface with business partners to understand new and continuing business needs. This policy shift was christened the "strategic restructuring plan" and was communicated to MM's employees with strong emphasis on how it was *the only* way to stay competitive in a "rapidly transforming business arena." Maintenance and enhancement of MAGIC first went to *New Age Systems* (NAS), one of SST's close competitors. SST wrenched the contract away from NAS a year and half later based on the value of what Samar called SST's "superior delivery plan." SST also offered an hourly billing rate that was 25 cents less than what NAS had been charging.

In addition to allowing users to apply for credit cards online, MM also wanted MAGIC to provide Web-based transaction reports. CPFG's business partners had long been clamoring for electronic statements. The competition had gone the e-statement route quite some time back, and MM was bleeding business fast without this feature. The numbers proved it. Roger, from MM's technology department, had made it clear when granting the contract to SST that electronic statements should be up ASAP.

Tina had been taking notes and asking questions in order to get a handle on the situation. Samar got up, checked that the door was closed and the phone turned off, lowered his voice, and said: "Now, there are some sensitivities with MAGIC which you...I mean which we should understand."

Tina had half expected this kind of thing to come up. It always did when one worked at client locations. Samar continued: "We are bidding on a couple of other projects NAS is currently doing for MM. Roger has told me MM is not happy with the way NAS ran MAGIC. If we can turn MAGIC around quickly, we will make a stronger case for winning the other projects. So if you find something in MAGIC that is not really up to the mark, we may be able to use it *diplomatically* to our benefit. But of course, don't just go up to Roger and say this and that is bad. We can't do that; after all, we have to work *with* the other contractors. But, of course, you know what I mean..."

"Oh, yes," said Tina.

12.4. AS THINGS SHOULD BE

As mentioned earlier, the "three amigos" identify the four main *phases* of the software development life cycle as *inception, elaboration, construction,* and *transition* (Jacobson et al. 1999). This is a broad categorization which groups activities based on the dominant theme in each stage of the development cycle.

The names are pretty descriptive, as are the names of the deliverables for each phase: *Life Cycle Objectives, Life Cycle Architecture, Initial Operational Capability*, and *Product Release*. Looking at the names, the naïve might be tempted to conclude: At the end of the *inception* phase, the stakeholders know enough about the overall vision of the project to decide whether it is worth commissioning. At the end of the *elaboration* phase, a software architecture (but not the *design*) is in place which can support the development activity; this is a skeleton, so to speak, which can be fleshed out to create the system. At the end of the *construction* phase, the software is fully functioning, not yet fine-tuned but ready for rigorous testing. At the end of the *transition* phase, the product is ready to go out to the market.

Are the grand names (and games) of the *inception, elaboration, construction,* and *transition* phases just a rehash of the waterfall way of doing things? After all, both seem to start with objectives and end with a product. But there is a difference — and a vital one: there are infinitely more feedback loops within these phases, which the waterfall model lacks. Iterative and incremental development ensures the users go along with the project throughout the process, so the product does not land like a meteorite at the end; instead, it grows all along, little by little, endorsed by user feedback.

Yet very few projects — even when run iteratively and incrementally — can be mapped one-to-one with the *inception-elaboration-construction-transition* phase scheme of things. And that is what the difference between theory and practice in software development boils down to.

12.5. AND AS THINGS USUALLY ARE

How is the real different from the ideal? I usually get chary when a speaker or writer lobs such a sweeping question. Such a question has no answer that satisfies everybody. In particular cases, however, one can come up with *some* answer. In enterprise software development, the real varies significantly — and invariably — from the ideal. Even iterative and incremental development, which comes far closer to reality than the waterfall method, still has several disconnects with the *real* real. Each development scenario is unique, each customer's quirks are unique, and each system is unique in its technological and business circumstances. The success of a methodology lies not in how well its prescription can deliver, but in how well its general precepts can be bent to fit a specific situation and still deliver. The best software engineers I have worked with never swear by one methodology or the other. They culture in their minds a chemistry of many best practices and the sense to decide which fits where and when.

But why do the rules need bending? This section covers the reasons why, which I find to be increasingly common across enterprise software projects. These factors, by themselves and in combination, call for this kind of customization of methodologies. They — and the difficulties arising out of them — are usually ignored in textbooks or, even worse, paid lip service that does a world of bad. Tina and her team will encounter many of these factors in MAGIC.

12.5.1. Legacy Code

"Legacy code" is a phrase widely heard in the industry, with little thought given to its meaning. Some people call legacy code the code which runs on mainframes, while others use it to mean any *leftover* programs from earlier versions which the current version of a system still needs to run. In these contexts, another phrase often used, usually longingly, is "greenfield project." This is usually taken to mean a software project which is starting from scratch, that is, the first time a business process is being automated through software. Young hotshot software engineers long for greenfield projects because they seem to offer so much scope in displaying one's unique talents in software building. The word "greenfield" has great visual appeal; it conjures up images of a lush green field waiting to host a magnificent software edifice. Not only are greenfield projects rare and becoming rarer, but they present some singular difficulties due to what I call *legacy thinking* (discussed in the next section).

Even a decade ago, greenfield projects were common as the penetration of software into the domains of health care, transportation, finance, etc. was just beginning. In the early 1990s, my brother was involved in the project to build the online passenger reservation system for Indian Railways. Now Indian Railways mimics India in its size and diversity, carrying more than a million tons of freight traffic and about 14 million passengers daily across 6856 stations (http://www.indianrail.gov.in/) and still counting. Before such a computerized system existed, all bookings were done manually over the counter. This was a greenfield project in the true sense of the term.

Once such systems are into production, future enhancements or modifications — even maintenance— will need to build on them. Most software development projects that are commissioned today build on existing systems. Legacy code cannot be thrown or wished away. It has to be incorporated, often via indelicate patches, into the new system and done in such a way that the whole works seamlessly. When there is an existing system that is delivering something — even if slowly, inefficiently, and with frequent outages, it never makes business sense to retire it altogether and start afresh. There are many reasons for that, primarily the demands of *business continuity*. Every enterprise is wary of a turn-off/turn-on scenario, when the old system is switched off and the new switched on. What if the new system crashes? Can the old one take over again? Hardly wishing to take such a risk, enterprises want the new to be rung in gently and transparently folded into the old. The bottom line is that legacy code (software from existing systems that supported and still supports business processes) will be there. How to handle legacy code remains a proverbial gray area of enterprise software development.

12.5.2. Legacy Thinking

Sometimes legacy thinking results in more pain than legacy code does. Whenever there is legacy code, there is legacy thinking. Even more disturbingly, even without legacy code, there can be legacy thinking. Legacy thinking, like other subtle ideas, is easier to understand than explain. Let me relate how a friend of mine awoke to the consequences of legacy thinking.

He was working on a project to develop a system to give credit-card holders Web-based access to their transaction histories. Before the Web age, cardholders accessed their data by installing on their PCs a piece of client software which periodically downloaded the information from the credit-card provider's servers. Once the information was on the local machines, the client software gave cardholders different ways to search and sort the data. Gradually, major problems arose with this client-server mechanism, including the need for many versions of the client software to run on different platforms and the frequent issues the cardholders had installing and configuring the software. All this was why the Web-based system was commissioned. Much communication went out to the cardholders *a priori,* touting how easy it would now be to access one's data — anywhere, anytime. Just go to the Web and bingo!

The new system my friend helped build did exactly what it was meant to, but within the first month there were complaints galore. Sorting the data took more time, searching was worse on the Web pages, reports took a long time to display if a cardholder tried to pull data for the last twenty months — the list was long and ugly. This was classic legacy thinking in play. The users were so used to the legacy system (accessing the data from their desktop computers) that their very thinking was tuned to its quirks. Sifting through data on a local machine is always faster than over a network, and when someone tries to pull details for several thousand transactions, the difference shows.

It took quite a bit of coaxing, and finally the threat of discontinuing support for the desktop software, to shepherd the cardholders to the online system. Legacy thinking is thinking and seeing a new software system in the light of an older one which users are used to. No methodology, to my knowledge, teaches you how to tackle legacy thinking.

12.5.3. The Myth of Transitioning

Today, very little enterprise software is developed in-house. Organizations like MM are finding it increasingly cost ineffective to maintain technology personnel whose skills and aspirations are not wholly aligned to the organization's main lines of business. On the other hand, computer companies are increasingly getting into software services, which means being hired to build and maintain software systems for customer organizations. Outsourcing comes from the confluence of these trends.

It is unfortunate that some circles view the "O" word in such a negative light, for many loaded reasons. When an organization *outsources* its software development, it does not usually contract with only one company. It is common practice to have several providers (variously called contractors, vendors, or, more flatteringly, technology partners) vie for the pie (just as SST had to). This fosters competition and ultimately helps all parties, most immediately the company outsourcing. It also prevents one contractor from gaining a total monopoly on the contracting company's technological know-how.

In such situations, it is not unusual to lose business to a competing company. Terms such as "outbid" and "reallocation" often are used to soften the blow. Your team may have nurtured a project from birth through infancy and adolescence, but just as it was blossoming into youth, another company is put in charge. What happens to all the project wisdom you acquired and which you feel is absolutely necessary to run the project, both technologically and managerially?

It is not uncommon to have one week, two at the most, to *transition* the project to the new custodian. Often, the new custodian is not a bird of prey but someone you met in the break room when both your teams worked side by side on the same floor. No matter how friendly you might have been in the break room, losing business is losing business, and transition never happens with great goodwill. Design documents are almost never passed on, and even if they are, no one can make heads or tails out of them. In the end, the incoming team is left holding just the code, for better or for worse. Inheriting other people's code (that is, code written by people with very different ways of thinking and building software) and understanding, running, bug-fixing, and enhancing it without a sliver of reasonable documentation to help you out is another fact of life in enterprise software development. Methodologies, in their ideality, seldom if ever account for it.

As an aside, cross-company transitioning is not the only thing that can leave you with no documents. Similar ills frequently abound within organizations. To someone who has given notice and is packing up for greener pastures, passing on the wisdom is not often the highest priority. It should be, as a basic professional courtesy, but as I said pretty early on, this book is about how things are, not how things should be.

12.5.4. Interfacing with Teams from Other Organizations

Somewhat linked to yet distinct from the previous point is the need to work with teams from other organizations to build software for the same customer. This is what the line "working in conjunction with other independent entities toward the furtherance of MM's business interests" boils down to. It is not unusual for teams from different contractors to work on modules that must finally come together in order for the whole system to work. It is sometimes difficult to work in these situations, as the success of your project may depend on a key deliverable from another team from another organization; you have no handle on the chain of command that team reports to. But working toward a common goal with personnel from other organizations is also an opportunity to learn about different company cultures and processes. Interteam dynamics remain an important reason why the real and ideal differ in software development; methodologies do not have a prescription for it.

12.5.5. Cross-Continental Teams

Globalization of the software trade has had some fallout: distributed teams. It is now almost the norm for one team member to interface with the customer at the customer's location, while the rest of the team works from another location, which can be the next building or on another continent. Often, teams function solely through the medium of long-distance conference calls ("con calls" as they are called, which fortunately has nothing to do with *conning*) without members meeting face to face.

It is certainly more difficult to keep motivation consistent across continents. When a major production issue arose with a New York–based client in late October, in perfect sync with the major Indian festival of *Diwali*, the project leader at the client site had a hard time galvanizing her team in Bangalore. Even for less cataclysmic or more routine work, distributed teams add a new level of challenge to enterprise software development. Software development methodologies have little if any advice for this increasingly common situation.

The above are just a few reasons why theory and practice differ in enterprise software development. But merely noting that theory and practice differ and leaving it at that does not help. Successful software building, like many other worthwhile things, happens when this breach is bridged.

12.6. SHALL THE TWAIN MEET?
THE STORY OF THE METRICS

The whole point of Part 3, and indeed of the whole book, is that using metrics can reasonably reconcile the chasm between the real and the ideal in enterprise software development. This assertion will be demonstrated through the case study. Methodologies are the distillate of many of the industry's best practices — lessons learned over many successes and many more failures. The case study will show how the metrics in this book can help derive the best out of the best practices in far from ideal circumstances. It contains a number of threads, some of which will be identified as we go along.

Tina, the tech lead in the case study, is a software engineering practitioner like all of us. We allow her one special gift: the use of the metrics developed in Part 2. In the following chapters, we will follow the MAGIC project as Tina and her team work on it. The case study medium is used to help avoid pontification about how to go about using the metrics.

The following narrative seeks to engage the reader through a story. Whenever something sublime or very important is discussed, a brazen point will be made of it. The next four chapters correspond roughly to the phases *inception, elaboration, construction,* and *transition,* but only roughly. Phases are only placeholders — something to help us better understand the software development life cycle. The customer paying to have software built does not care a bit if a phase is called conception instead of inception or instruction instead of construction, as long as the software is delivered on time and within budget. (In fact, I think it is good for both developers and customers if the vocabulary of the two groups does not overlap; customers have every reason to feel intimidated, then upset, and ultimately unhappy when too many software buzzwords are used, just as we are when we hear about sales targets and brand value.) In sum, let the puritans be warned that in the next four chapters we will not be too concerned with what should and should not go into a phase. We will go where MAGIC takes us.

Welcome to Tina's odyssey; it will be as much fun as it is real. Let the MAGIC be with you!

12.7. SUMMARY

The case study was introduced in this chapter. It also discussed why and how real enterprise software development deviates from the ideal situations assumed in methodologies. Over the next few chapters, which *loosely* map to the four phases of *inception, elaboration, construction,* and *transition,* the case study will illustrate how the metrics in Part 2 can help leverage the best practices of the trade.

REFERENCE

Jacobson, I., Booch, G., and Rumbaugh, J. (1999). *The Unified Software Development Process.* Addison-Wesley.

GETTING INTO
THE GROOVE

13.1. OVERVIEW

This chapter takes us deeper into the case study. As Tina and her team start working on the MAGIC project, we see when and where the *Correlation Matrix* and the *Mutation Score* come to the aid of the party. This is the first time we will see the metrics in action.

13.2. THE FIRST MEETING

Tina's first brush with the "weekly alignment meeting" was an interesting affair. Roger and Tracy were there, and so was Samar, as this was Tina's first time attending. There were also some people on the phone, introduced as Betty from the business unit, Kevin from customer service, and John from infrastructure. Quickly pressing the mute button, Roger winked and said these were *his* customers. In the first fifteen minutes a litany of complaints about the existing MAGIC system was voiced, mainly led by Betty, with Kevin and John chipping in. Three-quarters of an hour later, the meeting ended with high expectations for MAGIC 2.0 and a wish list for Tina:

- *Premium* users should receive electronic statement of their transactions, sent monthly via e-mail.

- *Contention* functionality needs to be added.
- The Transaction Summary Report "took ages" to load, and something had to be done about that.

This was the closest to requirement specification that existed at the time. Of course Tracy would help Tina "write things up" as the project moved forward. Toward the end of the meeting, Tina had raised, almost sheepishly, the question of a development methodology. Before she could get to the "incremental" in "iterative and incremental," Roger said they were fine with anything that delivered. Betty added "on time and within budget."

While walking back to their desks, Roger said the electronic statement, which he recommended should be called *ElectState* (the name had such a nice ring to it and it just came to him one morning while playing golf!), should be done using NIRVANA. "That's a smart piece of software; just plug-and-play for this sort of canned report. We paid two hundred thousand dollars for the license." When she arrived at her desk, Tina decided to look up NIRVANA.

13.3. TAKING STOCK

The next week was a busy one for Tina. She had a lot on her plate: understanding the existing version of MAGIC, getting up to speed on NIRVANA, and building her *offshore* team.

The current version, MAGIC 1.6, allowed users to see their credit-card transactions for any period within the past twelve months, pay bills, and update postal and e-mail addresses over the Web. There were two levels of users, regular and premium, with different facilities as decided by the business logic. The new contention feature, part of the wish list, would allow users to dispute any charge on their account online. Currently, all contentions were handled by customer service representatives over the telephone. User profiles, as well as credit-card transaction data, were stored in databases maintained by AXT, another of MM's contractors. MAGIC 1.6 was a J2EE-based system with business logic in Enterprise JavaBeans (EJB) and user interface in JavaServer Pages. The Transaction Summary Report Web page was indeed slow in loading and even frequently timed out when more than six months of data was being pulled.

Tina asked about the design documents for the existing version of MAGIC. Roger said Tracy was the one who knew all about them. Tracy said she had joined the project just a month earlier, when the previous system analyst left. She knew of a database where some of the documents might be and promised to forward the link to Tina. Tina went through the documents; she knew what to expect and got what she expected. There was a little bit of everything: requirements, use cases, Unified Modeling Language (UML) diagrams, and test scripts. None of the documents had been updated, and MAGIC 1.6 went way beyond what the requirements said it should be. Tina was seasoned enough not to complain about such a state of affairs. She went into the code to make sense of things.

On a different plank, NIRVANA appeared to be one of those commercial off-the-shelf software products that promised a "sure-shot solution to all your financial reporting needs." With the idea of electronic statements being floated around, MM allowed itself to be convinced NIRVANA was just what was needed. It bought the NIRVANA license for a price which would certainly affect Roger's appraisal if nothing came of it. Roger had led the MM team that "evaluated" NIRVANA before it was bought. From what Tina understood, NIRVANA had many useful features. It allowed large volumes of data to be quickly searched and sorted; lack of this feature was one of the major gripes the business unit had against the current version of MAGIC. However, no one seemed to have the faintest idea how to *integrate* NIRVANA within the MAGIC architecture. Roger said he had spoken with someone from NIRVANA who had promised to help in an effort to fulfill contractual obligations with MM, but the contractual obligations only included support for the NIRVANA product and did not cover "interfacing with existing infrastructure." So that was that.

Expectedly, existing MAGIC code was a tangled mass, liberally patched. A couple of years back, while still a tyro in enterprise software development, this sort of thing would have aggravated Tina. MAGIC code had all the symptoms of real-world systems, enhanced and modified by evolving business needs, and Tina now knew that evolving business needs have to be supported whatever its toll on the software system. There was repeated code galore; some components seemed to be doing a lot of disconnected things, while others had too little to do. It seemed a miracle, as it always does, that this kind of ad hoc implementation was doing anything meaningful. Yet it was, and MAGIC 1.6 was up and running, although churning a wake of complaints that grew shriller by the day. A few hours with the code convinced Tina that a quick fix to improve the response time of the Transaction Summary Report would most likely be neither quick nor a fix.

In the break room over coffee, Roger asked Tina how things were going. Tina said she was looking into the existing system and things would be easier if there were design documents. Roger said they should be there. Hadn't Jillian, the system analyst before Tracy, fixed all that? Tina knew she had to prepare well for the next meeting.

Before proceeding, a note on the nomenclature going forward: MAGIC 1.0 is the original version of the system, MAGIC 1.6 is the currently running system, and MAGIC 2.0 is what Tina and her team will build. When just MAGIC is used, it should be clear from the context which version is being referred to. Whenever a legacy/back-end/contention database is mentioned, it refers to the database where contention information entered by the users must be recorded, outside the MAGIC system. If some of these terms sound unfamiliar, stay tuned; you will soon be in the know.

13.4. CORRELATION MATRIX TO THE RESCUE

The MAGIC situation is common. A vast majority of software projects are commissioned to be built on existing systems. These systems usually evolve over multiple versions, worked on by different teams. Documentation is mostly missing, and what is there is vastly out of date with the running code. This should never be the case if software engineering best practices are followed, but it is the case here, and a key skill of enterprise software development is being able to deliver under — or in spite of — these circumstances.

We will now see how the metrics in Part 2 make life easier for Tina and her team and offer the customers better value. At the end of her reconnaissance, Tina made some decisions:

- From the wish list, it is clear the customers want some things badly, but are not exactly sure what they want. Waterfall is out of the question; MAGIC 2.0 would be best developed iteratively and released over increments. Only when the customers see something working will they be able to tell which way they *really* want to go.
- The state of the existing MAGIC has to be clearly documented and explained to the customers. This will help set expectations for MAGIC 2.0 and set the context for future projects for redesigning MAGIC. Improving response time of the Transaction Summary Report calls for a major overhaul and quick fixes cannot be promised.
- There are likely to be significant issues in integrating NIRVANA with MAGIC. A workable approach would be to do a small ElectState pilot with MAGIC 2.0 first.

Tina went over these points with Samar. He was half convinced, but also wondered how convincing the explanation of MAGIC's current (sorry) state

Table 13.1. Parts of *Correlation Matrix* **for the existing MAGIC system**

Artifacts	Requirements			
	R_01	**R_02**	**R_03**	**...**
Use case: Login	X			
Use case: View transactions		X		
...				
Code component: MainPage.jsp	X			
...				
Code component: LoginHandler.java	X			
Code component: DateCalculator.java				?
Code component: TransactionReporter.java		X		
Code component: GenericController.java				?
...				
Test case: View transactions		X		
...				

would sound to Roger and company. "We will use the *Correlation Matrix*," Tina told him. Samar said, "Okay, but let's look at this matrix of yours before the next meeting."

Table 13.1 gives parts of the *Correlation Matrix* Tina prepared for the existing version of MAGIC. The fields marked "?" denote some of the correlations that should have been there but were not. Conversely, there were artifacts which did not trace back to any requirements, so there were clear disconnects: either requirements did not reflect the current state of the system or the system did something beyond the requirements. Either way, the *Correlation Matrix* gives a quick and clear snapshot of the system.

This is a good time to highlight an important theme: artifacts which reflect metrics data are *living* as long as the project is alive. As Tina's team works on MAGIC, the *Correlation Matrix* will undergo changes, and it has to be kept updated.

Tina presented the *Correlation Matrix* at the next meeting. She pointed out the gaps where the documents and the code were hopelessly out of sync and how this would affect MAGIC 2.0. Betty said she knew all along MAGIC was not being handled in the proper way. Roger said there is always scope for improvement and added that the team now had the right leader in Tina. The meeting moved on to the next point on the agenda, expectations from MAGIC 2.0. It was Kevin's opinion that something also needed to be done about the MAGIC user interface. There were several complaints from users about not finding their way on the Web site. In addition, some users wanted to see the past three years of transaction history. Could that be done? And what about a new home page for MAGIC, one that was, well, more attractive? Betty chimed in, "How about giving all users, premium and regular, the electronic statement 'thing'?"

Tina was taking notes. She said she would look into each need and get back to Betty and Kevin. Roger agreed they would have some answers by the next meeting.

13.5. FIRST PASS

It was time to get into things more concrete. In Web-based projects, screen navigation is a major part of the overall user experience. The best way to get users to agree on navigation is to have the *wireframes* in place. Wireframes, sometimes called screen captures, help users visualize the navigation of a Web site.

Tina decided to have her offshore team start working on the wireframes. The team was just forming; Arvind in Pune was asked to take a look at the existing MAGIC pages and modify them to fit in the flow of the contention functionality. Meanwhile, Tina decided to dive into the first cut at specifying requirements.

Writing out requirements is officially the task of the system analyst, in this case Tracy. But requirements are not only about writing, not even about understanding. As discussed in Chapter 7, *elicitation* is a vital aspect of requirements. People who commission a project seldom have clear ideas about what they want built. Therefore, one of the most important tasks of the development team is to clarify for the users (or those representing the users, in this case Betty and company) what they can actually expect from the software system, given the outline of their needs. This task is best done by those accountable for delivering the project.

Table 13.2 is the first outline of the requirements document for MAGIC 2.0. Figure 13.1 gives a few wireframes and their navigation paths. As is evident, the wireframes capture only the essential elements of the Web pages. The pages have quite a bit of white space, often called "real estate," which later may be filled by pictures, verbiage, or whatever else the customer wants. For the time being, wireframes are exactly what they sound like, wire frames that contain only the skeleton of the user interface.

The requirements in Table 13.2 merit some reflection. The vital/essential/desirable column is to be filled in by the business unit. At this time, the requirements are at the high level; they outline broad directions of functionality without

Table 13.2. MAGIC 2.0 requirements: first cut

Requirement ID	Requirement description	Vital/ Essential/ Desirable?
M2_001	The system shall present a Contention Page for users to enter information relevant to contention processing.	
M2_002	The system shall offer a navigation path between the Transaction Summary Page and the Contention Page.	
M2_003	The Contention Page shall contain fields for transaction ID, transaction date, transaction description, and transaction amount and a text area for the user to enter the reason for contention.	
M2_004	The Contention Page shall contain fields for the user's mailing address, e-mail address, and daytime phone.	
M2_005	The system shall present a Confirmation Page to confirm successful submission of a contention.	
M2_006	The system shall offer electronic statements of monthly transactions to be sent by e-mail on a pilot basis to a group of not more than ten users.	
M2_007	The electronic statement shall present the same information as the paper statement, although not necessarily in the same format.	
M2_008	The system shall deliver electronic statements only to those users (within the pilot group) who have valid e-mail addresses in their user profiles. The system will have no functionality to validate e-mail addresses of the users.	
M2_009	To reduce the response time of the Transaction Summary Page to the extent possible with the existing software and hardware infrastructure, the system shall restrict users from selecting more than three months of past transaction data.	
M2_010	The system shall have a modified Main Page announcing the introduction of the new contention functionality.	
M2_011	The system shall support all other existing functionality of MAGIC 1.6.	

going into implementation details. There is no mention of specific GUI elements; font color and radio buttons will only muddy the waters at this time. Getting caught up in the details too early is an insidious trap. It gives the impression everybody is deeply into the project, racking their brains to get

MAGIC 2.0

Home
Account
Contention
Transaction
Logout

TRANSACTION SUMMARY REPORT — CARD XXXX XXXX XXXX 1234

Date	TXN ID	Description	Amount	Balance
12/01/2006	AX542	P for Pizza	21.34	279.1
12/02/2006	YJ765	The Best Collection	102.56	381.66
12/02/2006	HS457	XYZ Automobile and Service Center	55.19	436.85
12/03/2006	PQ238	Books! Books!	12.43	449.28
12/04/2006	UY564	Super-Duper Grill	62.98	512.26
12/05/2006	TW765	The Mom and Pop Market	104.45	616.71
12/06/2006	KL765	Corner Cafe	14.50	631.21
12/07/2006	CM765	Payment received —Thank You!	-257.76	373.45
12/08/2006	KJ345	The Big Store	34.26	407.71
12/09/2006	UR876	Neighborhood Grocers	9.96	417.67
12/10/2006	PW084	My Shop	71.23	488.9

Want to contend a charge? Click on TXN ID above. Page 1 of 4 >> next >> last

View Web Site Rules and Regulations, Trademarks and Privacy Statement of MAGIC 2.0. Copyright © 1995 - 2007 MM. All Rights Reserved. Users of this site agree to be bound by the terms of the MM Web Site Rules and Regulations.

MAGIC 2.0

Home
Account
Contention
Transaction
Logout

CONFIRMATION

Your information has been successfully recorded; the contention ID is **XYZ123**. Please allow up to 14 business days for the contention to be processed. You may contact magic@mm.com for further information. In all communication please quote the contention ID.

OK

View Web Site Rules and Regulations, Trademarks and Privacy Statement of MAGIC 2.0. Copyright © 1995 - 2007 MM. All Rights Reserved. Users of this site agree to be bound by the terms of the MM Web Site Rules and Regulations.

Figure 13.1. Wireframes and navigation paths

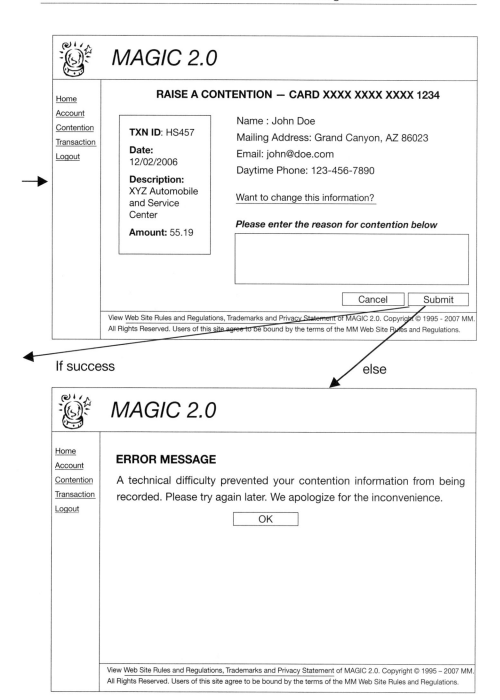

Figure 13.1 (continued).

things straightened out, while the real questions (and consequently their answers) remain obscured.

Obsession with *writing* requirements is also waterfall baggage. While it certainly helps to have worthwhile things written down, and written clearly, there is no point in being overly particular about documenting every detail in the iterative and incremental approach. From pretty early on, iterative and incremental development delivers working code for users to see, play with, and criticize. One benefit of writing requirements in excruciating detail is sometimes cited as its potential *legal* value. Should something go wrong with the project and issues escalate beyond amicable settlement, having everything written down and signed off on may help in a lawsuit. This is a specious line of reasoning. If a project fails, it makes more sense for the customer to move on to another development organization than to spend time and resources on courtroom battles.

Speaking of legality, requirements should *not* read like a legal document. Sentences should be short and clear, mostly in the active voice ("the system shall do…" instead of "…shall be done by the system"), and unequivocal in both their meaning and sense. This is not the same thing as trying to close every loophole and ensure the safety of one's posterior for every contingency. The main objective is to have the requirement documents read, understood, and endorsed by the stakeholders. This objective will not be fulfilled if readers are not comfortable with reading them in the first place. Also, of course, requirements should be described in prose, not poetry or pictures. (The same holds for use cases. Use-case diagrams [ovals and stick figures joined by arrows] remain one of the most useless and confusing UML artifacts. They cannot and should never substitute for use-case description in prose.)

Before forwarding the wireframes and the requirements to Betty et al., Tina had a meeting with Roger. Roger went over the wireframes and the requirements in one swift glance and said, "Looks good. Let's send them over." Tina drew his attention to requirement M2_006, the *pilot* aspect of the NIRVANA-based electronic statements. This seemed something of a dampener to Roger: "But NIRVANA is just plug-and-play; can't we roll it out to all the users? After all, that software cost us two hundred thousand dollars." Tina explained in brief what the difficulties with NIRVANA were, highlighting the main issue of integrating it into the MAGIC architecture. Roger still had his qualms: "But this is a big thing we promised to the business unit. Getting NIRVANA up would be a big boost to my…I mean a big win for all of us." Tina fished out the *Correlation Matrix*, touched upon the state of the current version of MAGIC, and said that including ElectState for all users — using NIRVANA — in MAGIC 2.0 would increase development time by a couple of months, with added risks to the contention functionality. Roger reflected for a while in half soliloquy, "Did they sell us a dud?" Tina kept quiet. Roger said, "Okay, but the pilot better be good." Tina said it would be, so the wireframes and the first cut at requirements were sent to Betty and Kevin for their feedback.

13.6. BACK AND FORTH

The next couple of days were busy ones, as e-mails flew back and forth and there were many ad hoc meetings. The wireframes and the requirement descriptions seemed to give Betty and Kevin many new ideas. They expressed surprise at some of the requirements and concern about others. Could the users change their contact details on the Contention Page (M2_004)? Pop-up boxes were so "cool" for running advertisements and user surveys; could the business unit ask for pop-ups to be added and taken off at a "couple of days" notice (*new*)? After raising a contention, users usually become anxious about the status of their case. Could the home page have a "Status of Contention" box (*new*)? Why have a pilot for ElectState? Why couldn't it be rolled out to all users? After all, NIRVANA would churn out the canned statements (M2_006, M2_007, M2_008), wouldn't it? Why did the date range need to be restricted to improve response time (M2_009)? The wireframes looked good, but the color scheme (or lack thereof) was kind of boring and the fonts too small, plus the page could use some more pictures. How about giving the Transaction Summary Page (M2_011) a whole new look and feel? The business unit said all these issues needed to be resolved before requirements could be marked vital, essential, or desirable. For now, all requirements were very important.

Every time there was talk of changing a requirement or a new requirement came up, Tina updated the requirement list and circulated it. The list was marked MAGIC2_Requirements_versionXX; every time it was updated, the version number was changed. Much has been written about version control of code, and it is very important, but version control of requirement documents is no less important, especially early in a project. It helps track the initial changes and their frequency. Version control tools are helpful, but just naming files consistently goes a long way.

Weeks rolled by without consensus being reached on the requirements. Tina was keeping track of how many times and how each requirement was changing. In the ideal world, requirements are taken as a given. In the real world, practitioners must ensure requirements make sense and are feasible to be implemented, at least on three counts: infrastructure, time, and budget. In the ideal, customers cannot change a requirement once they have signed off on it. In the real, customers do not see why they cannot. Our case study is about the real; it is about showing how the metrics can help us stay on course in spite of the copious (and inevitable) deviations of the real from the ideal in enterprise software development.

13.7. MUTATION SCORE: LET THE METRIC DO THE TALKING

At the juncture MAGIC 2.0 is now at, metrics come in handy. The difficult part in going back and forth with requirements is that customers seldom accept that *they* are going back and forth. The dexterity of eliciting requirements lies in *transparently* guiding customers with their requirements. This is not easy and calls for patience and practice. Customers and developers interact closely for the first time while requirements are being threshed out; this is a time to build relationships, not break them. Customers do not like being told what they need or, worse, hints that developers know more about *their* requirements. One has to be careful — discrete, perhaps is the word — in this phase of the development life cycle. Developers not only must understand requirements in their current form, but also must be able to internally (that is, *within* the development team) forecast how they might change in the future. Working with requirements calls for a range of skills, not the least of which is an understanding of human psychology.

Table 13.3 gives the *Mutation Scores* for the MAGIC 2.0 requirements. (Note that there are eleven requirements, which went back and forth between the development team and customers at least four times; therefore, $m = 11$ and $n = 4$, corresponding to the derivation in Section 7.6.2. Here we take iterations

Table 13.3. *Mutation Scores* for MAGIC 2.0 requirements

Requirement ID	Mutation Score
M2_001	3
M2_002	1
M2_003	2
M2_004	3
M2_005	1
M2_006	3
M2_007	3
M2_008	1
M2_009	2
M2_010	0
M2_011	2

to mean the cycles of revision the requirements are undergoing.) Tina presented the table at one of the meetings. It gave a snapshot of how many revisions each requirement had undergone since MAGIC 2.0 kicked off. There was nothing in the making of these numbers the stakeholders did not know, but seeing the *Mutation Scores,* clear and unwavering, had an effect. Everyone seemed more malleable to the point of view that it was time to agree on a core set of requirements and get development started. The meeting ended with agreement on the set of requirements for the first incremental release of MAGIC 2.0 (Table 13.4).

There is a point worth noting here. In deriving the *Mutation Score* (Section 7.6.2), we considered change over each iteration. Iteration then was taken in its broader, more formal sense: a time-boxed collection of activities that resulted in an incremental release of the system. There has been no incremental release of MAGIC 2.0 as yet, but the idea of iteration can be applied at many levels.

Table 13.4. MAGIC 2.0 requirements for first release

Requirement ID	Requirement description	Vital/ Essential/ Desirable?
M2_001	The system shall present a Contention Page for users to enter information relevant to contention processing.	V
M2_002	The system shall offer a navigation path between the Transaction Summary Page and the Contention Page.	D
M2_003	The Contention Page shall contain fields for transaction ID, transaction date, transaction description, and transaction amount and a text area for the user to enter the reason for contention.	E
M2_004	The Contention Page shall contain fields for the user's mailing address, e-mail address, and daytime phone. If the user wishes to modify any of this information, there will be hyperlink(s) to reach the User Profile Page of the existing MAGIC 1.6 application, which will enable the modification.	V
M2_005	The system shall present a Confirmation Page to confirm successful submission of a contention.	E
M2_006	The system shall offer electronic statements of monthly transactions to be sent by e-mail on a pilot basis to a group of not more than ten users. The group of users will be identified by the development team in consultation with the business unit, based on considerations most conducive to implementing the electronic statement functionality using NIRVANA.	V

Table 13.4. MAGIC 2.0 requirements for first release (continued)

Requirement ID	Requirement description	Vital/ Essential/ Desirable?
M2_007	The electronic statement shall present the same information as the paper statement, although not necessarily in the same format. The format for the electronic statement shall be decided by the development team in consultation with the business unit, based on considerations most conducive to implementing the electronic statement functionality using NIRVANA.	E
M2_008	The system shall deliver electronic statements only to those users (within the pilot group) who have valid e-mail addresses in their user profiles. The system shall have no functionality to validate e-mail addresses of the users.	D
M2_009	To reduce the response time of the Transaction Summary Page to the extent possible with the existing software and hardware infrastructure, the system shall restrict users from selecting more than three months of past transaction data.	V
M2_010	The system shall have a modified Main Page announcing the introduction of the new contention functionality.	Out of scope: see M2_012, M2_013 for requirements related to the Main Page
M2_011	The system shall not enhance or modify the functionality of the existing MAGIC system in any way not mentioned in these requirements.	E
M2_012	The system shall have the facility to display a pop-up box on the Main Page which will contain a message related to promotions, etc. The verbiage of the message will be provided by the business unit at least five days prior to the start date of the pop-up box display. The business unit will also specify how many days the pop-up will need to be displayed.	E
M2_013	The system shall display a "Status of Contention" box on the Main Page which will display the number of unresolved contentions currently existing for the user.	E

The act of revisiting a task, each time with newer information, experience, or insight, is also iterating. This is what has been happening so far with the MAGIC 2.0 requirements. The *Mutation Scores* are calculated based on this local perception of iteration vis-à-vis the global perception of iteration leading to an incremental release. This underscores an important attribute metrics must have in order to be widely used. The conditions for computing and using a metric should not be so stringent (or esoteric) as to preclude all but the most special cases. Specialization surely gives soundness and rigor, but sometimes it takes things too far. I recently read a paper, brilliantly written with extensive references, that derived *the* "metric for measuring cohesion in object-oriented online gaming software that use EJB and AJAX." The metric sounds good, but somewhat too specific. Essential features of usable metrics are their flexibility, customizability, and adjustability. Make a metric too specific, and you will hardly find a situation to use it.

13.8. BEFORE DEVELOPMENT BEGINS

Once the requirements for the first release are agreed upon, is it time to jump into the actual building? Yes and no. Yes in the sense that iterative and incremental development is all about starting to build working software as early as possible, building it bit by bit and getting user feedback at every release. A delivery that does not contain working code is no delivery, so the earlier one gets to building code, the better. But no in another, deeper respect. Rushing to code is a common syndrome, and no development methodology (iterative and incremental development included) offers immunity. Rushing to code has more to do with mind-set. It is about trying to get things going as quickly as possible; in short, it is about showing results. But how do we evaluate the results? This leads us to a key concern: setting up the success criteria.

Just as beauty is in the eye of the beholder, success criteria are whatever users deem acceptable fulfillment of each requirement. No matter how clearly requirements are written, and how well what is written is implemented, there will always be scope for misunderstanding. Take, for example, a hypothetical login requirement:

> The system shall allow the user to enter their user ID and password on the Login Page. Upon the user hitting the "submit" button, the system shall verify the entered user ID and password. Upon successful verification, the system shall present the Welcome Page to the user. Upon unsuccessful verification, the Error Page is displayed with the message "Login failed; please try again."

The success criteria for this seem pretty straightforward: pass if the system lets in a user with bona fide credentials; fail if otherwise.

But what if the system takes ten minutes to decide if a user can be let in? Even if the user is eventually let in after a ten-minute triage, would this be considered successful implementation of the login requirement? Probably not. The success criteria for the login requirement may actually read something like:

> The system needs to complete user ID and password verification within five seconds after the "submit" button is hit after entering user ID and password at least 95% of the time.

Notice how the notion of success is quantified — five seconds and 95% of the time. This is what success criteria need to be — putting down in black and white what would cause a system to fail (or, more optimistically, pass) when the users test it.

Setting up the success criteria *before* starting to build the requirements also offers the valuable opportunity to identify nonfunctional requirements. As discussed earlier (Section 7.3), nonfunctional requirements are not requirements not expected to function. Instead, they are requirements that do not link directly to any system functionality but concern overall system behavior. Usability, reliability, performance, and supportability are the commonly encountered nonfunctional requirements, but there can be other ones too, specific to a project. I know of a project where major production launches had to be over by 3:00 A.M. PST, because that corresponded to the time the first wave of East Coast users hit the site at 6:00 A.M. EST. This was certainly a nonfunctional requirement but had to be included in the success criteria!

Table 13.5 lists the success criteria for the first incremental release of MAGIC 2.0. Just because the iterative and incremental model is being followed does not mean the success criteria can also go back and forth. (Of course, new criteria will be added as new requirements for later increments come up, but there has to be very good reason to change criteria that have already been set up.) Setting up realistic success criteria and sticking to them as development moves ahead remains a key element of success in enterprise software projects.

Listing the success criteria is not the only list that needs to be made before build begins. If success criteria are what need to be met for a project to succeed, then the *risk list* is an artifact which identifies all the factors that can thwart success. The risk list is very much a living document, even within an iteration. Risks which look very menacing at the beginning often mellow as things move on, and new risks, unfathomable just yesterday, pop up. Each risk is given a severity level, and some mitigation strategy is indicated for it, if any exists at that time (if none exists, that has to be indicated as well). All risks must be tracked. Identifying risks is by far the only indemnity the development team can

Table 13.5. Success criteria for first release of MAGIC 2.0

Success criteria ID	Success criteria
SC_01	Modifications (if any) to mailing address, e-mail address, and daytime phone made by users on the Contention Page should be recorded.
SC_02	The contention information as submitted by the users should be recorded for offline processing.
SC_03	The number of unresolved contentions for a particular user are displayed on the Main Page.
SC_04	Electronic statements are delivered to the selected users in the pilot group at their e-mail addresses as recorded in the respective user profiles within the first ten days of a calendar month.
SC_05	The Transaction Summary Page loads within ten seconds of being requested.

expect to have for messing things up. Risk management in software projects has attained the status of a discipline by itself and is beyond the scope of this book. Table 13.6 gives the risk list for MAGIC 2.0.

Before development begins, several other tasks remain. Use cases need to be harvested from requirements, the customer has to be given precise time and effort estimations, and the development team needs to be built. In Chapter 7, the relationship between use cases and requirements was discussed in some

Table 13.6. MAGIC 2.0 risk list

Risk ID	Risk description	Severity	Mitigation strategy	Status
R_01	NIRVANA integration (for ElectState functionality)	High	Review NIRVANA's facilities	Open
R_02	State of the existing MAGIC 1.6 system (for performance improvement)	Medium	Scrutinize MAGIC 1.6 design and code	Open
R_03	MAGIC 2.0 interfaces with other applications	High	Analyze all dependencies of MAGIC 2.0 on other applications	Open
R_04	User expectations — Web-based contention functionality and ElectState	Low	Discuss need for end-user briefing with customer	Open

detail, and why our metrics are based primarily on the requirements was explained. In a nutshell, requirements are the primal artifacts from which use cases are derived. Notwithstanding how intuitive the use cases may be from the developer's point of view, customers relate to requirements more easily. This probably has its root in our shopping mind-set when we pay to have something delivered, and that is the way it is. However, use cases are important, as they drive the development process. As MAGIC 2.0 is the vehicle for illustrating the use of metrics derived in Part 2, we will base our discussion on requirements. We talked about time and effort estimation briefly in Chapter 9, but deeply enough to hint that these activities have ramifications beyond just the technical. Team building is also an interesting social and political exercise. Because these are beyond the scope of this book, we will consider them done.

13.9. GETTING ON WITH THE GAME

MAGIC 2.0 is now poised to move to the next level, into analysis, design, implementation, and testing. How long do the activities described in the previous sections take? There are no ready answers. It is important to do them with rigor, so that requirements, success criteria, and the risk list are in their proper places. It is equally important to do them quickly, so the initial momentum is not lost before development begins. "All we have so far is documents" is a bad thing to hear from a customer, but one does hear it sooner or later if indeed all the customer has so far (after funding the project for an appreciable time) is documents. Getting a piece of working software to the customer is a great psychological fillip — for both the developer and the customer. And believe me, psychology — or more pithily, *morale* — does play a role in enterprise software development.

In the next chapter, we will focus on how Tina and her team analyze the requirements and come up with a structural framework of the components — an *architecture*, if you will — and a detailed design. All the while, they will also be implementing, if only to prove the feasibility of things to themselves and get some initial feedback.

13.10. SUMMARY

This is the first chapter where we saw the metrics in action. We took the plunge into the MAGIC 2.0 case study. The growing pains of any enterprise software project — confusion about requirements, need to interface between diverse products and teams, modulating customer expectations, extending an existing system, as well as other personal and political issues — were touched upon. The *Correlation Matrix* helped establish to the customer how dated the artifacts of the existing system were. The *Mutation Score* attached a "number" to indicate how often requirements were changing. The case study moves forward in the next chapter, where use of the *Meshing Ratio* and the *AEI Score* is illustrated.

DIVING AT
THE DEEP END

14.1. OVERVIEW

The last two chapters built a case study — the MAGIC 2.0 project and its cast of characters — to demonstrate how the metrics in Part 2 can be applied in practice. The stakeholders have come to a point of *reasonable* consensus as to what should go into the first release, the success criteria, and the risk list. In this chapter, Tina's team gets deeper into development. How the *Meshing Ratio* and *AEI Score* come in handy during analysis and design is illustrated. The stage is then set to cast the design into code.

14.2. WHAT IS SO DEEP ABOUT THE DEEP END?

This chapter is called "Diving at the Deep End." The juxtaposition of diving and deep is more than just alliterative. Diving has an element of the unknown to it; deep relates to difficult or at least something that is not entirely trivial. The iterative and incremental model is *risk driven*, as has been said many times before. Simply put, risk-driven development is about tackling the riskiest part of the project first. This can be stated in simpler (and blunter) terms — if you must fail, fail early. The implicit (but unstated) corollary is — then you may live to fight another day. Going after the riskiest part first has two important obstacles, one technical and the other political.

First, it is never easy to identify the riskiest parts. It takes a lot of experience and insight to nose out the real risks in a software development scenario. As a rule of thumb, those factors which have the maximum number of unknowns are likely to be the riskiest. It is best to try to get to the bottom of the unknowns first, instead of budgeting for a nasty surprise later. Unknowns come in many flavors, all of which can be equally disconcerting.

Second, assuming all risks are identified and understood, does the development team have the political will to tackle the biggest risk first? This seems a rather insidious issue, and it is. A friend of mine was doing a project for a demanding customer. (Well, all customers are demanding, but every software engineer takes pride in calling his or her customer the *most* demanding.) The development team felt that showing quick results would staunch the daily demands for results. The project involved talking to a legacy database through a third-party middleware component, which no one knew much about. The project also had some easier parts, such as capturing user information and storing it. User-entered information and data pulled from the legacy database had to be checked against one another. Against wiser counsel, the team decided to quickly get the easier parts over with first, show the customer some "results," and then get into the uncharted waters. Thus the argument went: even if the development team got into trouble with the difficult part, the customer goodwill that the quick results should produce would see things through. It was a flawed decision, more unfortunate since taken after seemingly careful deliberation. And it backfired. The easy part was quick, but not quick enough to allow the hard part to be started sufficiently early.

This serves as an important lesson and sheds much light on the psychology of iterative and incremental development. It is true that this model allows incremental releases to get feedback from the customer. If the feedback is good, the development team feels better knowing customer satisfaction is also growing incrementally. But what the customer has commissioned is a finished software product. Only by delivering that cohesive whole (and *not just* bits and pieces along the way) can the development team hope to win the appreciation that will add to its reputation and result in more business. As the project moves on, setting the right customer expectation at each stage is vital. It is foolish to root for fulsome praise early on, thinking that will help tide over the darker things until later. Plunging into the riskiest part first, fully aware that it might entail some plain speaking to and from the customer, calls for confidence and maturity. And that is the way to go with enterprise software development. The MAGIC 2.0 team will tackle the riskiest parts first.

14.3. UNDERSTANDING THE INTERACTION OF REQUIREMENTS

Raw requirements from users read like a grocery list of items. But just as items on a grocery list have deep and subtle connections (depending on the menu being planned, food preferences, etc.), requirements also relate to one another. These relations are interactive: there are multiway dependencies between the requirements. Once requirements for a release are finalized, the development team's task is to find out how the requirements interact. Why are we interested in the interaction of requirements?

As noted earlier, a software system is a collaboration of components. Components deliver functionality, and functionality is driven by requirements. The best way components can collaborate is to execute the required functionality (along with nonfunctional needs) in the most optimal way. Optimality is a neat word, but it means many things in many contexts. It may be seen as a solution to a problem that maximizes the benefits while minimizing overhead. Overhead for software components can include repeated code, redundant code, needless function calls (especially *remote* calls in distributed system), etc. By sensing the interaction of requirements early, these can be minimized during design and implementation. Analysis is very much about sense and sensibility.

14.4. FROM REQUIREMENTS TO ANALYSIS: THE MESHING RATIO

Chapter 8 highlighted how and where analysis fits into software development. In a way, analysis is by far the most reflective of all the development activities. Much of it is thinking, with little tangible output. Yet analysis remains the vital bridge between the problem and the solution. The following discussion refers back to Table 13.4, where the requirements for the first release of MAGIC 2.0 are listed.

Who are the players? Tina brainstormed with her offshore team. The user interface players were easy to pick: Contention_Page, Confirmation_Page, Main_Page, Main_Page_Popup, and Transaction_Summary_Page. The business logic for contention had to be contained somewhere, so there had to be a Contention_Controller. A User_Input_Verifier was a handy player to have, since there are a number of places for user input, and wherever users enter information, it has to be checked. The user request for a particular service had to be received and delegated to the appropriate component. A generic User_Request_Processor could help. The contention information entered by the user had to be stored in the database. How would database access be coordinated? There had to be a Database_Accessor. The tricky part was interfacing with NIRVANA. The ElectState functionality ran somewhat parallel to MAGIC 2.0's other features: both shared the same database and had access to the same user profile information. How about a NIRVANA_Bridge that would make the two talk? But there is an even trickier part.

Existing MAGIC had to run the way it was currently running (M2_011). A full-fledged redesign of MAGIC was a project SST eventually wanted to bag, but that would come later. This was no time to explore existing code whose topography the team understood little. This is one of those golden rules of the software trade: code that is running is best left alone, especially if it is someone else's code. But MAGIC 1.6 and MAGIC 2.0 had to talk, and there had to be an interpreter. How about a player Legacy_Bridge?

Tina knew that in applications such as MAGIC, response times became a major issue. Response time was the time a Web page took to load on a user's browser. There was already talk of improving the response time of the Transaction Summary Page, and other pages were likely to have similar demands. Knowing which part of the code was eating up most of the round-trip time was essential in improving response times. *Code instrumentation* is a useful technique, and it is best thought about *a priori*. Code instrumentation, among other things, allows recording of events of interest as a piece of code runs; it can help identify bottlenecks in code that is part of an application, where most of the execution time is spent. There had to be a player Performance_Monitor, an instrument to collect and collate data for the entire application.

Several points need to be highlighted here. Because the players are placeholders for ideas, their names need to be explanatory. When it comes down to identifying the actual components, there may or may not be a one-to-one mapping with the players. As the project moves ahead, new players may arise and old ones may wither. Players are vital, but they are not cast in stone.

Analysis has identified the following players so far:

> Contention_Page
> Confirmation_Page
> Main_Page
> Main_Page_Popup
> Transaction_Summary_Page
> Contention_Controller

User_Input_Verifier
User_Request_Processor
Database_Accessor
NIRVANA_Bridge
Legacy_Bridge
Performance_Monitor

There are twelve players and, coincidentally, twelve requirements (M2_010 is out of scope). If every player meshed with every requirement, there would be 12 * 12 = 144 links, but that is not the case. By going over the list of requirements and the players, Tina and her team came up with the links in Figure 14.1. There are twenty-five links in all. It should be pointed out that Figure 14.1 (and Figure 14.2, which will be discussed later in this chapter) is not pretty as a picture. This is because the team is focused more on analyzing than drawing pretty pictures, and that is how it should be at this time.

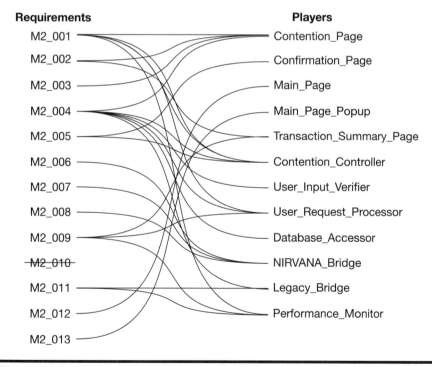

Figure 14.1. *Meshing Ratio*: first pass

Thus, for iteration 1 of analysis, the *Meshing Ratio* is given as:

$$MR(1) = 25 / 144 = 0.174$$

What does this number tell us?

Referring back to the discussion in Chapter 8, we observe that 0.174 is between $(12 * 12)/(12 * 12) = 1$ or $(1/12) = 0.083$. So happily, we are neither in a spider web nor an island scenario. But is a *Meshing Ratio* of 0.174 good or bad?

There are no magic numbers in software metrics. A metric value is only meaningful in its circumstances and has to be taken in that context. As an example, for a GUI-intensive application, there will be many user-interface-related requirements, meshing loosely with the corresponding players, but few requirements of a processing-intensive application can mesh closely with the corresponding players. The *Meshing Ratio* values will be low and high, respectively, for these two applications. For a particular application, variation of the values over iterations reflects how the tugs and pulls of interaction are being progressively resolved.

Many of the metrics developed in this book are internal metrics; their purpose is to guide development effort from *within*. Metrics may also have external roles to play, in streamlining customer expectation and management decisions, as demonstrated by the use of the *Correlation Matrix* and *Mutation Score* in the last chapter. Not all metrics, however, will make complete sense to the customer, and neither are they meant to. There is much debate as to who should or should not be privy to metrics data, and this is a debate of consequence. (These themes were discussed in detail in Chapter 5.) As stated strongly before, metrics should never be used to fix blame or, worse, fix individuals. Anyone who has used metrics to any effect in enterprise software development knows this. As their value in introspection and guidance becomes clear, developers will learn to love them, use them, and, most importantly, try to improve upon them. Even if the customer does not fully understand the logic behind the metrics or their exact use, the fact that you are calculating and collecting metrics (that is, tracking things precisely enough to quantify them) sends the message that you are in control of things.

14.5. FROM WHAT TO HOW: GETTING INTO DESIGN

What does the development team have at this point? The team has a set of reasonably firm requirements for the first release and has also harvested a set of players. Instead of getting bogged down in fine-tuning the players (which is rather unnecessary, as players are just placeholders and must finally give way to the components), Tina will now lead the team into design. However, before getting into the design scrum, it is worthwhile to check other undercurrents.

So far, Tina and her team have avoided delving into the design of the existing MAGIC system. The *Correlation Matrix* for MAGIC 1.6 (presented in the last chapter) established that the system had undergone the usual accretion of functionality over time, way beyond the scope of the original design. This is a common symptom in enterprise software, especially systems in actual use. Thus the team has to live with, and take in good humor, the precarious patches and nasty shortcuts that have kept MAGIC 1.6 running to date. When working with existing systems, it is always a good idea to look at requirements with a fresh eye and come up with one's own design. Getting too involved in the existing design to see how much of it can still be used takes one into the *refactoring* mode at best and a hopeless quagmire at worst. It may also foster dark feelings about fellow practitioners. After a design framework is in place, it is time to see how much of the existing components can be reused.

That brings us to reuse. Reuse often has been cited as the Holy Grail of software development, at least object-oriented software development. Since at least a decade ago, we have been hearing that the acme of reuse is just around the corner. Software engineers would no longer write code — just plug-and-play off-the-shelf code components, the same as a structural engineer builds a house from standardized bricks, beams, and brackets. That has not happened. Reuse is a complex issue. Reuse of code is just the proverbial tip of the iceberg. Possibilities for reuse are mostly nixed by incompatibility of contexts, and that is difficult to forecast or fix. Whether we like accepting it or not, the most endemic form of reuse is cut-and-paste. Getting its other more sublime forms to work takes a lot of thinking, planning, and investment in terms of time, which is seldom feasible in customer engagements. In projects such as MAGIC 2.0, the best reuse Tina can hope for is to utilize some of the user interface components, and even those would require quite some modification.

Before getting into the details of design, the architecture has to be in place. Almost everyone seems to agree on that, but there is no such consensus about what architecture is for software systems. The phrase "software architecture" began to be used in earnest around the mid-1990s. In fact, the November 1995 issue of *IEEE Software* remains the fountainhead of many enduring architectural credos. Incidentally, *IEEE Software* published another "architecture issue" in March 2006, reflecting how relevant the decade-old ideas remain and offering recent insights.

Most authors agree that architecture goes deeper than design. But how deep? And deep in what way? The word "framework" explains to some extent what software architecture is: it can be thought of as a system's skeleton to which flesh is added as the project moves on. Given a skeleton, there is much that can be accomplished by fleshing it, but there is also much that cannot be done, like making a human out of a mouse skeleton. Thus the structure of the system, as well as its possibilities and limitations, is decided to a very large extent by the architecture. The architecture for a system has to be chosen with care. The word "chosen" has been chosen deliberately. Enterprise software projects, thankfully, do not need to conceive or construct architectural frameworks that often. If reuse (reuse at a higher level of wisdom and experience, not just code cut-and-paste) has been achieved to any reasonable extent anywhere in software development, it is with software architecture. These components of architectural reuse have been variously called *patterns, frameworks,* and even *libraries,* but all of them exemplify Alexander's (1979) notion of "a three-part rule, which expresses a relation between a certain context, a problem, and a solution."

Let us take as an example the architectural idiom Tina thinks will suit MAGIC 2.0 best: *model-view-controller* (MVC) (Sun 2002). It describes the structure of software systems where there is persistent data (model), user interface (view), and a mechanism to regulate data access and modification by the users (controller). Many Web-based enterprise software projects fit snugly into this MVC template. There is no need for Tina to reinvent the proverbial wheel; the development team can base its design on MVC. Many a time, architectural ideas like MVC are available for a project to use. Sometimes a team can get into trouble trying to think of new architectures when deadlines loom large. I know of projects which got in deep creating their own frameworks; near the delivery date, they had frames but nothing that really worked. Developing architectural frameworks that do justice to the gravity of "architecture" takes much iterating across many organizations and projects to stabilize. Architectures are best begged, borrowed, or stolen. Fowler's (2003) book *Patterns of Enterprise Application Architecture* gives a hit parade of such ideas one can appropriate.

Another closely related pitfall can be described as *future proofing.* It is enchanting to shoot for a design that will withstand the onslaught of change for the next twenty years, but there can be no such design. A common affliction of the tyro designer is to vie for the most *general* design, where every change can just be plugged in. In a given set of constraints, I will not say such design is not possible, but the overhead — mainly due to the experimentation that must go on — is usually prohibitive for an enterprise project. Forecasting future change is very tricky, mainly because of what Fowler (2003) has so pithily called "business illogic" of enterprise applications. Another category of users for MAGIC, in addition to regular and premium, may be added in the future. Should Tina build that possibility into the design so that other categories can be quickly and painlessly included in MAGIC? But when that change occurs, if it does at all, will the current design still be around? This is a tough call to make. I have found it useful to never assume future changes; only if Tina has been told there will be another user category significantly soon (within the time of the current contract) would it make sense for the project to design for it.

The next task is to decide on the most important demands on MAGIC 2.0's design. Before that, however, initial organization of the design on the MVC pattern is needed. As stated earlier, J2EE technology will be used for MAGIC 2.0. MVC and J2EE are the broad parameters; now the team has to decide how code components will actually interact.

In my undergraduate study of electrical engineering, the first jab at an unknown system was to see what excitation led to what response. Given a particular stimulus, how did the system react? I find this approach helpful with software systems too. Most interactive software systems (and the Web-based systems are certainly interactive) are user driven. That is, the system must respond to user inputs in expected ways and behave gracefully for unexpected inputs. User actions (excitations to the system) and system reactions (responses from it) are identifiable from requirement narratives or use-case scenarios.

What are some of the excitations to MAGIC 2.0? They include users clicking a hyperlink on the Transaction Summary Page to be taken to the Contention Page, users entering the contention information and hitting the "submit" button, users clicking a hyperlink on the Contention Page to be taken to the User Profile Page, and users selecting a date range to access transaction data on the Transaction Summary Page. All of these can be construed as *requests* from the user, to which the system must *respond*. One group of players can be called the request processors. They are in overall charge of getting things done, and they can command (or commandeer!) other players and give them things to do. But how is a request sent to the right request processor? The users should not care, as all of these inner mechanisms are transparent to them. There has to be another player that coordinates between the user (that is, the user interface) and the request processors, making sure each request gets handled by the processor meant to handle it. This is a key player which contains much of the delegation intelligence. Let us call this player the *task manager*.

The above discussion, almost imperceptibly, brought in the *layering* view. Layering is a powerful abstraction; it finds use in many computer-related areas, from software development to network protocols. In fact, a layered view of things is not just computer related; Tagore's essay "Tin Tala" ("The Three

Storeys") analyzes the layers of human perception (Datta 2004). Layers are also called *tiers* — the basic notion being slicing a system into logical parts for easy understanding and implementation. Often, a constraint imposed on the layered model is that only adjacent layers can communicate; layer 1 cannot talk to layer 3, bypassing layer 2, and vice versa. In MAGIC 2.0, the user interface components along with the task manager would be one layer, the request processors another, the contention controller another, and the data accessors with the database yet another. Due to layering constraints, the task manager cannot directly call the contention controller, and the data accessors cannot be called by the request processors. These protocols of interaction are a part of the system architecture and will be honored by the design.

However, not all parts of the system fit this easily into the user request–system response stereotype. What about the ElectState functionality? The users will receive monthly statements delivered via e-mail without prompting on their part, but there are covert stimuli for the system to generate and send out the electronic statements: a particular day of the month or some other system that updates the database with the last month's transaction data. It is difficult to model this scenario in the MVC way of doing things, and there is no need to. ElectState is nearly independent of other MAGIC 2.0 functionality — nearly, but not fully. Thus the need for a bridge has already been identified as a player.

14.6. THE GUTS OF DESIGN

Before getting into the guts of design, it pays to identify the major objectives, or *intents,* of the design. What are the aims of MAGIC 2.0? Here is the first cut:

- Allow for transfer of data from the back-end database to the user interface within specific time constraints
- Allow for updating of the back-end database with user inputs and provide confirmation of successful updating
- Allow for verification of user input based on specific criteria
- Allow for periodic delivery of electronic statements to a group of users on or before a specific date
- Allow for integration of the contention business logic within the MAGIC 2.0 system

From the above, it is clear that MAGIC 2.0's design must support data transfer between the back-end database and the front-end user interface, in both directions. Additionally, it must also verify user inputs and provide for the delivery of the electronic statements. The electronic statement facility will be handled mostly through NIRVANA, so it needs to be as decoupled as possible from other parts of the system. All database access logic is best encapsulated in separate components with an interface to the business objects. This will ensure the business objects will be insulated from databases changes in the future. User verification is also a job that depends on rules which may change, so a separate component(s) should handle it.

That leaves the core business logic of the contention process — rules which guide how the business unit handles contention cases, what steps are taken to resolve a contention, and how the status of a contention is decided. A bit of crystal-ball gazing is needed here. From the MAGIC 2.0 requirements, it appears all the system has to do now is record the contention issue from a user input, update the database with that information, and return the number of unresolved contentions for a particular user, to be shown on the Main Page when the user logs in. In future releases, however, things will certainly go deeper than that. Tina recalled that the business unit was already talking about showing more contention information on the Main Page, so this would become a full-fledged requirement sooner or later. What exactly is a contention and how do MAGIC's business processes work on it? Tina set out to find out.

Tina's quest to find out about contention will help us see how the understanding of business processes, often called *domain knowledge,* plays a crucial role in software design. Some methodologies, especially the high-ceremony ones (refer to Chapter 6), make a strong pitch for building *business cases* and a *domain model* at the outset. This is sound advice, but not always feasible, due to a reason we will soon discover.

Roger said, "Contention? Doesn't that have something to do with cardholders complaining about a charge or something? Tracy should have the details." Tracy, who was still learning about how things were done, did not have much to add. Tina was finally able to find out from Betty, Kyle (who was in Betty's position earlier), and a couple of others deep inside MM's departmental maze how a contention kicked in and how it was handled.

A contention can be raised by a user who wants to contend a particular transaction charge that appears on his or her statement. Once a contention is raised, it is given a contention ID, which is the corresponding transaction ID appended with a five-character randomly generated number. Once raised, a contention is handled by someone in the customer service group, who investigates the issue and has to resolve it within fourteen business days. This group apparently works on "green screens." Currently, users can only raise contentions over the telephone, talking directly to the customer service agents. Green screens obviously meant some kind of legacy systems, which may have been running for several decades. A contention could have one of four statuses: *open, in process, resolved,* or *reopened.* MAGIC 2.0 must not only capture the contention information from the user, but should also ensure it gets recorded in the customer service databases and fetch the number of contentions for a user. In the next release, the status of the contentions may also need to be fetched. Building an *adapter* component from scratch for MAGIC and the customer service group's legacy systems to talk to one another was going to be a tall order.

Further foraging across MM's departments brought some succor though. It seemed such an adapter component existed and was being used by another group to talk to legacy systems. It was called the *Information Access Utility* (IAU) and, to Tina's utmost relief, offered a Java Application Programming Interface (API). Therefore, MAGIC had to have a player to talk to IAU: the Data_Transfer_Coordinator.

Tina now had a working knowledge of the contention business process to keep moving with the development of MAGIC 2.0. It has been my experience that instead of worrying too much about domain models and business cases at the beginning, it is more useful to hunt down information on a need basis. Those who commission a project often do not have adequate domain knowledge to share, and that can be frustrating and misleading. The rules and processes that drive an organization's business are seldom, if ever, archived and annotated for ready reference (although, like many other good things, they should be). That knowledge usually remains distributed in bits and pieces in people's heads. It is best to go head-hunting when you know what you are looking for.

A subtle shift has already occurred in our terminology; this is a good time to point it out. We have moved from talking about requirements and players to components, APIs, interfaces, objects, and adapters. This change, like adolescence, brings itself to the fore only after it happens. And like adolescence, this is a point of inflection in the life cycle. From now on, practitioners find themselves thinking more in terms of the solution than the problem. Requirements should have sunk in sufficiently by now for design and then implementation to take center stage.

14.7. DESIGN ELEMENTS

Related to the above discussion, Tina and her team came up with the following components:

- JavaServer Pages (JSP)
  - ContentionPage.jsp
  - ConfirmationPage.jsp

- ☐ MainPage.jsp
- ☐ MainPagePopup.jsp
- ☐ TransactionSummaryPage.jsp
- ■ Java servlet
  - ☐ TaskManagerServlet.java
- ■ Java classes
  - ☐ ContentionRequestProcessor.java
  - ☐ UserInputVerifier.java
  - ☐ DatabaseAccessor.java
  - ☐ NIRVANABridge.java
  - ☐ LegacyBridge.java
  - ☐ PerformanceMonitor.java
  - ☐ DataTransferCoordinator.java.
- ■ Enterprise JavaBeans (EJB)
  - ☐ ContentionBean.java
  - ☐ ContentionHome.java
  - ☐ Contention.java

We have started speaking the language of implementation, so the components are named as per Java naming conventions. There is really only one EJB, and the three Java classes refer to the enterprise bean class, the home interface, and the remote interface, respectively. In addition, the MAGIC database now has to have a contention table, with the fields ContentionID (primary key), TransactionID, TransactionDate, TransactionAmount, CauseOfContention, and ContentionStatus.

Components by themselves do not deliver, but their interactions do. Software design is about figuring out the most optimal way components can interact. At this stage of the MAGIC 2.0 project, all the contracts between components are not yet in place, but a general idea of how components collaborate is slowly emerging from the discussions.

A quick digression on designs and diagramming is appropriate. The adage "a picture speaks a thousand words" is very true in software design. A drawing (even if nothing more than a few boxes, circles, and lines) explains a design more succinctly than words can. Unified Modeling Language (UML) has a number of powerful diagrams, but not all UML diagrams are useful for all projects; one needs to pick and choose only those which add value to a particular case. Moreover, UML diagrams make sense only to the initiated. It is not a good idea to take them to the customer. That will only shift focus from the real item of delivery — working code, which needs user feedback to grow. At the "drawing board" stage, UML diagrams may help find design issues that are more costly to resolve later. It is helpful at times to brainstorm on a paper napkin, but passing an idea through the UML formalism helps make it more resilient. Besides, paper napkins are difficult to preserve. Yet even the best of diagramming techniques can only mitigate, and not obviate, the effects of software's oddities: invisibility and unvisualizabilty (Brooks 1995). Diagrams are often made more useful by embedding annotations. UML diagrams now have wide-ranging tool support, much of which is open source. With the increased thrust toward model-driven development, this is the time to utilize modeling language constructs.

14.8. AEI SCORE: OF CHECKS AND BALANCES

Tina and her team have had a first go at analysis and design. The *Meshing Ratio* has been calculated for the first run of analysis. Now let us see what light the *AEI Score* can shed.

As discussed earlier, the *AEI Score* is based on a questionnaire tuned to the project. Earlier in this chapter, the objectives of MAGIC 2.0's design were identified. The *AEI Score* questionnaire is primarily based on these. Table 14.1 shows the calculation of the *AEI Score*. The answers Tina and her team gave (as objectively as they could) for each question are as follows:

- **Question 1** — Some (2). The players sometimes arose out of discussions with the customer. Not all the players, however, will make sense to the customer.
- **Question 2** — Some (2.5). Some of the analysis artifacts (that is, players) had to take into account design constraints such as integrating NIRVANA.
- **Question 3** — Some (2.5). We were talking in terms of the Java platform as we went into design.
- **Question 4** — Yes (1). Related to question 3.
- **Question 5** — Yes (10). Database access logic is confined to two components, one for the MAGIC database and the other for the legacy system.
- **Question 6** — No (1). This is important because either the user-entered data have to be persisted or the whole transaction rolled back, but transaction integrity has not yet been factored into the design.
- **Question 7** — Yes (10). The UserInputVerifier.java is supposed to accomplish this.
- **Question 8** — No (1). NIRVANA as yet remains much of a black box; integration is yet to be done.

Table 14.1. Calculation of *AEI Score*

ID	Question	Yes	No	Some/ sometimes
1	Can users readily relate to the *raison d'être* of every player identified during analysis?	**3**	1	2
2	Do the analysis artifacts mention any design component?	1	**5**	2.5
3	Do the design artifacts depend on any implementation detail?	5	**10**	2.5
4	Does analysis or design build on ideas specific to a particular language, platform, or technology?	1	**3**	2
5	Is the database access logic concentrated in one or a group of closely cohesive components?	**10**	1	5
6	Does the database updating process ensure transactional integrity?	**10**	1	5
7	Is every user input verified before being passed on to the next layer?	**10**	1	5
8	Is the electronic statement delivery integrated within the MAGIC infrastructure?	**10**	1	5

Adding the values in parentheses, we arrive at the *AEI Score*:

$$2 + 2.5 + 2.5 + 1 + 10 + 1 + 10 + 1 = 30$$

The numbers in bold in Table 14.1 indicate the values of the most desirable answers to the questions. Adding the best possible values, we have:

$$3 + 5 + 10 + 3 + 10 + 10 + 10 + 10 = 61$$

so the *AEI Score* for the first iteration of design, AEIS(1), is

$$30/61 = 0.49$$

This is roughly half of 1, the value if all the questions had the most desirable value.

Once again, the value of the metric is not worth worrying about, but what is of concern is what caused the score to be the way it is. Responses to which questions pulled down the overall score? The worst were the ones which scored the lowest: questions 4, 6, and 8. There is nothing that can be done about question 4, as once the development technology has been decided, it is in fact good to start thinking along those lines. Ideally, analysis and design should be as detached from the implementation technology as possible, but that is not always the case practically. Questions 6 and 8 are indeed areas of concern and need to be looked into.

The *AEI Score* serves as a sanity check for the development team, at a point where design is still on paper; the die, as they say, is yet to be cast. A very low value for the *AEI Score* can raise a flag to indicate to the development team that design is getting too narrow in scope; variations in the value across iterations can also point to trends in design.

Who comes up with the questions on the *AEI Score* questionnaire? It is best done by someone outside the development team. Someone who knows the general architecture well and has been briefed on the project specifics can suggest the areas to watch out for. Tina asked her friend and colleague Naresh, the lead on another project in the MM portfolio, to create the *AEI Score* questionnaire for MAGIC.

14.9. MESHING RATIO: ANOTHER PASS

Now that the initial design is somewhat in place, how about another look at the *Meshing Ratio*? We now replace the players with the actual components to see how closely the design meshes with the requirements.

There are seventeen components and twelve requirements (M2_010 is out of scope). If every player meshed with every requirement, there would be 17 $* 12 = 204$ links, but from Figure 14.2 we can see that there are twenty-seven links.

Thus, for the second iteration of analysis and design, the *Meshing Ratio* is

$$MR(2) = 27/204 = 0.132$$

Comparing MR(2) with the value of MR(1) = 0.174 calculated earlier, we find that the extent of meshing has in fact *gone down* as players were crystallized into components. Is this good or bad?

The only certainty in enterprise software development is change. If the enterprise for which the software is being built stays in business, the requirements will change. Changing requirements mean the design has to be modified — either by reorganizing components and their collaboration or by bringing in new components. Is there a way to quantify the effect of changing requirements on components and their interaction? Datta and van Engelen (2006) suggests

Requirements
Players

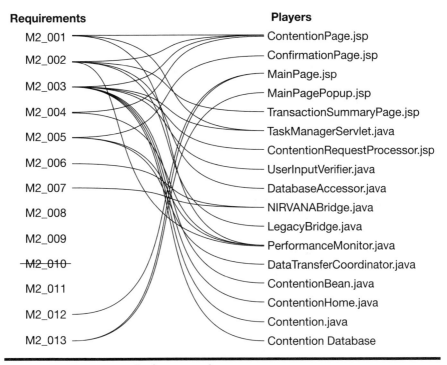

Figure 14.2. *Meshing Ratio*: second pass

a set of metrics toward this end. As the design evolves over time, a decreasing *Meshing Ratio* value indicates that component interactions are better understood and optimized. As described earlier, islands and spider webs indicate the boundary conditions of *Meshing Ratio* values.

14.10. KEEPING THE USER IN THE LOOP

An oft-cited benefit of iterative and incremental development is that users are on the "same page" all along. Thus, there is less chance for "delivery blues," and "big bangs" and "nasty surprises" are not saved until the end. Extreme Programming takes the idea further by advocating a user representative always be present *within* the development team. (Perhaps in a similar spirit, *embedded* TV crews have become popular in modern warfare.) I am not sure how much value an embedded customer can add; it is very easy to get hopelessly in the way. In my experience, customers with a smattering of software development knowledge are far more difficult to handle than those who are totally ignorant. A friend of mine once worked with a customer manager who took much pride in having been a "techie" once upon a time. Those atavistic talents gave him the leeway to beset the development team with suggestions (increasingly strident) on how to go about building "his" system. Everything displayed on a browser was, to him, just a "value in a JSP" and could be changed on the fly. My friend aggravated him no end by pointing out that things went a bit deeper.

Keeping users in the loop is difficult business, and it calls for discretion. Customers (and sometimes users) have an understanding of the business processes (which are seldom, if ever, *documented* anywhere), and it helps to tap into that. I find it useful to do a high-level *walkthrough* of the overall design with the business partners: many a time, these sessions reveal gaps in the design which only a business eye can detect. One question on the *AEI Score* questionnaire asks whether users can relate to all the players: this is meant to check early on whether all major business concerns are in focus.

14.11. STARTING TO BUILD IN EARNEST

Design is only tested through running code. This sounds rather sweeping and very much like an excuse to jump into coding after giving design short shrift. Maturity in software development is about avoiding this and doing a sincere job in design and then verifying via code.

The trickiest part of the MAGIC 2.0 design is still how NIRVANA will be fit in. True, Tina had negotiated only a ten-user pilot for the first release, but getting NIRVANA to work on the real scale meant a lot to Tina's immediate customers. If SST hoped for a bigger part of the MM pie, Tina's team would have to deliver on NIRVANA. There is no point in designing on paper for NIRVANA; there are still too many unknowns. Tina deputed Arvind and Shanker, from the offshore team, to get into NIRVANA and make it work. Arvind and Shanker loved this kind of challenge; less than a year out of college, software engineering for them was making things run. The other members of the team, Prabha, Rahul, and Indrani, were to start implementing the design for the rest of the system.

14.12. SUMMARY

This chapter followed the MAGIC 2.0 development team as it went from requirements to the first cut of design. This was by no means a straight-line path.

There were several twists, and turns were missed. That is okay, and that is the way it is with enterprise software development. The *Meshing Ratio* and the *AEI Score* gave valuable insights into the direction of development.

In the next chapter, we take up the challenges of implementation, and we will see how metrics help tackle them.

REFERENCES

Alexander, C. (1979). *The Timeless Way of Building.* Oxford University Press.

Brooks, F. P. (1995). *The Mythical Man-Month: Essays on Software Engineering, 20th Anniversary Edition.* Addison-Wesley.

Datta, J. P. (2004). Santiniketan Lectures by Rabindranath Tagore: Translated from Bengali by Jyoti Prakash Datta. http://www.parabaas.com/rabindranath/articles/pSantiniketan_storeys.html.

Datta, S. and van Engelen, R. (2006). Effects of changing requirements: A tracking mechanism for the analysis workflow. In Proceedings of the 21st Annual ACM Symposium on Applied Computing (SAC-SE-06), vol. 2, pp. 1739–1744.

Fowler, M. (2003). *Patterns of Enterprise Application Architecture.* Addison-Wesley.

Sun (2002). Model-View-Controller. http://java.sun.com/blueprints/patterns/MVC-detailed.html.

BUILDING TIME

15.1. OVERVIEW

Over the last few chapters, we followed Tina and her team as they worked on the MAGIC 2.0 project. We went through requirements, analysis, and design; learned how interconnected yet distinct the activities are; and saw how the metrics in Part 2 endow the team with insights and control in the development process. In this chapter, we delve into the actual software building. No matter how clear requirements are, or how consummate analysis and design have been, the act of construction is bound to throw surprises, often unpleasant ones. In this chapter, the *Specific Convergence, Morphing Index,* and *Interface Map* will be applied to show how such surprises can be better managed and to ensure many more do not arise later.

15.2. DISSECTING THE DESIGN

Once there is an initial design, and before implementation, it does a world of good to step back a little for a perspective view of things. Often, what seemed absolutely watertight on paper springs several leaks in code.

The first step in plumbing the depths of design is to start identifying the *Deliverable Units* (DUs), dealt with at length in Chapter 9. Thinking about DUs helps focus on what finally matters to the users, and it may uncover aspects not considered before.

What are the candidates for DUs in MAGIC 2.0? Evidently, the whole chunk of ElectState is a DU — implementing it will offer value to the user, and the implementation of it is fairly independent of other parts of the system. Identifying the other DUs is less intuitive, but more important. We will soon see why it is less intuitive. As has been pretty clear all along, the electronic statement feature is more or less stand-alone, thrown into MAGIC 2.0 for reasons other than any unifying thread of functionality. Other requirements, however, have so far been closely intermingling; it will take some doing to thresh them apart.

I cannot help digressing here to put in a quick comment. It is about a software development phenomenon no textbook mentions but every project encounters. The word "project" is usually used to convey a set of connected and coordinated tasks toward a clear-cut goal. Shopping for groceries may mean visiting three stores, but it is a project, as activities are linked in a common goal — stocking up on supplies. But shopping for groceries, doing the laundry, and going to the bank — even when squeezed into one Saturday morning — can hardly be called one project. These are diverse tasks, and a common goal is hardly discernible. One could say that doing all of these accomplishes a better way of living or at least domestic harmony for the weekend. But that is stretching the imagination too far, and this kind of stretching happens many a time with software development projects. I know of engagements that involved Web development, performance tuning of databases, and migrating to a new application server, all as tenuously linked as grocery shopping is to lawn mowing, but lumped together as a "project" the customer is willing to fund. Something similar has happened in MAGIC 2.0.

As we are seeing, electronic statement generation using NIRVANA is a totally different line of functionality than Web-based transaction reports or contentions. Yet these have been bundled in the same development life cycle and must be delivered together. It is important to ensure the ball is not dropped for any of these parallel chunks of functionality. It helps to have teams within teams to handle these tasks (as MAGIC 2.0 is doing), but still have close coordination among the subteams (which Tina hopes to do).

In every enterprise with more than one person, delegating work is a challenge. It is even more of a challenge in software building, differing as it does from the assembly line model of other production systems (refer to Section 3.2.2 for discussion of production of software versus a cheeseburger). In building a car, separate components, such as the chassis, doors, and steering wheel, can be manufactured separately and then fit together. This fitting together of parts to make the whole occurs in far subtler ways in software, which are very difficult to conceive and control. DUs help break up the system into smaller, more manageable, and logically related units. These units can then be delegated to individuals or teams.

One school of thought recommends distributing development work along use cases. This works for certain kinds of projects where users know for sure how they want the system to work. The use cases come naturally here and can be used for allocating work.

How should the DUs for MAGIC 2.0 be determined? The development team should look around for the "chunks" of functionality that stand apart and are more or less on their own, "talking" to the other chunks through clearly definable interfaces. The whole ElectState feature is a DU — it is an independent mechanism for generating and delivering the electronic statement that shares only the common database with MAGIC. Let us call ElectState DU_1. Along similar lines, is the whole of the contention functionality a candidate DU? Yes, but we can do better than that. The issue of *granularity* often comes up in software development. Simply put, it is about deciding how large or small a unit of attention needs to be.

In one project I know of, the writing of use cases was entrusted to the junior-most member of the team. (This is always a bad thing to do, but it is often done, due mostly to the stigma attached to "documentation" in software engineering. See the sidebar titled "Software Engineering and Documentation in Chapter 8.) The individual came up with a single use case (with a maze of myriad streets and alleys), and it encompassed the entire application's functionality. When asked to make the use cases more fine-grained, he came up with nearly a hundred of them, with specimens such as "enter user ID and password," "wait for credentials verification," etc. This is a classic granularity problem. There must be in each grain enough so that it makes sense in a broader context, but not too much so that it may lead to missing the trees for the forest. This is tricky. For use cases, the discriminator between too fine and too large a grain is often the catchphrase "of sufficient value to the user." But sufficiency and value are again deep and subjective notions, so the waters get deeper and deeper. However, the beauty of subjectivity is that experience makes it more objective. After observing and participating in a few fine-grain/coarse-grain decisions, one develops an *intuition* for the granularity that best fits a situation. This helps a lot in software engineering, as it does in other engineering disciplines.

Contention as a whole for a DU is too coarse-grained. One part of the contention functionality is about letting users enter their contention information, verifying the inputs, and recording them in the MAGIC database. Another part is to ensure this information goes to the back-end database where the contention will finally be processed, fetch the contention ID, and show a confirmation to the user. How about breaking the functionality into DUs by layers? Let DU_2 be the contention user interface, DU_3 be the contention business logic and MAGIC database access, and DU_4 be the bridge between the MAGIC Web-based system and the back-end contention database.

Delegating work by layers of the system — going inward from the user interface layer — works well when the development team is a potpourri of varied skills and experience. Enterprise software development teams usually are like that. What constitutes the perfect software team has been studied a lot (Brooks 1995; Humphrey 2006), with hardly any consensus. Too many experts on a team is often as bad as too many neophytes. The latter are ready to go the extra mile (sometimes several) to add to their learning, but lack maturity and intuition. On the other hand, experience gives the experts vision and a strong feel for which way a project is heading, but may also foster a "slogging-is-for-someone-else" attitude. The best situation is to have the *right* mix of youth and experience, but as in life, the right mix is elusive. Given a choice, I would always prefer to have more eager young people on the team than mavens.

Software development is no rocket science (DeMarco and Lister 1987), and the ropes can be learned pretty quickly, if one wants to. A friend of mine was once the junior-most member of a team of seven. In addition to being called "the kid" (with rights and privileges appertaining), she also had a ringside view of the big battles. Four members of the team thought their seniority should warrant the lead role. The situation came to the point that tasks were only done when requested by e-mail. When done, completion was announced by e-mail, with copies to a host of honchos. Ironically, the team was built that way because the module seemed most complex and needed the most experienced people. It is true that tasks like implementing business logic, tuning databases, specifying major interfaces, etc. call for the depth of understanding that experience — and only experience — can give, but everything in a project is not that involved.

Identifying DUs by layer ensures that it is easy to delegate the less intense parts to those with less experience and the more intense ones to those better equipped. Every software system can be broken down into the logical layers of *display, processing,* and *storage,* and system functionality remains distributed across these (Datta and van Engelen 2006).

So far, Tina and her team have identified the following DUs for MAGIC 2.0:

- **DU$_1$: ElectState** — Electronic statement generation and delivery to the pilot group of users.
- **DU$_2$: Contention user interface** — All the Web pages and related components that facilitate user interactions.
- **DU$_3$: Contention business logic and MAGIC database access** — It is worthwhile to make a point here in passing. In enterprise systems, business logic and database access are closely linked. Business logic is

ultimately about making decisions, and decisions depend on data. Information entered by a user almost always has to be weighed in light of already persisted data to make a decision. As a common example, every online application for a credit card needs the user to provide his or her social security number. Whether or not the application is approved (a business decision) depends on a credit history check (accessing persisted data), using the social security number. Business logic and database logic go hand in hand; one cannot function without the other. This is the reason why both have been included in the same DU.

■ **DU_4: The bridge between the MAGIC Web-based system and the back-end contention database** — So far, one component has been identified as LegacyBridge.java; DU_4 will include this, but other components may be needed as development proceeds.

Tina and her team next have to decide on the *Risk Factor* and *Effort Factor*. The major concerns in determining risk and effort were covered at length in Chapter 9. As indicated, estimation of risk and effort remains one of the most subjective acts in software development. Many methods have been suggested, but none serves across the spectrum. Gilb has come up with his *Juicy Bits First* principle (Gilb and Gilb 2006). He observes that if the "juiciest" bits of the project are delivered first, then the development team may be forgiven for not providing all the customers had dreamt about or not delivering strictly on time and within budget. Juicy Bits First sounds succulent and has the kind of common sense appeal which usually works wonders, but deciding on the juiciest bits is the hard part. Asking the customers does not help. Customers will not have an answer right off the bat; different groups within the same customer organization may have different views on *the* juiciest. After all, one individual's juice may be another's bile. I once worked with two customer managers, both of whom had different though related stakes in a project. Each consistently called the other's most important requirement "trivial."

But there is hope. With experience and intuition, software engineers are able to perceive what would *finally* seem most juicy to customers and act accordingly. Experience has to be endured, and intuition harvested, by living life. There are shortcuts to neither, but metrics can help practitioners reuse some of the experience and intuition. As stated in Chapter 9, deciding on the *Risk Factor* and *Effort Factor* for each DU also calls for experience and intuition, and once determined, they facilitate better choices for future projects.

To decide on the *Risk Factor* for each DU, the team will need to refer back to the risk list in Table 13.6. Getting NIRVANA to fit into MAGIC as well as setting the right user expectations for electronic statements are risks directly associated with DU_1. Integrating MAGIC 2.0 with the existing MAGIC framework is a concern that affects all DUs. It is time for a mitigation strategy.

Integrating code with existing code developed by those who are no longer associated with the organization is thorny. Everything that may go wrong with the new code can be blamed on the old, but the buck cannot be passed, as there is no recipient of the blame. The lure of reuse often draws teams into such a quagmire, more often with undesirable results. Reusing code not meant for reuse is far worse than writing code from scratch. Refactoring, that is, improving the design of existing code, should only be undertaken when stakeholders know what refactoring may mean in terms of time and effort. Refactoring is a powerful idea, but I have had occasion to wonder how and where the lines are drawn between refactoring and recoding. One thing is for certain: refactoring is very much an expert's cup of tea. Lower levels of expertise may lead to the refactored code being worse than it earlier was and efforts at re-refactoring, re-re-refactoring, *ad nauseam.*

In view of these concerns, Tina took the tactical decision to leave the existing code alone and build a parallel framework for MAGIC 2.0. Users clicking on a hyperlink on the Transaction Report Summary Page to lodge their contentions would be entering the new MAGIC 2.0 system. Tina discussed her decision with Roger, outlining future plans to integrate MAGIC 1.6 into MAGIC 2.0. Integrating the two versions of MAGIC appealed to Roger, who said, "Anything for a great user experience." Maintaining two systems for the same Web site needed approval from the infrastructure group; Roger was able to accomplish that with a few e-mails by citing "urgent user need."

Next, the risk of interfacing with other applications had to be addressed. One of the major risks as noted in the risk list has been mitigated by bypassing. Bypassing is clearly the best way to address some risks, but not all risks can be bypassed, like "interfacing with other applications" in the risk list. Note that the specific need to pass on user-entered contention data to a legacy database was not even known when the risk list was initially drawn up (in Chapter 13). Experience, however, told Tina that "other applications" would pop up as development proceeded, and she used that particular risk as something of a placeholder. Among the DUs, communicating to the legacy database will certainly prove to be fraught with the highest risk.

Reviewing the DUs, ElectState is risky because it was being done for the first time and there is limited understanding of the workings of NIRVANA. However, the electronic statement generation and delivery is understood to be on a pilot basis, so the customer sees it as not being mission critical. Building the contention user interface is pretty straightforward, although it calls for close attention. I have found working with user interfaces rather intense. It is the first thing customers see, and most of the initial nit-picking goes on there. I have seen people spend days, if not weeks, early in their projects straightening images or modifying text on Web pages. I have also seen e-mails go back and forth over whether a period should come before or after a close quotation mark. (One of the correspondents went so far as to say, "I have an M.A. in classical languages, so I should know where to put a period." And that was it; the period went where she wanted it.)

Contention business logic and MAGIC database access are complicated in their own ways. Ultimately, the existing MAGIC 1.6 will need to be subsumed within MAGIC 2.0; that means its design and implementation must look beyond just the current contention functionality. It would finally have to support the large data transfers associated with the transaction reports. In addition, designers also need to know how the business logic may change in the near future and provide for that. This is not an easy thing to do; the biggest threat comes from getting sucked into the quicksand of future-proofing, as discussed earlier (refer to Section 14.5). Still, this needs to be done to the best extent possible. Discussion with the customers helps, or just picking up the chatter about the "next big thing the business unit wants" can keep these issues in perspective. Business logic follows no pattern and is determined by market forces, acquisitions, mergers, opening new lines of business, and the like.

All this must finally be translated into the symmetry and structure of code. As business processes evolve, it becomes increasingly difficult to keep on "patching" the code to support the latest logic. This evolution is the root of software decay, and it is also the reason why enterprise software systems need to exist. If businesses did not grow and change, there would be no need to build software to support them. Very interestingly, Booch (2006), in a recent article, said: "For my purposes, an interesting system is one that has significant economic value."

Thus MAGIC 2.0 must provide for the eventual integration of MAGIC 1.6's functionality and also have some hooks for attaching newer functionality in the future. A line of new functionality that Tina heard mentioned in several meetings is allowing new users to apply for credit cards online. It might be a good idea to have that in focus as low-level design and implementation proceeds. However, not being able to communicate to the contention database is a potential showstopper for any functionality, current or future. The entire success of the online contention feature hinges on it, and that can make or break MAGIC 2.0. Therefore, the bridge between the MAGIC Web-based system and the back-end contention database is the riskiest DU of all.

Based on the above discussion, the following *Risk Factors* (RF) correspond to the DUs:

$$RF_1 = 3$$
$$RF_2 = 1$$
$$RF_3 = 2$$
$$RF_4 = 4$$

Chapter 9 examined some of the methods (or lack thereof) for coming up with effort estimates. As discussed, although there are formal approaches to effort estimation, "sizing" is usually informal and ad hoc, due to factors more political than technological. We will now see how the *Effort Factors* for each DU can be arrived at.

Let us assume Tina and Samar followed organizational best practices. I cannot help but put a word (several actually) in here about "best practice." The phrase "best practices," or for that matter "organizational best practices," is bandied about freely in enterprise software circles. I have often wondered what they could really mean. They can, of course, mean what they say: a set of proven techniques carefully culled from the organizational history. But not every organization has the foresight or capability to maintain such a repository. (Some organizations, though, do that and reap the expected benefits.) Sometimes best practice is a euphemism for short-circuiting processes. Some processes may need to be short-circuited at some times, but not all processes at all times. Therefore, best practices should be carefully reviewed before being applied; good and best, after all, are strongly relative. Best practices will remain, varying from organization to organization. When working with a new organization, it is often best to warm up to the best practices fast; that is taken as a sure sign of acclimatization.

Tina arrived, via best practices, at the following *Effort Factors* (EF) corresponding to the DUs:

$$EF_1 = 400$$
$$EF_2 = 300$$
$$EF_3 = 250$$
$$EF_4 = 350$$

Comparing these with *Risk Factor* values given before, we notice that DUs with higher risk do not necessarily entail higher effort. DU_1 has a lower risk than DU_4, yet the effort needed to deliver the former is estimated to be higher than that for the latter. Interestingly, the *Effort Factors* may not be distributed across a wide range of values. If they are, such as one DU has an *Effort Factor* of 10 while another has 1000, it may be a good idea to review the composition of the DUs. DUs should roughly be of comparable scope and expanse — the idea is to distribute the overall functionality as *equally* as possible. A wide variation in the *Effort Factors* indicates a skewed distribution. As a rule of thumb, a difference of more than an order should be seen as a flag.

The product *Risk Factor* ∗ *Effort Factor* for each of the DUs is

$$DU_1 \quad RF * EF = 3 * 400 = 1200$$
$$DU_2 \quad RF * EF = 1 * 300 = \ \ 300$$
$$DU_3 \quad RF * EF = 2 * 250 = \ \ 500$$
$$DU_4 \quad RF * EF = 4 * 350 = 1400$$

In the next section, we get down to calculating *Specific Convergence*. It will help guide the sequence in which the DUs may be taken up.

15.3. CONVERGENCE: QUEST FOR THE HOLY GRAIL

As derived in Chapter 9, *Specific Convergence* gives an idea how much the implementation in an iteration contributes toward convergence. Given the DUs, there are usually several ways to jump into building them, depending on how strongly one feels about doing one DU before another. Given the scope of the MAGIC 2.0 release, Tina decided it will need about three iterations to construct the system. Which DU should go into which iteration? This is exactly what *Specific Convergence* will help the team decide. First, however, the options need to be laid out. Plan A and the proverbial Plan B, as well as a possible Plan C, are the different sequences of addressing DUs over iterations.

In Plan A, the team would focus on getting electronic statements working in the first iteration, since this has little or no dependency on the other DUs, and then follow up with DU_4 in iteration 2 and DU_2 and DU_3 in iteration 3. Plan B is about doing DU_4 first, then DU_2 and DU_3, and then, once the core contention functionality is in place, getting down to doing DU_1. Plan C envisages getting the low-intensity things done first — DU_2 and DU_3 in iteration 1, and then taking on the deeper waters — DU_4 and DU_1, respectively — in iterations 2 and 3. At face value, choosing one among Plans A, B, and C is far from trivial. Each has its bright pros and commensurately dark cons.

Before calculating and examining the *Specific Convergence* values for each iteration, let us review the sequence of DUs per iteration for the three plans:

	Iteration 1	*Iteration 2*	*Iteration 3*
Plan A	DU_1	DU_4	DU_2, DU_3
Plan B	DU_4	DU_2, DU_3	DU_1
Plan C	DU_2, DU_3	DU_4	DU_1

Specific Convergence for the kth iteration, that is, $SC(k)$, was defined in Chapter 9. Intuitively, we divide the sum of *Risk Factor* $*$ *Effort Factor* for the DUs that will be complete at the end of iteration k by the sum of *Risk Factor* $*$ *Effort Factor* for all the DUs planned to be implemented across all iterations. To illustrate, calculation of $SC(1)$ for Plan A and $SC(2)$ for Plan B is as follows.

For DU_1, DU_2, DU_3, and DU_4:

$$RF * EF = 1200 + 300 + 500 + 1400 = 3400$$

At the end of iteration 1 of Plan A, only DU_1 will be completed. For DU_1:

$$RF * EF = 1200$$

Thus, for Plan A:

$$SC(1) = 1200/3400 = 0.35$$

On the other hand, at the end of iteration 2 of Plan B, DU_4, DU_2, and DU_3 will be completed. For these three DUs:

$$RF * EF = 300 + 500 + 1400 = 2200$$

Thus, for Plan B:

$$SC(2) = 2200/3400 = 0.64$$

Table 15.1 gives the *Specific Convergence* values for iterations 1 to 3. The numbers in Table 15.1 are plotted in Figure 15.1. Evidently, Plan B gets most of the work done in iteration 1, followed by iteration 2. Compared to the other plans, Plan B sticks closest to the credo of tackling the difficult parts (in terms of risk and effort) earlier. From plotting the *Specific Convergence* values, Plan

Table 15.1. *Specific Convergence* **values**

	SC(1)	SC(2)	SC(3)
Plan A	0.35	0.76	1
Plan B	0.41	0.64	1
Plan C	0.23	0.64	1

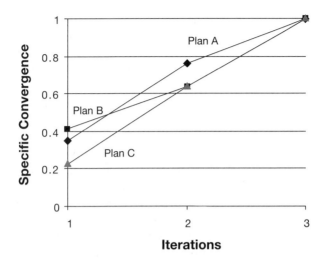

Figure 15.1. *Specific Convergence* **versus iterations: Plan A, Plan B, and Plan C**

B appears most expedient to the development team. If new DUs are discovered during development, the $SC(k)$ values for future iterations will change and the development plan will have to be modified accordingly.

15.4. DESIGN DRIFT

It is time now to get into design, in earnest. Design is a plastic word, one which has many meanings and many contexts. For some, design connotes aesthetics; for others, utility. Design is sometimes regarded as essence and sometimes accidence. There is certainly some quality — something that is readily recognized when seen or felt, but rarely identified otherwise — which sets apart *good* design from *bad.* Alexander (1979), in his book *The Timeless Way of Building,* calls this "the *quality* without a name." He considers several words which come close to describing the quality without a name, but do not quite capture it — words like *alive, whole, comfortable, free, exact, egoless, eternal* — and then declares: "The quality which has no name includes these simpler sweeter qualities. But it is so ordinary as well, that it somehow reminds us of the passing of our life." Norman's (1990) *The Design of Everyday Things* places similar attributes of design in the context of our everyday usage of "things," objects and articles which we use and depend on, often unconsciously, in our very existence. The idea of design is profound. It is where ingenuity and invention combine to reconcile our existence and our environment.

Design has no definition and no recipe. This may be taken to mean anything goes in the name of design. When I joined the software industry fresh out of college, one guy I worked with behaved as if he was pretty much ahead of us in all respects. He was smart, no doubt. One evening, the rest of us had left the office for the younger pleasures of life, but the smart one stayed around, drawing rectangles and ovals on the board in a conference room with glass walls. His enterprise, expectedly, did not go unnoticed. When asked by the boss what he was doing, the reply reportedly was: "I am trying out different designs for our project." (First of all, *projects* cannot have designs, unless one is using the word in a sense similar to "evil designs"; second...) Another grander anecdote: An Indian leader of much erudition and statesmanship was once pictured standing beside a river, apparently thinking. The caption is said to have ran "...contemplating the design of a dam." So design may mean many things to many people. Enterprise software design was reflected on to some extent in Chapter 8.

Software design does not happen with a bang. It is a gradual process — of internalizing, visualizing, and iterating. Perhaps no other development activity is as evolutionary as design. Design may start with the first customer meeting and may not end even when the product is rolled out. True, design artifacts are created in a specific phase of the development life cycle, but design artifacts are not design (refer to the sidebar in Section 8.6). They are only the vehicles for *communicating* design amongst practitioners. Maybe in the future, design artifacts will help communicate design ideas to software that will construct the software being designed. Being evolutionary, design needs to absorb and adapt to continual change.

As much as every design activity must start with a clear goal, it must also remain sensitive to the inevitable *drift* that will creep in over time. There is no easy way to define *design drift*, but everyone who has spent time in the trenches of enterprise software development knows what design drift is. Design drift is about starting with a set of parameters for design and seeing the parameters morph as newer inputs come in. These inputs may be changed user requirements, but not necessarily only that. They can also be deeper understanding of the system's circumstances — as happened to Tina as she realized that talking to the back-end contention database had to be built into the Web-based contention functionality. As design progresses iteratively, it is very important to track how it morphs. In Chapter 8, the *Morphing Index* was defined; we will now see it applied in a MAGIC 2.0 scenario.

What do I mean by a "scenario"? In this context, the word refers to a sequence of user inputs and system responses that together deliver a functionality of value to the user. Naturally, scenarios are closely aligned to use cases. Scenarios may be expressed in sequence diagrams. Sequence diagrams, like other Unified Modeling Language (UML) artifacts, can be used to address several different levels of system behavior. They can be used to show the messages going back and forth between system and user "black boxes"; they can also depict the collaboration amongst individual objects. As design evolves, components and their collaborations also change. Being able to monitor this change is vital in tracking the general direction of design. Design drift is one of the most insidious of software development problems, and being ignorant of its extent can cause major rework, not to mention rancor.

Understanding and measuring design drift can only occur after construction has started. Design at its most minute melds into implementation; it is only when code is written out line by line that design is finally realized. Interestingly, "cutting code" is an expression often used to describe the real writing of code. Some commentators have discussed the scientific, technical, and societal ramifications of cutting code (Mackenzie 2006). I wonder how the expression came about; there is no incision or laceration in the act of programming. In fact, programming in high-level language is closer to stitching things together than cutting them apart.

In object-oriented systems, objects are the components and they collaborate via messages. Messages are passed by invoking methods of one object invoked by another; this *caller-callee* interaction is at the root of programming. Some of the preliminary components of MAGIC 2.0 have been identified during analysis and preliminary design. It is now time to reflect on their interaction.

To illustrate the use of the *Morphing Index,* the following MAGIC 2.0 scenario will be used: A user wishes to contend a particular transaction. The system allows the user to enter contention information, verifies the input, submits the information, and returns a confirmation page with a contention identifier. In a nutshell, this is the core contention functionality that MAGIC 2.0 must implement. It involves user interfaces, business logic, and database access — both the MAGIC database as well as the legacy contention database.

It should be noted that this scenario stretches across several DUs. What, then, is the relationship between scenarios and DUs? Earlier in this chapter, we discussed one way of choosing DUs. DUs are best chosen according to circumstances specific to a project; if every member can handle every layer, DUs can very well align with the scenarios. As shown before, the idea of DUs along with *Specific Convergence* is useful in iteration planning, whereas scenarios are the basis for calculating the *Morphing Index*. Each metric has its niche; for metrics to really aid in the development process, their contexts have to be taken into account.

In the scenario chosen, the *Morphing Index* will help us explore how the design changes as components and their collaborations are modified. Low-level design starts off with the high-level design artifacts, by examining components that came up during initial analysis and design. On closer scrutiny, some of the aspects are found to have been overlooked or misunderstood. Thus the fine-graining starts. It is healthy if these lacunae are found now. If they are not, either the high-level design was too detailed — eating up too much time and resources at the beginning of the project, which is bad — or the scrutiny at this eleventh hour is not close enough — which is worse.

All design is inherently iterative, and this holds just as well for software as it does for the conventional engineering disciplines. My father started his engineering career more than forty years ago. His first job was designing mining machinery with a large public sector company in India. An expert from the (erstwhile) Soviet Union was a consultant to the company's projects. The ingredients for good design, the expert used to say, are a running supply of pencils, a clean eraser, and a reliable pencil sharpener. Those were the days when drawing boards meant drawing boards. Even now, the best software design ideas flow first through pencil onto paper or through marker onto white board. With digital cameras everywhere (I just got a cell phone with one, and have been feeling rather smart ever since), it is easy to capture the first drawings and convert them later into design documents. Nothing harms design more than feeling pressured to get it right the first time. Good design is all about changing and absorbing change, but it is important to know which way the change is going, and this is where the *Morphing Index* comes is. Before getting into the specific MAGIC scenario, I will relate a story about the permanence of design.

I know of a project where the design drift was getting to be too much. Too much was what the team in fact felt; there was no way to objectively see why the drift came about or what it was doing to the project. The development team privately blamed the customer for being too capricious; the customer publicly blamed the development team for negligence in meeting "real" customer needs. Matters came to the point where the team was given a week to show something — which meant something that worked, not just documents — or face the music — which meant getting the boot. Monday of that week, the whole team was huddled in a conference room with a big white board, and the final design was drawn. There was to be no change to it, the leadership announced. After three-and-a-half hours of brainstorming, the final design was on the board by lunch-time. In poetic justice, this finality was drawn in indelible, permanent markers, instead of dry-erase markers, by mistake! I find paper-pencil-eraser-sharpener design to be very humbling and uplifting; drawing and erasing and drawing again reminds one of the evanescence of things and that life is full of second chances, or third, or fourth, or....

The following discussion will refer to Figure 15.2 and then Figure 15.3. These are along the lines of UML sequence diagrams. They highlight how components interact; each block is a component, and the vertical line beneath it is its so-called "lifeline" — indicating the time for which the component lives. Knowing how long a component lives is fraught with subtleties; it depends on factors such as explicit destruction of objects, garbage collection, etc. An easier way (with risk of oversimplification) is to view lifelines as times for which the components are available for interaction with other components to fulfill some system functionality. In sequence diagrams, time flows from top to bottom, vertically down the lines for each component. We are more accustomed to seeing time flow from left to right along the horizontal x-axis. Sequence diagrams are *not* very good at depicting conditional branching of functionality. If much branching needs to be shown in one sequence diagram, it is a good idea to fine-tune the scenario the diagram depicts. Breaking up a use case into smaller use cases somewhere upstream will help create a more cohesive scenario. This again is an issue of granularity. In Figures 15.2 and 15.3, we slightly abuse the notation, most notably by attaching dog-eared "notes" to components and messages to show their types and corresponding weights. Some liberty has also been taken with names of the components and their lifelines.

Figure 15.2 shows the scenario for contention as it appeared during early design. The functionality was to accept contention information from the user, pass it down the layers of the system, and persist it in the MAGIC database. The user inputs on the ContentionPage.jsp are being serviced by the TaskManagerServlet.java, which invokes the ContentionRequestProcessor.java. The request processor component creates the Contention Enterprise JavaBean (EJB), which calls the database accessor to communicate with the MAGIC database. The sequence of return messages from DatabaseAccessor.java to the Contention Page completes the round trip for the scenario. This is the simplest view of the contention functionality and one that was apparent early in the life cycle. In light of subsequent understanding, this appears not only naive but incorrect as well. The process of design, however, is like peeling an onion; it gets deeper by the layer. Therefore, we will address the subsequent understanding subsequently.

To calculate the *Morphing Index* (refer to Chapter 8), we label components *primary, secondary,* or *tertiary* and the messages between components *creational, computational,* or *transmissional.* Section 8.8.5 underscored the motivations

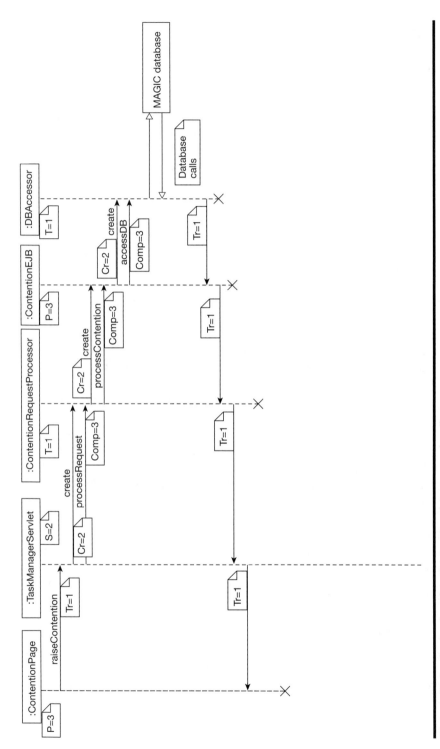

Figure 15.2. Designing for the contention scenario: first pass

behind these groupings. Note that each type of component or message has the following weights:

Components	Messages
Primary (P) = 3	Computational (Comp) = 3
Secondary (S) = 2	Creational (Cr) = 2
Tertiary (T) = 1	Transmissional (Tr) = 1

The *Morphing Index* for a given scenario is the ratio of the sum of weights of all components to the sum of weights of all the messages in a particular iteration of design. The ContentionPage.jsp and the Contention EJB have been marked *primary* as they encapsulate most of the functionality specific to the contention business case. As discussed earlier, the TaskManagerServlet.java delegates tasks to appropriate components based on a user request. The servlet's charter cuts across specific lines of functionality; it is like the MAGIC 2.0 system's gateway to the outer world. Due to its scope, TaskManagerServlet.java has been labeled *secondary*. The ContentionRequestProcessor.java and the DatabaseAccessor.java are marked *tertiary,* as they have supporting roles in the execution of the contention functionality.

Among the messages, *creational* ones are easiest to identify; they are the invocation of constructors on each of the classes. It is important to note that no *creational* message is being called on the TaskManagerServlet.java; it is created when the application server starts. Some of the messages to ContentionRequestProcessor.java, Contention EJB, and the DatabaseAccessor. java are marked *computational.* With the ubiquity of computers, "computation" has broadened in meaning. It no longer means just calculation, but also includes decision making based on information. The contention functionality does not call for involved calculation — there are no differential equations to be solved, but it calls for accessing persisted information and persisting user-entered information and facilitating decisions. *Computational* in this context is thus method calls that initiate execution of code that contains business logic. Other messages marked *transmissional* are pretty straightforward; they are the vehicles for transferring information from one component to another. Note that the first message (that is, earliest in time, the first one from the top) in the sequence diagram from the ContentionPage.jsp to the TaskManagerServlet.jsp is a *transmissional* message. It informs the servlet that a user is accessing the contention functionality, and the servlet delegates the request accordingly.

The classification of the components and the messages is not cast in stone. As the design evolves, components change and so do their collaborations; it is not unusual for a *primary* component to lose its primacy in a later iteration or vice versa. We will see the effect of such change on the *Morphing Index* value as we go deeper into the design.

Referring to the sequence diagram in Figure 15.2 as the scenario of interest in iteration 1 of MAGIC 2.0's design, we calculate the *Morphing Index* for the first iteration, RI(1), as:

$$RI(1) = (3 + 2 + 1 + 3 + 1)/(1 + 2 + 3 + 2 + 3 + 2 + 3 + 1 + 1 + 1 + 1)$$
$$= 10/20$$
$$= 0.5$$

As said earlier, Figure 15.2 represents an initial design. This was before contention functionality was understood in all its nuances and complexity. The flow had seemed straightforward: present a Web page to the user, accept inputs, and persist the information. More digging unearthed deeper currents. Was there a single discovery that changed the whole view of the system? Usually it does not happen that way and this time was no exception. The complexity of enterprise software does not hit like a rock, but rather seeps in like water. It is often fruitless to expect something like a eureka moment, as when buoyancy hit Archimedes in his bath.

For the MAGIC system, realizing how contentions were actually handled by the customer service representatives using the so-called legacy contention database was an eye-opener for the development team. The knowledge was not written down anywhere; it had to be eased out of people's heads, in the true spirit of requirements *elicitation*. The MAGIC 2.0 contention functionality was about webifying the contention business process; the information entered by the users had to end up at a place where the process of resolving a contention could commence. This is essentially a business process. Amid all the hype and hoopla about technology, which very often goes to the heads of software engineers, it is very important to remember that enterprise software is finally about facilitating business. Software may make things faster and easier, but it will ultimately have to help business processes, not hinder them.

As a young software engineer, I learned a lesson that has stayed with me. It was at the time when middleware products were making their mark. Very many people talked about middleware, and very few could get it to do useful things. To tide me over during the monotonous few weeks of "bench life," I read up a bit on the primary middleware product of the day and taught myself some of the ropes. The next project called for me to write software that allowed two applications to communicate via messages and message queues. Getting the infrastructure in place was a pain, and configuring it more painful, but finally it was up. I wrote up a Java application which allowed messages to be put on and taken off queues. It was tested by exchanging messages between two computers that ran the Java code ("my code," I remember calling it rather unabashedly), and it worked. As far as I was concerned, putting messages on and getting messages off the middleware queue was all the application was supposed to deliver, and it did. I was pleased to the point of even volunteering to document "my" code. When it was delivered, the customer made a comment about expecting something that could accept messages from several sources and put them on different queues based on some criteria, something like a *message broker*. Given the business context, that made perfect sense. But it made sense only when given the context, and I, in my white heat of inspiration, had blinkered myself to the context of the code and produced something almost useless in circumstances of its intended use. I had not worried about who would put messages on that would have to be gotten off or what business purpose this putting messages on and getting messages off served. And in these issues lay the whole point why the development effort was commissioned. That I lived to fight another day and, more practically, deliver code that fit the bill goes to the credit of my superiors and the organizational culture. The lesson came to me loud and clear: when building enterprise systems, assume nothing, and always be sensitive to what makes business sense.

With this wisdom, Tina and company went deep into the contention business process and arrived at Figure 15.3. We will now briefly discuss how the contention scenario is being planned to be implemented.

Comparing Figures 15.2 and 15.3, the first thing that comes to mind is there are wheels within wheels. Indeed there are; design artifacts give a view where certain details are highlighted and others are hidden. Every detail is not manifest until implementation begins; even then, details reveal themselves in layers. Figure 15.3 clarifies certain aspects of the design which were glossed over in Figure 15.2. The contention functionality does not kick off from the ContentionPage.jsp; it starts when a user clicks a hyperlink on the TransactionSummary.jsp page, wishing to contend a transaction. This user request is intercepted by the TaskManagerServlet.java and delegated to the most appropriate request processor, to wit, the ContentionRequestProcessor.java. Now the ContentionPage.jsp has to be presented to the user, for him or her to be able to enter the contention information. But what information needs to be present in the ContentionPage.jsp at the time it is presented to the user? The details of the transaction being contended (such as transaction ID, date, description, etc.) must be shown to the user. All of this can be found in the MAGIC database. So even before the user enters any of his or her contention data, there has to be a database call to fetch the background information. To make this happen, the request processor instantiates the Contention EJB, which in turn creates the

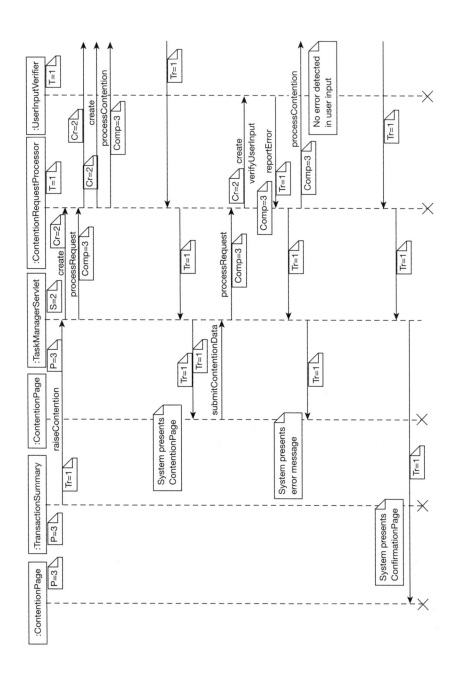

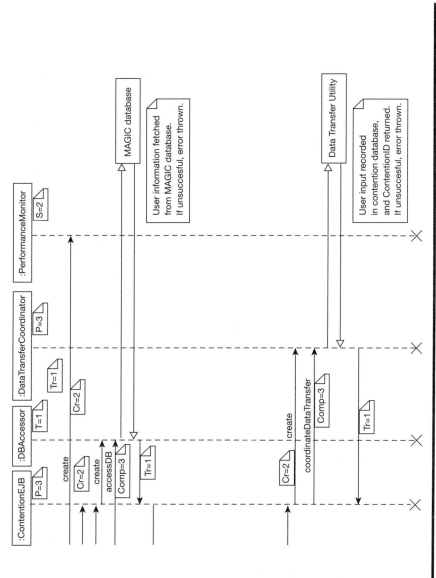

Figure 15.3. Designing for the contention scenario: second pass

DatabaseAccessor.java, which finally fetches the data from the MAGIC database and sends it back to the servlet, which throws the ContentionPage.jsp to the user, populated with the data.

Arvind, the youngest on Tina's team, railed against the stupidity of having so many databases. Why have a MAGIC database and another contention database, on diverse platforms, necessitating so much intricacy in code? Why on earth not just have a single database, with all the data stored? This was righteous indignation, and Tina addressed it with care, and a smile. MAGIC 2.0 was not a "greenfield" project; they were not building from scratch. The challenge was to build within the existing system's constraints. The MAGIC database was fed with transaction data by a batch process running on another system, and the contention database had no Web interface. There had been skepticism about "business value" when the idea of allowing users to see their transaction data online was first debated. That was early in the Web age. Then the Web and business merged, bringing with it changes in business logic, and the need to "webify" contention arose. So there they were, trying to marry two different lines of functionality. Systems never meant to talk to one another now needed to combine in a seamless interface to the world. This is much of what enterprise software is about: combining the hodgepodge of new and existing systems into a coherent design. Multiplicity of databases, incongruity of subsystems, diversity of platforms — these are the birds and bees of enterprise software development; facts of life that have to be lived with and made the best of.

Returning to the contention flow, once ContentionPage.jsp is presented, users can enter their contention information. Hitting the "submit" button on the ContentionPage.jsp brings the "control" back to the request processor, which then creates UserInputVerifier.java. If the latter finds something wrong with the user input, an error message is generated, with which the Contention Page is displayed again. Only when what the user enters is in acceptable format is it allowed to percolate to the EJB. The user input must finally be recorded in the contention database; by way of confirmation, a contention ID is returned to the user.

As discussed earlier, talking to the contention database is not just about issuing database calls; the data transfer utility (DTU) brokers in between. The MAGIC component interfacing with the DTU is DataTransferCoordinator.java, so the EJB instantiates the latter, passes on the user-entered information, and waits for a reply. This waiting is an important aspect — communication between MAGIC and the contention database is meant to be synchronous. The DTU is supposed to return with a response (that is, the contention ID) from the contention database within a specified time. The DataTransfer-Coordinator.java waits that amount of time on the call, and if there is no response, an error is reported. This design choice ensures there is no disconnect between the MAGIC Web-based system and the legacy contention database. The user is given a yes or no answer then and there to indicate whether the contention was successfully lodged or is asked to "please try again later." The most important part of the contention functionality is accepting information from the user and making sure it is recorded in the contention database, so the contention resolution process can start. Once the contention ID is available (or there is reason for an error message), it bubbles up to the user through ConfirmationPage.jsp. PerformanceMonitor.java is instantiated from the request processor when the latter is first invoked; it keeps recording the time taken in the execution of various parts of the code. This completes the sequence of user actions and system response that makes up the contention functionality.

Evidently some issues have been elided: How does the servlet decide which request has to go to which request processor? How does presenting a Web page to the user actually get done? But all this goes on at the framework level, and if the application servers are sound, developers need not worry about these details.

To measure how the design in Figure 15.3 differs from that in Figure 15.2, we calculate the new *Morphing Index* for the second iteration of design, RI(2):

$$
\begin{aligned}
\text{RI}(2) &= (3 + 3 + 3 + 2 + 1 + 1 + 3 + 1 + 3 + 2)/(1 + 2 + 3 \\
&\quad + 2 + 2 + 2 + 3 + 2 + 3 + 1 + 1 + 1 + 1 + 1 + 3 \\
&\quad + 2 + 3 + 1 + 1 + 1 + 3 + 2 + 3 + 1 + 1 + 1 + 1) \\
&= 22/48 \\
&= 0.46
\end{aligned}
$$

Comparing RI(1) with RI(2), we see the value has decreased. This is expected as design becomes more detailed, components exchange more messages, and ways of their collaboration change. From high- to low-level design of a given scenario, the *Morphing Index* should have a diminishing trend. As we go deeper into designing, we find more need for collaboration, and components may be split into smaller ones. Instead of many components with very little interaction, there has to be a trade-off between the number of components and the way they collaborate. The *Morphing Index* helps to see the pattern of this trade-off across iterations.

We have so far been concerned with the development team's point of view. We now turn to the vicissitudes of the individual practitioner.

15.5. THE BUCK STOPS HERE

When the *Interface Map* was introduced in Chapter 9, it was given a proletarian spin by calling it "an artifact for the foot soldier." The foot soldier is the developer who has to write the code. Note how it is just plain "write the code," and not *development* or *construction* or even *implementation.* For the foot soldier, the world is *coding,* writing line after line of instruction in a programming language and — most importantly — unit testing the code. I am chary of analysts, designers, and (especially!) managers who have never been foot soldiers. The view of software development one gets from being down in the trenches cannot be matched by seeing people toil in the trenches or by reading books. The only way to know the hazards of coding is to have coded by one's own hands at some point in one's software engineering career, and the earlier, the better.

Enterprise software components live and work in a state of great connectedness. No snippet of code is "independent" in the sense it does not need to interface with other entities in the system. Thus a key concern for those who write the smallest units of code is to understand how the code interfaces with other parts of the system. As examined earlier, interfaces are vital in the functioning of enterprise software systems. In a way, they are the contracts which have to be honored by the components if the system is to deliver. The *Implementation Unit* (IU) was introduced to specify the *atomic* elements of code that are implemented, usually by individual developers. The *Interface Map* relates the IUs to one another through their dependencies. Intuitively, for each IU, the *Interface Map* specifies the other IUs it needs to interface with, to fulfill its responsibilities. The dependencies for an IU usually cause the biggest bottleneck. The coding of an IU is accomplished with reasonable effort. Most of the time and frustration are spent in trying to have an IU deliver in combination with the other IUs. The *Interface Map* helps keep the dependencies in perspective and documented. This seems like a trivial exercise, assuming things will go right. Battle-scarred practitioners do not make such assumptions.

A friend of mine was once coding some components which needed the services of another set of components being built on another continent. Everyone assumed all knew what to give and take. Considering the intercontinental recriminations they ended up having, matters would have been better if only an *Interface Map* was maintained for each IU. Then again, continents apart, interfacial altercations are sometimes more acidic between one cubicle and the next!

We will now build the *Interface Map* for a sample IU in the MAGIC 2.0 system. How do we select an IU for our purpose? Remember that an IU is the atomic element of implementation. It is an aggregation of code that is sufficiently complete in itself, adds to the functionality of a DU, but is manageable enough to be entrusted to a few developers, usually one. DataTransfer-Coordinator.java is a viable IU. It plays a crucial role in bridging the MAGIC system with the contention database; there are bound to be some thorny interface issues. DataTransferCoordinator.java is also the type of component that is best built by one experienced developer. The adage about the deleterious effects of a multiplicity of cooks on the broth has a nasty habit of turning out to be true in these kinds of IUs. Let us analyze how this IU depends on other IUs and how other IUs depend on it.

DataTransferCoordinator.java is invoked by the Contention EJB. The former's task is to facilitate transfer of information both to (user-entered contention information) and from (contention ID) the contention database. Facilitation is one of those broad, general words; it is terribly vague, but gives one a feeling of control. What is facilitation here? Well, a lot.

DataTransferCoordinator.java (hereinafter referred to as "coordinator," as they say in legalese), as its name suggests, coordinates between the MAGIC system and the contention database. How does this happen? The coordinator expects to be given the user-entered data by the EJB which invokes it. It has to transfer the data to the contention database. As proof of a successful transfer, it needs to further fetch a contention ID, which has to be shown to the user by way of confirmation. The passing of the data from the Contention EJB to the coordinator is pretty straightforward, but the journey onward from the coordinator is far from trivial.

The contention database cannot be accessed directly through database calls; all communication to it is brokered by the DTU. What sort of creature is this DTU? MAGIC 1.6 has had no occasion to make the DTU's acquaintance, so poring over old code did not help.

Tina tried finding out who else in the organization has used the DTU to talk to the contention database. There was one group within MM, Corporate Research and Reporting Services (CRRS), that confessed to having used the DTU. A part of its charter was to generate reports on demand on the status of contentions (how many raised, how many resolved, how many still open, how many reopened after resolution, etc.) for higher management. CRRS had its application written in Visual Basic, and it spoke to the DTU through the latter's Visual Basic interface. Getting the interface to work, it was reported, "was quite a pain in..." well, somewhere. Talking to other groups, Tina tried to confirm whether a Java interface for DTU existed.

Approaching the team which managed the DTU was Tina's last option. After countless e-mails and many more conference calls, the DTU team agreed to provide an interface for data exchange with MAGIC, but the biggest bottleneck was the need for synchronous interaction. One option was to do away with this requirement. After submitting the contention information, the users would be shown a message that it is being processed, and the contention ID would be e-mailed to them later. But this would have complicated matters more, necessitating separate calls to fetch the contention ID later and requiring a mechanism for the timely delivery of e-mails with the contention ID. Moreover, the business unit gave a clinching reason why it wanted all of this in a single round trip: the competition had been offering something similar for over six months. After much brainstorming, it was decided that message queuing was the only way to go. The coordinator and the DTU would be talking through messages placed on queues. The DTU team said it had, in fact, been using this communication model with another application, and with some tweaking, the same queues might be used by MAGIC for the time being. Due to the "time being" clause, MAGIC would have to have its own message-queuing infrastructure set up later. Roger said, "Once online contentions kick in, the business unit will loosen the purse strings, and we will get that going."

The DTU team also added that it needed messages from MAGIC in a specific format. Whatever data came and went out had to be one long string, with fields separated by delimiters. As designed, however, the Contention EJB transferred data to and from the coordinator as data objects or data beans, so the coordinator would have to ensure some parsing and formatting take place to bridge the incompatibility of data representation. Moreover, the contention database would need the data to persist in a specific format and would return the contention ID in a specific format too. Thus, the round trip of information passes through diverse components, platforms, and formats. DataTransfer-Coordinator.java is the sole arbiter of this interaction — a crucial cog in the whole wheel of things.

For practitioners coding IUs like this, the *Interface Map* is a basic survival tool. With so many demands to meet, without clear specification of which IU must give what and get what in return, developing and testing could be, well, hell. It should be pointed out that quite a bit of low-level designing has been going on since we started dissecting this particular IU. A whole new paradigm of communication, using messages and queues, had to be looked into and accepted for implementation. This again is typical of real projects; implementation opens up newer vistas of design.

Let us see what all the coordinator needs to function. DataTransfer-Coordinator.java serves as a conduit for data and, more importantly, formats data to make sense to the entities at either end, which speak in different terms. The coordinator needs the data to be sent to the contention database from the Contention EJB. It needs the existence of a working message-queuing infrastructure and details of the specific queue(s) to put messages in and get messages from. It also needs the DTU to be *polling* a certain queue(s) for messages (which contain contention data from the user) the coordinator will put in and needs the DTU to put messages (which contain the contention ID) back into a certain queue(s) before a specified time-out period.

In addition, there are certain other facilities the coordinator needs to provide to itself. First, there should be a way to convert the data passed by the Contention EJB into the message format the DTU understands; let us call this *formatting*. Second, there should be a way to extract the contention ID from the message returned by the DTU; we will call this *parsing*. Thus, the coordinator has to have a formatter and a parser.

There is still something more. The element of *waiting* for a specified time for the DTU to respond is vital in this design. Waiting for a message is supported by the middleware which will host the queues, but some of the middleware's Application Programming Interface (API) must be invoked through MAGIC's components for the waiting to happen as the code executes.

Where does the code to interact with the middleware's API lie? Putting it within the DataTransferCoordinator.java is not a good design choice. If the middleware is changed in the future (this happens often, due to licenses expiring, new acquisitions, or just better advertising), any middleware-specific code within the coordinator will need to be changed. One principle of good design is to disengage — as much as possible — the ideas behind the design from the implementation of it. Ideas are usually more resilient to change than implementation details. The latter, after all, depends on the state-of-the-art, and the state-of-the-art is a pretty volatile state for software (and hardware) technologies.

Along this same logic, code for the formatting and parsing functions better not be embedded within the coordinator; these are ultimately helpers to the main contention functionality. A danger for components like the coordinator is to degenerate into what may be called a "miscellaneous class." I hate having a "Misc." folder on my computer (and always end up having one), because after a while the miscellany of it gets maddening; it can hold anything from a grocery list to a chess program to a tax spreadsheet. Something similar can happen with software components too; something being called a coordinator can jolly well end up as a Man-Friday, doing bits and pieces of everything, and these components are rife in enterprise systems. I once had a hard time trying to refactor a single class that issued three different database calls, did some evilly complex string manipulations, decided whether a given year was a leap year, and calculated profit after tax.

In our case, a cleaner design would be to spawn three new components out of the coordinator: formatter, parser, and communicator. These will serve as adjutants to the coordinator, doing tasks specific to this implementation. Let us give them formal names: MessageFormatter.java, MessageParser.java, and MiddlewareCommunicator.java. Surprisingly, we are still designing. This level of design detail can only occur close to implementation, almost during it. Trying to think through all of this earlier gets the team needlessly bogged down.

The IU that started with just the DataTransferCoordinator.java now stands expanded to: MessageFormatter.java, MessageParser.java, and Middleware-Communicator.java. But all this still remains one IU, and the components must be implemented closely, hand in hand, in a style of over-the-shoulder interfacing that Berners-Lee (1999) describes so evocatively in his *Weaving the Web*.

We will now draw up the *Interface Map* for the IU. Let us rename this IU Contention_Database_Access_Facilitator. The following discussion is with reference to Table 15.2.

Several points are worth special mention. This is the first time we are talking about error messages. Thinking about errors and error messaging is sometimes considered a needless distraction. If design is good, there will be no errors, per conventional wisdom. Conventional wisdom is often so steeped in conventions that it has little room for wisdom. Good software design makes allowances for errors before they occur. It is not about if errors will happen; it is about what one does when they happen. The disturbing part of not war-gaming errors beforehand is that when errors hit (and they eventually will), there is no clue as to what is going wrong. I know of a system which had logging code interleaved with application code. The log files were bulky, and the team thought the bulk was worth it; it came in handy when things went wrong. There was some talk of the log files being a security threat. Against wiser counsel, the decision to remove all logging statements from the code was made and executed. The next time an error occurred, it took the team nearly a week's effort

Table 15.2. *Interface Map* for the Contention_Database_Access_Facilitator IU

	User-entered contention data	Message queue information	Contention ID	Time-out error	Database error	Java API
Contention EJB	X					
Configuration.xml		X				
Contention database			X		X	
DTU						X
Middleware platform				X		

to simply know what was wrong. The moral of the story is that it is very important to put in place an error management framework even before writing of "business" code starts. With some attention, it is easy to implement a switching mechanism into the logging. Varying levels of logging details can be turned on or off at the flip of a flag in some configuration file.

Drawing the *Interface Map* for each IU offers the last and final chance to think about error handling, and this should not go to waste. Error handling does not work as an afterthought, and this has been brought home to many practitioners in hindsight. This issue will be discussed in more detail in the next chapter.

Table 15.2 specifies what all the IU Contention_Database_Access_Facilitator needs from other IUs to deliver its functionality. This IU will appear in the *Interface Maps* of other IUs as well, as and when they need something from it.

Table 15.2 is simple, and that is good. Collaboration of components can happen with minimal glitches only when interfaces are simple and clearly specified. An IU whose *Interface Map* is chockablock with Xs is indeed a well-connected IU, maybe a bit too well. Looking at the *Interface Map,* the amount of coupling for a particular IU can also be gauged. Too much coupling or lack of cohesion affects the long-term health of enterprise software systems and in the shorter term negatively impacts a system's ability to respond to (inevitable!) change. There is still scope to make changes to design, as we did in bringing in the parser, formatter, and communicator components. From now on, the opportunities will be harder and costlier to come by.

Even in iterative and incremental development, with all the facilities of going back and forth, committing a design to code is a major transition. Any subsequent change to the code due to design improvements (on the same requirements) is rework. The *Interface Map* may also be taken as an interface between design and code, the last chance for a sanity check before casting the die. As shown while working on the *Interface Map* for one IU, we faced and made a number of design choices that can only rear their heads as one gets closer and closer to implementation. The full import of design hits home only when individual practitioners sit down to code — foot soldiers get on their feet to march. The *Interface Map* rises to that occasion.

15.6. SUMMARY

This chapter traced MAGIC 2.0's odyssey through the *Specific Convergence, Morphing Index,* and *Interface Map.* Along with illustrating their use in the specific context, we also reflected on themes common to all of enterprise software development.

The next chapter demonstrates how the *Exception Estimation Score* can help us test our systems better.

REFERENCES

Alexander, C. (1979). *The Timeless Way of Building.* Oxford University Press.

Berners-Lee, T. (1999). *Weaving the Web: The Original Design and Ultimate Destiny of the World Wide Web by Its Inventor.* Harper San Francisco.

Booch, G. (2006). The accidental architecture. *IEEE Softw.,* 23(3):9–11.

Brooks, F. P. (1995). *The Mythical Man-Month: Essays on Software Engineering, 20th Anniversary Edition.* Addison-Wesley.

Datta, S. and van Engelen, R. (2006). Effects of changing requirements: A tracking mechanism for the analysis workflow. In Proceedings of the 21st Annual ACM Symposium on Applied Computing (SAC-SE-06), vol. 2, pp. 1739–1744.

DeMarco, T. and Lister, T. (1987). *Peopleware: Productive Projects and Teams.* Dorset House.

Gilb, T. and Gilb, K. (2006). Gilb community. http://www.gilb.com/community/tiki-page.php?pageName=Methods.

Humphrey, W. S. (2006). *TSP: Leading a Development Team.* Addison-Wesley.

Mackenzie, A. (2006). *Cutting Code: Software and Sociality.* Peter Lang.

Norman, D. (1990). *The Design of Everyday Things.* Currency.

16

FEEL OF THE WORLD

16.1. OVERVIEW

Over the last few chapters, we traced the life cycle of the MAGIC 2.0 project, emphasizing how the metrics in this book help practitioners in development activities. This chapter shows the use of the *Exception Estimation Score* in allocating testing effort to the *Deliverable Units*. Before getting to the metric, we will connect the dots where we left off in the last chapter. We will then briefly review how implementation and testing mesh together in a project and explore how common and uncommon testing activities are in enterprise software projects. Finally, we will take leave of Tina and her troop.

16.2. WHAT HAPPENED AFTER THE INTERFACE MAP?

Later parts of the last chapter demonstrated how the development team segued from design to implementation through the *Interface Map*. By the time *Interface Maps* for each *Implementation Unit* (IU) are in place, practitioners should know what to implement. This knowing hinges on understanding the scope of the allied IUs, as well as the vision of the architects and the designers. "Control, management, education and all the other goodies…are important; but the implementation people must understand what the architect had in mind." This blunt and pithy statement comes from an ancient age, uttered by Ian P. Sharp at the 1969 NATO Conference on Software Engineering Techniques (Kruchten et al. 2006). It was at this conference that the phrase "software architecture" was probably used for the first time in public discourse. "What the architect had in mind" is another way of referring to something that has been called the *intent* of software design in this book.

As stated before, a useful abstraction of software design is to see it as a collaboration of components. The tricky part is assigning responsibilities to components and deciding how they collaborate. Once this is done, however, all that remains is specifying and communicating the interfaces, unequivocally. Thus design at its most atomic is a set of interfaces, one fitting into another like a jigsaw puzzle. Implementation must ensure the code behaves in such a way that it always ends up honoring its interfaces. The *Interface Map* helps bridge this chasm between design and implementation.

With the *Interface Map* for each IU in place, the development team got into coding in earnest. Some feel coding is the "real thing" about development, but we know better, and a large part of this book has been devoted to making us know better. There are several macro metrics for coding effort, like number of lines of code written per unit of time. Though these have statistical value, they can hardly affect the quality (or even quantity!) of coding in an ongoing project. There are also dangers in wagging too many such figures in the faces of de- velopers. Unnecessary tension creeps in, which may hamper the development effort. As pointed out a long time ago in *Peopleware* (DeMarco and Lister 1987), and mentioned in Section 3.2.2, there is a basic difference in the pro- duction techniques of software and cheeseburgers. Computer programs cannot be measured by assembly line metrics. I am personally against *metricizing* the coding activity. Every developer has a personal style, which should not be stifled as long as it is not at odds with widely accepted good programming practices. For example, class-level declaration of variables in Java can have very serious consequences, and no such instance may be allowed. But giving programmers room to exercise their coding idioms is usually a good thing. It engenders a sense of belonging with the code, and a sense of belonging brings with it care for the code. Each IU is bound by its interfaces; as long as implementers stay true to the interfaces, they are meeting the basic demands and may be trusted to be creative from then on.

16.3. IMPLEMENTATION AND TESTING

The implementation of the MAGIC 2.0 system proceeded by IUs, which were then aggregated into the *Deliverable Units* (DUs). Unit testing is the best an- tidote for coding errors at the component level. There are several frameworks which support unit testing, but unit testing *always* adds to the time and effort of the coding activity, however clever the framework might be. This has to be understood by the development team at the outset and the customer must be briefed accordingly. Added time and effort bring with them added cost, and this is a cost customers must be willing to pay for quality. Unit-testing gurus, driven by idealism or commerce, sometimes give an impression that unit testing is just a matter of getting into the habit; once the habit has been gotten into, it can be done seamlessly with coding. This is far from the case. Any nontrivial testing takes quite some reflection to identify circumstances that need to be tested most. There is no point in testing for testing's sake; it eats up resources at the cost of other life cycle activities. There was a project where a team member was found to be running unit tests on the Java hash table's Application Programming Interface (API). Upon interrogation, it was revealed he had taken the team lead's direction to unit test each and every piece of code a little too much to heart! Ideally, unit testing should be a part of every implementer's personal discipline. Just as a pharmacist checks the expiration date of every medicine that is handed to a patient, every software engineer must unit test the code that he or she releases. But the ideal is ideal and the real is real, and the twain unlikely to meet. Therefore, the habit of unit testing has to be drilled into practitioners by lure or duress.

Unit testing, however, can do just as much as testing a unit of code in isolation. It can test whether each unit of code is living up to its interfaces and (with some clever instrumentation) may tell you how well algorithms are performing. It can also weed out obvious bloomers like division by zero. What it cannot do is place a piece of code in the context of the overall functionality the code lives to support. It is not uncommon to have cases where every unit test has been run, yet the end-to-end functionality is breaking.

Let us look at an example. An authentication utility has to provide a twenty-character alphanumeric user identification number every time a new user successfully logs into the system. This ID is used at several places in the code to execute business logic. After the system runs into a major outage, the error, after some hair-raising debugging, is detected. It appears the authentication utility was passing a blank user ID. Code which trimmed trailing white spaces from the "usual" IDs had cut this blank down to nothing, and that led to an ugly array index exception. Unit testing could never have uncovered this.

The idea behind the *Exception Estimation Score* is to help make an informed judgment on which part of the system is most prone to exceptions and accordingly distribute testing efforts. We will now begin to calculate the *Exception Estimation Score* for the DUs of the MAGIC 2.0 system.

In Chapter 10, the *testing dimensions* were identified as technical, behavioral, political, and environmental. These are the major lines of concern for functional testing outcome. Each dimension was discussed at length earlier and shown to relate to different stakeholder constituencies. Calculating the *Exception Estimation Score* for a DU involves grading it on a scale of 1 to 5 for each dimension, adding the scores into its *Total Testing Score,* and then taking the ratio of its *Total Testing Score* to the sum of the *Total Testing Scores* for all DUs. Chapter 15 identified the following DUs for MAGIC 2.0:

- DU_1 — Generation and delivery of the electronic statements
- DU_2 — The contention user interface
- DU_3 — The contention business logic and MAGIC database access
- DU_4 — The mechanism for talking to the contention database

A bit of background for the *Exception Estimation Score* is appropriate at this point. An enduring theme of iterative and incremental development is keeping closely engaged with the customer, but not as closely as prescribed by some of the more radical of the agile methods, where the customer may be allowed to look over the developer's shoulder. Customer engagement in iterative and incremental development means ensuring the customer and the development team are on the same page at every project milestone, cognizant of the progress so far and the challenges ahead. At no point in the life cycle is the customer as important as at the start of testing. Up to that point, the development team somewhat owned the system, designing, building, and manipulating it to best fit requirements. This included effective unit testing. Then the system is given to the real users, that is, users who will use the system without the need or desire to know how it was built. No one knows the real users better than the customer (sometimes they are the same), so it is essential to have customers on board while end-to-end testing is planned and performed. This is difficult, for a strange reason.

As a business systems analyst, I was often involved in planning user acceptance tests. I frequently encountered a particular customer attitude which in our little circle was called the "hands-off" syndrome. Just because they are paying for the software to be built, many customers absolve themselves from all involvement with the development process. The thinking goes: "Well, I am footing the bill to get the finished product, and the perfect product, so why all this noise about participating in testing?" I have heard such refrains many times, and in all such instances each release was greeted with scores of bug reports within the first couple of days. The "hands-off" syndrome is a serious issue. At its core lies a peculiar pay-forget-get mind-set: pay for something, forget all about it until it is to be delivered, and expect to get exactly what you wanted (or think you want at the time of delivery). This may work for certain commodities like a tailor-made suit (still, good tailors insist on a trial) or a birthday cake, but software is not one of those commodities. For enterprise software systems — with so much business interest at stake — to be successful, the development team has to seek and receive continual feedback from the customer. This interaction with the customer is at its most intense during testing. After being mulcted several times by the "hands-off" syndrome, I now make it a point to clarify during the inception phase how much customer attention is needed during functional testing. If the customer seems to be uncomfortable with this, I have gone so far as to write it down as a project risk — and it has worked. The bottom line is: customers have an important role to play in functional testing and thus calculation of the *Exception Estimation Score*, and they need to play it. We will now see how the *Exception Estimation Score* is calculated for MAGIC.

Let us first consider DU_1, generation and delivery of the electronic statement using NIRVANA. This has considerable technical challenges, given the development team's unfamiliarity with the medium and no precedent of using NIRVANA in the customer organization. Many a time, a major technical challenge eases up if you can find someone who has worked on a similar problem before and remembers (and is willing to share) the wisdom from roadblocks and workarounds. Sometimes teams from different organizations working for the same customer are ready to share their know-how in a particular technology. The readiness, though often prompted by "political" motives rather than love and affection for a competitor, is nonetheless very helpful. The biggest benefit an organization gets from outsourcing its technical operations to a number of contracting companies is the rich mix of technical expertise that comes to it. Although Tina and her team are implementing ElectState as a pilot, for a handful of "representative" users, getting NIRVANA integrated within MAGIC is a major undertaking in itself. Once that it done, scaling up to larger user pools will expectedly be less painful. Thus DU_1 gets a score of 4 out of 5 for the technical dimension.

The ElectState feature is minimally interactive. It is an electronic delivery mechanism for the same information contained in paper statements. Although users can change their e-mail addresses online, this is a part of existing profile management and *not* directly linked to the ElectState functionality. It is easier, from an implementation standpoint, to arrange periodic delivery of large amounts of data than to provide online access to the data. As far as DU_1 is concerned, there is not much *excitation* from the users to which the system must *respond*. Therefore, DU_1 gets a score of 1 out of 5 for the behavioral dimension.

The political dimension, as always, is the most subjective. True, politics is a big part of why the MAGIC project was left holding the NIRVANA bag in the first place (refer to Chapter 12). Sound technological advice might have been the last thing to have influenced the purchase of the NIRVANA license. But this is the way things have been, are, and will be with enterprise software projects: software has to support the enterprise, not the other way around. The question now is how much of that politics will stand to affect the delivery of ElectState. Curiously, sometimes in situations like these, past politics plays in favor of the development team. (This is not to suggest that past politics is good or will never be to the development team's detriment.)

I know of a project which involved trying out a new application server. There had been much friction in the customer organization over switching to the new product from an earlier one. The customer manager had been an ardent supporter of the changeover, and he was itching to prove a point. The day servers were switched only in the *development* environment (still far from production), after which a lavish party was thrown and, amidst much wining and dining, the "resounding success with the new infrastructure" announced. The customer proved to be pretty easy for the remaining part of the project as well; it was a case of politics going the development team's way. Tina could sense something along similar lines for the ElectState functionality. Thus, DU_1 gets a score of 2 out of 5 for the political dimension.

The environmental dimension for DU_1 is closely associated with the technical dimension. Once the NIRVANA infrastructure was integrated within MAGIC, environmental factors were unlikely to play much of a role. Given this is a pilot, there should not be any issues with overloading the servers. Accordingly, DU_1 gets a score of 1 out of 5 for the environmental dimension.

The *Total Testing Score* for DU_1 is

$$TTS(DU_1) = 4 + 1 + 2 + 1 = 8$$

We next turn to DU_2, the user interface for the contention functionality. For GUI-intensive applications, user interface programming can be very involved. The contention user interface is, thankfully, not that complex; it only involves presentation of dynamic content, accepting user input, verifying that input, and passing the data on to the next layer of request processor. There are many technologies for creating sophisticated user interfaces. The *Struts* framework (Apache 2006), based on the same model-view-controller architecture MAGIC 2.0 is using, provides a smart way of creating Java Web applications. Asynchronous JavaScript and XML, better known as AJAX (Murray 2006), is another hot new area of Web programming. For the time being, MAGIC will stick with good old JavaServer Pages (JSP). (Only yesterday, JSP was the hot new area of Web programming. Alas, hot becomes cool — something to do with the second law of thermodynamics, I guess.) In this case, the decision to stick with good old JSP is driven by pragmatism more than love for antiquity.

There are always technologies around that can do a lot more than what one needs. These are often the current craze and called "the thing," with concomitant hype. Choosing them over more mundane but apt solutions is not only overkill, but has other insidious effects. Somehow one feels obligated to use the more obscure features and ends up losing focus on the objective. In the late 1990s, Enterprise JavaBeans (EJB) was hailed as "the thing" to have happened to enterprise software. Knowing what the acronym stood for was taken as a sign of great expertise. Back then, often an organization's internal projects such as a library management system choked themselves with EJBs. Thus the message is that technology should fit business needs, not vice versa. Choose whatever technology fits the system best, even if nerds call it passé.

Use of JSP makes the user interface development of MAGIC 2.0 straightforward. Given the team's experience with it, pitfalls can be seen in advance and worked around. Thus DU_2 gets a score of 1 out of 5 for the technical dimension.

User interfaces must absorb all sorts of user behavior, including the malicious. Unexpected and potentially harmful inputs have to be filtered out as near the system's surface as possible. Inadvertent user input errors like alphanumeric data for numeric fields, if not handled, can cause whole systems to trip. User interface development is not only about accepting and verifying user inputs. The craft is in predicting what kind of inputs can cause things to go wrong and putting mechanisms in place to prevent them. As a simple example, date formats are important for processing user-entered information. The system expects users to read (and heed!) directions for whether the date is to be mm/dd/yyyy or dd/mm/yyyy (in many countries other than the United States, the latter is the norm). Rather than rely on user compliance with diktats, days, months, and years can be shown as drop-down lists from which users make a selection.

These seem like minor issues of user interface design, almost trivial, but without attention to these details, user interfaces fare badly in terms of *usability*. Usability is among the important "ilities" of a system, the "U" in FURPS (Datta 2005), and user interface is almost the only aspect by which users judge the usability of a system. Every DU that involves user interfaces claims to have at least a score of 3 out of 5 for the behavioral dimension, depending on the complexity of the user interface. As the MAGIC user interface is not especially complicated, it gets a score of 3 out of 5 for the behavioral dimension.

There is not much to the political dimension of DU_2, but one must be careful about the text that is displayed on Web pages. Usually referred to as "verbiage," every word must be endorsed in writing by the customer before being released on the Web. There may be certain business or cultural sensitivities not readily apparent to the development team, especially if the team is located on the other side of the world. Overall, DU_2 gets a score of 1 out of 5 for the political dimension.

The environmental dimension for DU_2, however, is far from trivial. User interfaces on the Web are notoriously browser dependent, and you can trust users to have a wide range of favorite browsers. Some browsers are very forgiving of ill-formed HTML and such aberrations, while other browsers are not. Many Web sites carry disclaimers like "this Web site is best viewed by so and so browser and so and so version." Even then, there is no guarantee users will not try a different browser, have problems, and log complaints. It is best to have the customer agree up front what browser(s) must be supported and rigorously test with all of the supported browsers. Different browsers can give a different look and feel to the same content, and the difference can affect how users feel about the system.

It takes much effort to build Web sites which are supported by browsers "across the board," and the board is getting broader by the day. I usually recommend ensuring compatibility with at least one open-source browser in addition to whatever the customer wants; users can then be advised of a free download of that if nothing else works. Naturally, given the fragmented browser space, use of client-side scripting for special effects or even user input verification is better not done, but there may be rare occasions when such scripting cannot be bypassed. On one Web page, the target of a hyperlink had to be dynamically decided based on something the user entered on that page. This was almost five years back, and JavaScript was as sophisticated as the development team got. But these are rare occasions, and they must remain rare. DUs involving user interfaces may run into environmental issues mainly due to browser incompatibilities. Thus DU_2 gets a score of 4 out of 5 for the environmental dimension.

We next move to DU_3, contention business logic and MAGIC database access. Intuitively, this seems to call for a high score for the technical dimension. After all, this is where all the business logic lies. On a closer look, things are far more "gettable." MAGIC 2.0 does not have very involved business logic as yet. The main area of concern is accessing and working with different data sources and formats. As mentioned earlier, in enterprise systems, business logic and data access mechanisms often are closely intertwined. In this case, though, DU_3 embodies a very important aspect of the overall MAGIC functionality and its technology is well understood by the development team. Computationally complex enterprise systems are far from common; it is not every day one comes across the need to solve an NP hard *business* problem. (Many classic NP hard problems involve business though, like the traveling salesman problem or the optimal scheduling problem!) DU_3 gets a score of 3 out of 5 for the technical dimension.

User behavior cannot affect the functioning of DU_3 much. Assuming all the user input verification is handled by DU_2 (DU_2 got a score of 3 out of 5 for the behavioral dimension), DU_3 should only receive user input data that have been checked and deemed fit for getting deeper into the system. To guard against something that still might spike things, it is advisable to have generic exception handlers at crucial points in the code in DUs such as DU_3. Overall, DU_3 gets a score of 1 out of 5 for the behavioral dimension.

How does DU_3 fare in the political dimension? There is indeed no dearth of political will to see the contention functionality succeed on the Web platform. But are there any crosscurrents? What about the customer service representatives who have been handling contention manually so far? Usually this kind of change does not go down well with service personnel. Given the outsourcing concerns endemic today, it is more than likely the representatives who have been taking the contention calls from customers will see the webifying of the functionality as a threat to their jobs. There is nothing the development team can do to assuage these fears. The team has been hired to execute what essentially is a management decision by the customer organization. But saying and seeing this does not help in such situations. I know of projects where customer representatives have felt (and said that) their employment was in danger because the development team was hired to do what the reps called "our jobs." It is not really the best of working environments; sticking close to the project's brief helps somewhat, as does consciously avoiding arguments on the issue. Working in cross-cultural and cross-political environments is the first lessons today's peripatetic software engineers have to learn. The political dimension for DU_3 justifiably gets a very high score, 5 out of 5.

Success of MAGIC 2.0 depends largely on how smoothly the transition goes from manual resolution of contentions (recording them over the telephone and subsequently resolving them) to lodging of contentions over the Web and subsequent manual processing. The smoothness depends on how well the service representatives work with the new system. Evidently, this has many human issues, and cynically, human issues are ultimately political issues. The political dimension is something on which the development team has very little handle; no amount of effort on the team's part can guarantee there will be no surprises on this count. Therefore, giving this dimension a high score does not suffice; the customer should also know what is being seen as a potential issue. Tina found a sympathetic audience in Roger, who assured her of his full support in overcoming these "glitches."

The environmental dimension for DU_3 is also fraught with possibilities. Contention functionality per se is unlikely to be very load intensive, but the application server is already loaded due to the large volume of transaction data being pulled (recall that the slow response time of the Transaction Summary Page was a reason why electronic statements are being looked into). Also, there is no way to know for sure how the application server would behave under the additional load of the online logging of contentions.

There is another, more insidious, slant to the environmental factors. The environment, almost by definition, is a shared commodity. Sharing is fine, as long as stepping on one another's toes does not hurt. It is usual for different applications in the same organization to share computing infrastructure. This sort of sharing has its own troubles, which are often very hard to pinpoint (without finger-pointing!). I was once part of a team looking at serious performance issues for an application. It was an interesting exercise, and I had an opportunity to evaluate how aspect-oriented programming (AOP) can be used to instrument code. That experience helped later in examining how AOP can be used in the design of enterprise systems (Datta 2006). Finally, we ended up tweaking some database access code to enhance performance by a notable amount. Within a week after our changes were rolled out, performance was back to where it had been — bad. It seemed another application sharing the same database had launched and had the interesting effect of rolling back the improvements we had so painstakingly made. That required some explaining.

Sharing infrastructure is a fact of life, given the need to optimize enterprise resources, but it can and does lead to problems. In the MAGIC 2.0 system, the sharing points are the data transfer utility (or DTU, a generic gateway for applications to talk to legacy systems, including the contention database) and the application server on which it will be deployed. Both of these can cause serious performance issues, but before MAGIC 2.0 establishes its value, there is little hope of convincing the customer to buy a dedicated infrastructure. This is another one of those chicken-and-egg problems life at large and life at small are full of. Tina's brigade needs to shoot for the best performance given the current environment, so that MAGIC 2.0 will put up a good enough show to justify its own environment in the future. Thus DU_3 gets a score of 4 out of 5 for the environmental dimension.

We now turn to the last of the DUs. DU_4 involves building a mechanism for the MAGIC Web-based system to connect to the legacy contention database. As we found out in the last chapter, this DU covers several loosely coupled although strongly cohesive areas of functionality: talking to the DTU, passing and formatting messages back and forth, implementing a way to "wait" for an answer from the DTU, etc.

In the technical dimension, DU_4 presents major challenges. It has to run smoothly for the Web-based contention functionality to function at all. DU_4 has very little business logic in the conventional sense, but the functionality MAGIC 2.0 needs to support depends vitally on DU_4. Another curious aspect of DU_4 is that it arose only due to the requirement to be able to raise contentions online. In the earlier scheme of things (when users called the help line and the customer service representatives directly recorded the information in the contention database), there was no reason for something like DU_4 to exist. Thus DU_4 bridges the old and new ways of doing business, and bridges are difficult to build, especially between the old and the new. Building something like DU_4 is more difficult because it will be entirely invisible to the customer, who may ask: "Do we *really* need this? We didn't have something like this *before*." When it is hard to make customers see the very *raison d'être* for something like DU_4, one cannot expect much help from them in functional testing. Given the involved design and implementation of DU_4 discussed earlier, it gets a score of 5 out of 5 for the technical dimension.

Moving on to the behavioral dimension, DU_4 does not stand to be affected directly by user behavior. It lies so deep inside the system that it cannot reasonably be assumed all extraneous noise (in the form of bad input, etc.) has been filtered out. Whatever user behavior can cause damage to DU_4 will have a similar effect on DU_2 and to some extent DU_3, so these DUs in effect insulate DU_4. Still, it is important for DU_4 to carefully examine the information it is sending to the DTU, because if a message causes the DTU to trip, or causes even some minor problems, the members of the MAGIC team will be left with very red faces.

Finger-pointing goes on widely (and even wildly at times) when teams from competing organizations own subsystems that must work together in order for the bigger system to work. One needs to guard against finger-pointing. Conversely, it is a good idea to check the information received from the DTU before passing it on, just to be sure there is nothing unexpected. Overall, DU_4 gets a score of 1 out of 5 for the behavioral dimension.

Thankfully, the political dimension does not influence DU_4 much. If it remains by and large transparent to customers and users, the invisibility can give at least some detachment. And detachment keeps politics at bay. The political dimension may be of some concern though. The DTU is run by a group from another contractor organization. To be able to run smoothly, DU_4 has to mesh well with DTU's interface. What is called "mesh well" in one sweeping phrase is the result of numerous parleys among teams, sometimes calling for changes to low-level design and implementation. This parley business calls for close interaction, which is not always easy among competing organizations. (Remember that Tina's team and other contractor teams are vying for an increasing share of the customer's pie, naturally at a cost to each other.) To work around these situations, Roger, MAGIC 2.0's manager, has to remain in touch with his counterpart on the DTU side and see that the teams work together. Thus DU_4 gets a score of 2 out of 5 for the political dimension.

The environmental dimension for DU_4 can be seen at two levels. Since components such as the DTU have been around for a long time, and interface with several different systems, they must be relatively stable and immune to environmental changes. In other words, the software and hardware environments for the DTU cannot be changed without accounting for the far-reaching consequences that may entail. Some of this environmental stability would also rub off on DU_4, and any change to its environment will first need to be seen in light of the impact that may have on its interfaces. However, as discussed in the last chapter, DU_4 also needs to use message-queuing facilities from middleware. The middleware used is a third-party product which may be changed in future versions, so DU_4 code needs to be generic enough and not tied to a particular product API. Java Message Service acts as a "wrapper" around the middleware, decoupling its API from the application code. Without this indirection, environmental factors will affect the stability of DU_4 to a large extent. Overall, given these concerns, DU_4 gets a score of 3 out of 5 for the environmental dimension.

16.4. CALCULATING AND APPLYING THE EXCEPTION ESTIMATION SCORE

We are now ready to calculate the *Exception Estimation Score* for each of the DUs. DU_1 has a *Total Testing Score* of:

$$TTS(DU_1) = 4 + 1 + 2 + 1 = 8$$

Similarly, DU_2 has a *Total Testing Score* of:

$$TTS(DU_2) = 1 + 3 + 1 + 4 = 9$$

The *Total Testing Score* for DU_3 is

$$TTS(DU_3) = 3 + 1 + 5 + 4 = 13$$

and for DU_4 is

$$\text{TTS}(\text{DU}_4) = 5 + 1 + 2 + 3 = 11$$

The sum of all the *Total Testing Scores* is

$$\begin{aligned} \text{TTS} &= \text{TTS}(\text{DU}_1) + \text{TTS}(\text{DU}_2) + \text{TTS}(\text{DU}_3) + \text{TTS}(\text{DU}_4) \\ &= 8 + 9 + 13 + 11 = 41 \end{aligned}$$

Thus, by the formula for the *Exception Estimation Score* given in Chapter 10, we have for each DU:

$$\text{EES}(\text{DU}_1) = 8/41 = 0.20$$

$$\text{EES}(\text{DU}_2) = 9/41 = 0.22$$

$$\text{EES}(\text{DU}_3) = 13/41 = 0.32$$

$$\text{EES}(\text{DU}_4) = 11/41 = 0.27$$

Table 16.1 summarizes the data for calculating the *Exception Estimation Scores.* What do these numbers indicate? In order of descending *Exception Estimation Score,* the DUs can be arranged as DU_3, DU_4, DU_2, and DU_1. Thus DU_3 deserves the highest testing attention, followed by DU_4, DU_2, and DU_1, in that order. This should result in allocating time and resources for testing accordingly.

Complete testing is an oxymoron; testing can never be complete. Merely counting the number of paths in the code is enough to convince everyone that all of those paths cannot be tested within project constraints. And this is just unit testing, which should be addressed from *within* a practitioner's personal discipline. Humphrey's seminal works, *Personal Software Process* (Humphrey 2005) and *Team Software Process* (Humphrey 2006), discuss practitioner preparation and its positive impact on software development enterprise with great elan and insight.

Table 16.1. Calculation of *Exception Estimation Score*

	Technical	Behavioral	Political	Environmental	TTS(DU_n)	EES(DU_n)
DU_1	4	1	2	1	8	0.2
DU_2	1	3	1	4	9	0.22
DU_3	3	1	5	4	13	0.32
DU_4	5	1	2	3	11	0.27
				Total TTS	41	

The main concern of functional testing is allocating attention; both *overtesting* and *undertesting* need to be guarded against. It is widely accepted that undertesting is bad. A large percentage of postproduction bugs are commonly bunched under the root cause "inadequate testing." Even though hardly ever acknowledged, however, overtesting is just as bad. How do we identify overtesting? Cycles of testing without finding significant bugs indicate overtesting is under way. Overtesting is bad not just because it gives a false sense of assurance to the developers. Overtesting usually means undertesting is going on somewhere else in the system. Given limited time and resources, and the impossibility of complete testing, overkill somewhere must mean underkill elsewhere. Calculating the *Exception Estimation Scores* for the DUs gives an idea which areas of the system are most likely to be problematic and allows testing attention to be distributed accordingly.

As has been stated several times earlier, this is a book about using metrics from *within* the development process. The *Exception Estimation Score* is another stride in that direction, as it helps development teams decide on the relative testing focus each DU needs.

16.5. SUMMARY AND TAKING LEAVE

This chapter illustrated the calculation and interpretation of the *Exception Estimation Score*. It explained how the *Total Testing Score* for the MAGIC 2.0 system was arrived at, based on scores for the technical, behavioral, political, and environmental dimensions. Finally, it discussed how the *Exception Estimation Score* helps to moderate testing effort.

It is now time to take leave of Tina and her troop. MAGIC 2.0 gave us an arena — a sandbox, if you will — to see our ideas in play. Its "characters" also offered a peek into the human angles of enterprise software development. Enterprise software is not built in laboratories or by programming wizards in basements. It comes out of the mix of many talents, traits, and expectations and not a few frailties. These are words we readily associate with ourselves and the people we know; these are human characteristics. The entire point of the case study is to show, at least in part, how the metrics developed earlier in the book can help practitioners build enterprise software in the *real world*.

REFERENCES

Apache (2006). Struts framework. http://struts.apache.org/.
Datta, S. (2005). Integrating the FURPS+ model with use cases — A metrics driven approach. In Supplementary Proceedings of the 16th IEEE International Symposium

on Software Reliability Engineering (ISSRE 2005), Chicago, November 7–11, pp. 4-51–4-52.

Datta, S. (2006). Crosscutting score — An indicator metric for aspect orientation. In Proceedings of the 44th ACM Southeast Conference (ACMSE 2006), pp. 204–208.

DeMarco, T. and Lister, T. (1987). *Peopleware: Productive Projects and Teams.* Dorset House.

Humphrey, W. S. (2005). *PSP: A Self-Improvement Process for Software Engineers.* Addison-Wesley.

Humphrey, W. S. (2006). *TSP: Leading a Development Team.* Addison-Wesley.

Kruchten, P., Obbink, H., and Stafford, J. (2006). The past, present, and future for software architecture. *IEEE Softw.,* 23(2):22–30.

Murray, G. (2006). Asynchronous Javascript Technology and XML (AJAX) with the Java Platform. http://java.sun.com/developer/technicalArticles/J2EE/AJAX/.

EPILOGUE

You have come to this point either after reading the whole book, before reading any of it, or by a random selection of pages. In any case, the epilogue will either confirm what you already think about the book or provoke you to go back and read it, either for the first time or afresh. For me, this is another chance to say what I mean.

This book shows how simple, intuitive metrics can help the development of enterprise software systems. We started by reviewing the journey of software metrics and issues faced in taking projects the metrics way. Then we walked through the major activities of the software development life cycle: specifying requirements, analyzing, designing, implementing, and testing. Along the way, the *Correlation Matrix, Mutation Score, Meshing Ratio, AEI Score, Morphing Index, Specific Convergence, Interface Map,* and *Exception Estimation Score* were unveiled. Each of these has a place in the life cycle, helping uncover information or organize what is known so that new insights are revealed. The case study illustrates the use of these constructs in a typical enterprise software project scenario. Sometimes the metrics agreed with what was expected and sometimes they sprang the unexpected. Sometimes they made decisions easier for practitioners, and sometimes they helped customers see (reasonably more!) reason.

If increasingly powerful, complex, usable, and elegant software is to be built, then software engineers will have to share their experience and intuition among peers and across generations. Metrics offer a great way to do this. The metrics in this book are open to be used and improved upon. But the most important message is that metrics are a great way to formulate and test a practitioner's own understanding of the discipline. Every software engineer who has thought about software engineering while practicing it can come up with his or her own metrics. And metrics work best when practiced, not preached.

If this book inspires or instigates you to try out your own metrics or to apply the metrics given herein (if only to prove me wrong!), I look forward to hearing from you.

INDEX